Step by Step Cooking Course

Step by Step Cooking Course

Margaret Wade

Galahad Books · New York City
in association with Phoebus

Contents

Editor **Sarie Forster**
Designer **Roger Hammond**
Editorial assistant **Lesley Toll**

The cover picture shows Duck à l'Orange.

© 1977 Phoebus Publishing Company/BPC
Publishing Limited, 52 Poland Street, London
W1A 2JX
Reprinted 1979

Library of Congress Catalog Card Number:
77-75296

ISBN 0-88365-395-8

Printed in Great Britain by Redwood Burn Limited

Introduction

The Step by Step Cooking Course provides a clear and helpful approach to all areas of cooking and covers a wide range of recipes. You will find dishes suitable for all occasions from light snacks and economical family meals to the most festive of celebrations. There are also chapters on appetizers, pasta and rice dishes, vegetables and salads, cooking with eggs and cheese, and cakes and bread. As well as suggestions for new ways with old favorites, like roast pork stuffed with prunes, there are dishes from other countries, such as Jambalaya, a savory rice dish from the Caribbean, and Kugelhopf, a yeast cake from Austria, which will add new dimensions to your cooking.

This book will show you how, with skilful blending of flavors or the inclusion of an unusual herb or spice, you can transform simple dishes into something quite special.

The step by step photographs, which cover both basic technique and some individual recipes, should ensure success for both the beginner and the more experienced cook.

Pâté de Campagne.

Appetizers

Pâté de Campagne

½ lb veal
½ lb pork
¼ lb ham
¼ lb pigs' liver
¼ lb pork fat
1 clove garlic
allspice
salt and pepper
½ wineglass brandy
1 bayleaf
clarified butter

1. Set the oven at 350°F.

2. Assemble all the raw ingredients on a wooden chopping board and cut the meat into pieces.

3. Grind the meat and the pork fat and turn into a mixing bowl.

4. Mix the meats together well and then add the garlic clove, allspice and salt and pepper. Pour in the brandy and mix well.

5. Turn the mixture into a terrine, press the meat down well and smooth over the surface. Place a bayleaf on top.

6. Put on the terrine lid and lower the terrine into a roasting pan with a little water in it. Cook in the pre-set oven for 1½ hours or until the pâté is firm to the touch.

7. Remove from the oven, take off the lid and cover pâté with a sheet of waxed paper. Press the pâté under a weight of 2 lb until cool. Cover with clarified butter and keep in a cool place until required.

Appetizers

Rabbit Pâté.

Rabbit Pâté

1 lb raw rabbit or hare meat
¼ lb raw lean pork or ham
½ lb raw unsalted pork fat
1–2 cloves garlic
1 mild onion
6 tbsp dry sherry
1 small egg
salt and pepper
approx 8 thin slices of pork fat for lining
   dish

To serve
hot buttered toast
few sprigs of parsley
pickled gherkins and onions

Any kind of game may be substituted for the rabbit or hare suggested in this recipe. To obtain 1 lb meat, you will need to buy a large animal weighing at least twice this amount.

1. Cut the meat and pork fat into cubes. Peel and crush the garlic. Peel the onion and chop roughly.

2. Grind all these ingredients together, then put in a bowl. Stir in the sherry and egg with salt and pepper to taste. Stir well to mix.

3. Set the oven at 350°F.

4. Line the base and sides of a 4 cup loaf or pâté dish with the slices of pork fat. Spoon in the prepared pâté mixture, pressing it down well with the back of a spoon.

5. Cover the pâté with buttered foil and stand in a roasting pan half filled with hot water. Bake in pre-set oven for 1–1½ hours or until the pâté shrinks away from sides of pan or dish, and the juices run faintly pink when the pâté is pierced in the center with a skewer.

6. Remove the pâté from roasting pan and leave to cool. Place weights on top of the foil and chill in the refrigerator overnight. Turn out onto a heatproof plate or dish. Score the fat in a criss cross pattern and put under a hot broiler until browned.

7. Leave to cool, then arrange on a serving platter. Garnish around the pâté with sprigs of parsley and serve with hot buttered toast and pickled gherkins and onions, if liked.

Fine Liver Pâté

1 lb pork liver
milk
½ lb raw unsalted pork fat
1–2 cloves garlic
6 tbsp Madeira, port or full bodied red wine
⅔ cup fine fresh brown breadcrumbs
2 eggs
½ tsp grated nutmeg
salt and pepper
approx 8 thin slices of pork fat for lining
   dish

To serve
hot buttered toast

1. Cut the liver into slices, put in a bowl and cover with milk. Leave for at least 30 minutes.

2. Drain the liver and grind with three quarters of the pork fat. Put in a bowl. Peel and crush the garlic and add to the ground mixture with the Madeira, port or wine, breadcrumbs, eggs, nutmeg and salt and pepper to taste. Stir well to mix.

3. Work the mixture in a liquidizer until fine, or strain through a sieve.

4. Set the oven at 350°F.

5. Line the base and sides of a deep ovenproof serving dish with the slices of pork fat. Spoon in the prepared pâté mixture, pressing it down well with the back of a spoon.

6. Cover the pâté with buttered foil and stand in a roasting pan half filled with hot water. Bake in pre-set oven for $1-1\frac{1}{2}$ hours or until the pâté shrinks away from sides of dish, and the juices run faintly pink when pâté is pierced in the center with a skewer.

7. Remove from roasting pan and discard foil. Cut remaining pork fat into very thin slivers and put in a heavy based pan. Melt over a low heat until the fat is runny but not colored. Pour over the pâté in the dish, leave until cold, then chill in the refrigerator overnight.

8. Serve from the dish with plenty of hot buttered toast.

Fish Roe Pâté

4 oz smoked cod roe
½ lb soft herring roe
2 slices white bread
water
⅔ cup corn oil
juice of 1–2 lemons
cayenne pepper

To finish
few black olives
⅔ cup unset aspic

1. Skin the smoked cod roe, slice roughly and place in the top of a steamer. Cover with a lid and steam for 15 minutes. Add the herring roe and steam for a further 10 minutes.

2. Meanwhile, remove the crusts from the bread and discard. Soak the bread in a little water for about 5 minutes, then squeeze dry and put in a mortar or bowl.

3. Remove the roe from the steamer, leave to cool a little, then put in mortar. Pound the mixture with a pestle or kitchen mallet until smooth and well mixed. Add the oil a drop at a time, beating vigorously after each addition until the mixture becomes thick. Beat in lemon juice and cayenne pepper to taste.

4. Spoon the pâté into a serving dish, smooth the top and sprinkle with a little cayenne pepper. If liked, the pâté may be decorated with a few strips of pitted black olive and coated in aspic. Chill in the refrigerator until serving time. Serve with hot buttered toast.

Clarified Butter

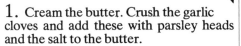

1. Cut up 1 cup butter and put in a thick saucepan. Melt it slowly over a very low heat and once melted, continue to cook until foaming well.

2. Skim and strain through a piece of muslin into a bowl. The liquid will settle leaving a sediment at the bottom. The clarified butter can then be carefully poured off into another container.

Garlic Butter

¼ cup butter
2 tbsp fresh parsley heads
2–3 cloves garlic
1 level tsp salt

1. Cream the butter. Crush the garlic cloves and add these with parsley heads and the salt to the butter.

2. Beat the ingredients together and refrigerate in an airtight container for use as required.

Fish Roe Pâté.

Appetizers

Mussels with Cream

3 dozen fresh mussels
juice of 1 lemon
⅔ cup light cream
salt and pepper

To finish
finely chopped parsley

1. Scrub mussels thoroughly under cold running water. Discard beards and any mussels that are open.

2. Soak the cleaned mussels for 1 hour in cold water, then drain and place in the top of a steamer. Cover with a lid and steam over a high heat for 5–10 minutes until the mussels open.

3. Discard any that are still closed. Scrape mussels from their shells and arrange in a serving dish. Sprinkle over the lemon juice. Season the cream with salt and pepper to taste and pour over the mussels in the dish.

4. Chill in the refrigerator for 2 hours, then sprinkle with parsley just before serving.

Mushrooms in Sour Cream

1 lb fresh button mushrooms
juice of ½ lemon
⅔ cup cultured sour cream
salt and pepper

To finish
paprika

1. Wipe the mushrooms clean with a damp cloth, but do not peel. Slice thinly into a bowl and sprinkle with lemon juice to prevent discoloration.

2. Add the sour cream with salt and pepper to taste and mix gently, until the mushrooms are coated in the cream.

3. Transfer to a serving dish and sprinkle with paprika to taste. Chill in the refrigerator and serve as required with French bread.

Artichokes with French Dressing

4 artichokes
½ lemon
French dressing made with 1⅓ cups oil

1. Cut the stalks off the artichokes, then remove any tough or damaged outer leaves. Cut off the top peaks of the petals. Wash thoroughly under cold running water and drain. Rub all cut surfaces with lemon.

2. Put artichokes in the top of a steamer or in a pan of boiling salted water, and steam or boil young ones for 25 minutes, older ones for 30–40 minutes, depending on age. The artichokes are ready when an outer leaf can be pulled out easily. Remove from steamer or pan, turn upside down to drain and leave to cool.

3. Pull artichokes open gently with the fingers to expose the centers. Pull out the 'peaked caps' from the centers by twisting slowly. Set aside. Scrape out the hairy chokes underneath with a teaspoon and discard.

4. Replace the caps upside down in the center of the artichokes, then arrange on individual serving plates. Pour French dressing into the center of each artichoke just before serving.

1. Pull the artichokes open gently with the fingers to expose the centers.

5. Using your fingers or a teaspoon, carefully scrape out the hairy choke.

2. Continue until you expose the peaked cap which is slightly paler in color.

3. Pull out the peaked cap from the center by twisting slowly.

4. Set the cap aside, as this is edible. The inedible hairy choke is now exposed.

Artichokes with French Dressing.

Appetizers

Stuffed Peppers

4 green sweet peppers
6 eggs
3 tbsp tomato paste
1 tsp paprika
6 tbsp chilled butter or margarine
1 small onion
salt and pepper
2 cooked new potatoes
1 cooked carrot
⅓ cup cooked peas

1. Cut the tops off the peppers and reserve. Scoop out the pith and seeds using a
grapefruit knife. Wash thoroughly under
cold running water, then pat dry with absorbent paper. Set aside.

2. Beat the eggs in a bowl with the tomato paste and paprika. Grate 2 tbsp butter or margarine into the egg mixture.

3. Peel the onion and chop very finely.
Melt the remaining butter or margarine in
a pan, add the onion and fry gently until
soft and golden. Pour in the egg mixture
and scramble over a high heat, stirring
constantly. Season to taste with salt and
pepper. Remove from the heat and leave
to cool.

4. Dice the potatoes and carrot very finely, then add to the scrambled eggs with the
peas. Stir well and mix. Taste for seasoning.

5. Spoon the mixture into the prepared
pepper cases and replace tops. Chill in the
refrigerator until serving time.

6. Arrange on serving dish(es) and garnish with lettuce leaves or macedoine of
vegetables. Serve with hot garlic or French
bread.

Avocado Vinaigrette

2 avocados
½ lemon
French dressing made with 1⅓ cups oil

1. Cut the avocados in half lengthwise,
using a silver knife. Remove the seeds and
rub the exposed flesh with the cut surface
of the lemon to prevent discoloration.

2. Arrange an avocado half on each individual serving plate. Pour French dressing
into avocados and serve as soon as possible.

Variation:
As an alternative, substitute Madeira for
the French dressing. Cut the avocados in
half as above, then score the flesh in
diagonal lines. Arrange on individual
plates, pour 1–2 tbsp Madeira into each
avocado half and leave to steep for 1–2
minutes before serving.

Avocado with Crab

6 rounded tbsp mayonnaise
4 drops of Tabasco sauce
½ tsp paprika
scant 1 tsp lemon juice
salt and pepper
scant ¾ cup frozen crabmeat, thawed
2 avocados
½ lemon

1. Blend 4 tbsp mayonnaise thoroughly
with the Tabasco sauce, paprika and
lemon juice and season to taste with salt
and pepper. Mix the white and dark crabmeat and fold into the mayonnaise.

2. Cut the avocados, remove the seeds
and rub with lemon as for Avocado Vinaigrette. Spoon the prepared crabmeat
mixture into the avocados and if liked,
pipe rosettes around the edge of each
avocado half with the remaining mayonnaise. Serve as soon as possible.

Variation:
Shrimps can be substituted for crab.

Stuffed Peppers.

Avocados shown with Crab, French Dressing, Shrimps and Madeira.

Appetizers

Melon and Orange Cocktail.

Melon and Orange Cocktail

1 large honeydew melon
4 large oranges
2 tsp medium or dry sherry
½ tsp ginger

For sweet orange sauce
juice of 4 oranges
1 tbsp light brown sugar
½–1 tsp cinnamon

1. Cut a slice of the base of the melon so that it will stand upright, Cut melon into a basket shape with a handle by removing 2 sections from the top, leaving a thin strip of skin in the center. Take out the flesh with a melon scoop or sharp knife, dis-carding all seeds. Snip the edges of the melon with scissors to make a zigzag pattern. Set aside.

2. Skin the oranges and divide into segments. Remove all pith and seeds. Put in a bowl with the melon flesh, sprinkle with the sherry and ginger and leave to marinate for approximately 15 minutes, stirring occasionally.

3. Meanwhile, make the sauce. Put the orange juice and sugar in a pan and heat gently until the sugar has dissolved. Increase the heat and boil rapidly for 1–2 minutes, then remove from the heat and leave to cool. Fill melon baskets with fruit and serve separately.

Béchamel Sauce

2½ cups milk
1 stalk of celery
1 onion
1 bayleaf
¼ cup butter or margarine
¾ cup flour
salt and pepper
nutmeg

1. Heat the milk with the celery, onion and bayleaf for a few minutes. Take off the heat, leave in the pan for about ½ hour, then strain and add enough milk to make up the 2½ cups again.

2. Melt the butter or margarine in a pan. Stir in the flour with a wooden spoon and cook gently for 1–2 minutes until the mixture forms a soft ball. Stir constantly.

3. Remove the pan from the heat and gradually stir in the hot milk, beating vigorously all the time to obtain a smooth sauce. When all the milk is incorporated, return pan to heat and bring to the boil stirring constantly. Simmer and stir for 3–4 minutes, adding seasoning and a dash of nutmeg if required.

4. Remove from the heat and use immediately, or cover sauce with a piece of dampened waxed paper and leave until required. Reheat gently before serving.

Mornay Sauce

¼ cup butter or margarine
¾ cup flour
dry mustard
2½ cups hot milk
¾ cup grated cheese

1. Melt the butter or margarine in a pan. Stir in the flour and a dash of dry mustard with a wooden spoon and cook gently for 1–2 minutes until the mixture forms a soft ball. Stir constantly.

2. Remove the pan from the heat and gradually stir in the hot milk, beating vigorously. When all the milk is incorporated, return the pan to the heat and bring to the boil stirring continuously. Simmer and stir for 3–4 minutes, and stir in the grated cheese with seasoning. Remove from the heat and use immediately, or cover as for Béchamel Sauce.

Cucumber Tubs

1 large cucumber
salt
2 rounded tbsp mayonnaise
¼ tsp cayenne pepper
¾ cup shelled and veined shrimps

To finish
4–5 fried bread croûtes
4–5 strips of tomato
1 large bunch parsley

1. Cut both ends off the cucumber and discard, then cut cucumber into 4 or 5 equal portions. Cut a very thin slice off each one and set aside.

2. Make cuts from top to bottom of each portion using a canelle knife. Hollow out the insides with a grapefruit knife. Sprinkle with salt, leave to drain in a colander or sieve for 30 minutes, then wipe the insides dry with absorbent paper.

3. Blend the mayonnaise with cayenne pepper. Chop the shrimps roughly, setting aside 4–5 whole ones for decoration. Fold chopped shrimps into mayonnaise.

4. Arrange croûtes on a serving dish. Place one cucumber portion on each, then carefully spoon in the mayonnaise mixture. Garnish the top of each portion with reserved cucumber slices and whole shrimps and decorate with strips of tomato.

5. Surround cucumber with sprigs of parsley, then chill in the refrigerator until required.

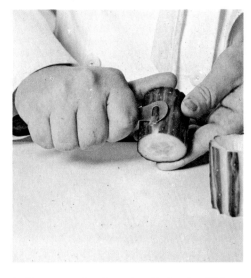

1. Cut cucumber into 4 or 5 chunks. Using a canelle knife, cut vertical strips of peel from chunks of cucumber.

2. Scoop out a hollow from the top of each cucumber chunk.

Cucumber Tubs.

Vol au Vents or Bouchées

These little cases for individual servings are a good party way of using up small quantities of leftover cooked meat or fish, bound with a white sauce or, sometimes, a hollandaise or mayonnaise sauce. A 2 cup quantity of puff pastry will yield 12–16 vol au vents or double this amount of bouchées. Bouchées incidentally, or 'mouthfuls', are simply tiny vol au vents.

1. Set the oven at 425°F.

2. Remove pastry from refrigerator and roll out into a rectangle $\frac{3}{4}$ inch thick.

3. With a cookie cutter approximately 3 inches in diameter, stamp out bases and transfer to a dampened cookie sheet.

4. With a 2 inch diameter cookie cutter, cut each round until almost through.

5. Brush with beaten egg and bake in the pre-set oven for 15–20 minutes, or until golden brown and cooked.

6. When cooked and cooled, remove top neatly with a teaspoon, leaving a cavity to be filled.

1. Dip cookie cutters in boiling water each time you use them.

2. Using the larger cookie cutters, cut out circles and place them on a dampened cookie sheet.

Kidney and Mushroom Filling

4 lambs' kidneys
2 cups button mushrooms
2 tbsp butter
¼ cup flour
1–2 tbsp dry sherry
⅔ cup stock
about ½ cup heavy cream
salt and pepper

1. Skin and blanch the kidneys and leave in a pan of hot water for 15 minutes. Wash and finely slice the mushrooms.

2. Melt butter in a pan over a gentle heat, remove kidneys from the pan and dry with absorbent paper. Slice finely. Sauté in the butter for 2–3 minutes, then add flour and stir until blended. Add sherry, and, gradually, the stock, stirring all the time. Finally add the mushrooms and stir in the cream.

3. Taste for seasoning and continue to simmer gently for 3–4 minutes over a gentle heat. Do not allow kidneys to overcook.

4. Fill vol au vent cases with mixture, replace tops and heat through in the oven for a few minutes. Serve hot.

Vol au Vents with Kidney and Mushroom Filling.

3. Using the smaller cutters, press very nearly through the pastry circles.

4. When the vol au vents are cooked, the lids will have shrunk and be easy to lift off.

Chicken and Mushroom Filling

½ cup cooked chicken
½ cup button mushrooms
1 tbsp flour
1 tbsp butter
⅜ cup dry white wine
⅛–¼ cup milk
⅜ cup light cream
salt and pepper

For garnish
1 cooked carrot
1 tbsp cooked peas
1 tbsp cooked green beans
1 or 2 stuffed green olives
aspic

1. Chop the chicken meat, finely dice mushrooms and shred the carrot. Dice the green beans, slice the olives and prepare the aspic.

2. Melt the butter in a pan and add the flour when melted. Stir to a straw colored roux (this should take about a minute), then add the wine. Blend well, stirring vigorously, then add milk and bring to the boil. Using a balloon whisk, whisk up the sauce until it is smooth, then add cream and continue whisking. Add the mushrooms, cook for a few minutes before adding chicken and seasoning to taste.

3. Allow to cool before filling the cases and garnish each one with a sprinkling of diced vegetables, topped with a slice of stuffed olive. The topping can be kept in place with a little aspic. Otherwise replace the lid as usual and omit the garnish.

Seafood Filling

1 cup shrimps
1 tbsp flour
1 tbsp butter
⅜ cup dry white wine
⅛–¼ cup milk
¼ cup light cream
salt and pepper

For garnish
parsley
watercress

1. Make the white sauce as for the Chicken and Mushroom Filling.

2. Add the shrimps and season to taste.

3. Allow to cool before filling the cases and garnish.

Appetizers

Peperoni Croûtes

½ lb onions
1 lb red and green sweet peppers
scant ½ cup cooking oil
1 level tsp ginger
1 lb tomatoes
¾ cup light brown sugar
⅔ cup raisins or seedless raisins
1 tsp mixed spice
1 clove garlic crushed with a little salt
1¼ cups wine vinegar
1 tsp dried tarragon
bread croûtes

1. Peel and finely chop onions. Remove core and seeds from peppers, and dice.

2. Heat oil in a skillet and add the peppers and onions. Fry gently over a low heat, until onions are transparent. Place lid on skillet and continue to cook for a further 7–8 minutes.

3. Add the rest of the ingredients, stir gently until mixed, and cook for a further 10 minutes until thoroughly cooked and mushy. Remove the lid and cook for a further 10 minutes.

4. Prepare the croûtes. Cut rounds from 3 or 4 slices of bread with a 3 inch diameter plain cutter. Fry rounds in a little oil or butter until golden brown and crisp and drain on absorbent paper.

5. Pile mixture on top of croûtes and serve hot or chilled.

Peperoni Croûtes.

PEELING PIMIENTOS

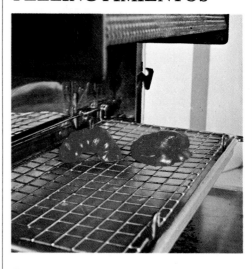

1. Halve the pimientos and remove pith and seeds. Place under a very hot broiler.

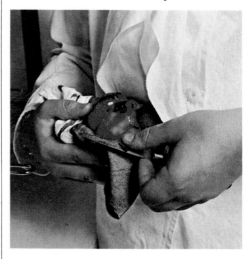

2. When the skin has blackened and cracked you can peel it away.

Austrian Liptauer Cheese

4 oz cream cheese
½ cup sweet unsalted butter
1 tsp paprika
caraway seeds
5 capers
1 anchovy fillet
milk
1 tsp Dijon mustard
salt and pepper

1. Put the butter in a warm place to cream; chop the caraway seeds; drain and chop the capers finely; soak the anchovy fillet in a little milk to remove excess saltiness, then chop.

2. Beat the warmed butter until light and fluffy, then beat in the cream cheese slowly. When the mixture is smooth, add the paprika, caraway seeds, capers, chopped anchovy fillet and mustard. Continue beating. Taste for seasoning and adjust, if necessary.

3. Shape into a rectangle or square and chill before serving on triangles of brown toast, dark rye bread, pumpernickel or pretzel biscuits.

Variations:
This is an Austrian version of the classic Hungarian recipe. Chopped chives, or garlic or finely chopped onion are alternatives to add as variations. Liptauer cheese is good spread quickly over warmed water biscuits, if rye bread etc. is not available.

Salmon Asparagus Rolls

¼ lb smoked salmon cut into slices
1 small can asparagus tips, or fresh asparagus if available

For garnish
thick mayonnaise
lemon wedges

1. Drain asparagus tips and pat dry on absorbent paper, or cook and drain if fresh. Roll each tip in a slice of smoked salmon and place the rolls on a serving dish.

2. Pipe rosettes of mayonnaise on each roll to garnish. Surround with lemon wedges.

Bouchées à la Grecque.

Bouchées à la Grecque

1 cup large dry beans
1 onion
2 cloves garlic
powdered coriander
8 slices white bread from sandwich loaf
1 tsp baking soda
salt and pepper
parsley to garnish

1. Soak beans overnight. Remove crusts from slices of bread and soak bread for a few minutes. Peel onion and garlic.

2. Pass soaked beans through a mincer or mouli sieve, with the onion and garlic. Pound with a pestle in a mortar with the soaked bread, or use a liquidizer, to achieve a smooth paste.

3. Pound in, or add, a dash of powdered coriander and baking soda, season and chill mixture for 2 hours.

4. Roll into small balls and deep fry until golden and crisp. Drain on absorbent paper and serve immediately on cocktail picks. Sprinkle with chopped parsley if wished.

Tomato Sauce with Herbs

1 lb ripe tomatoes
1 clove garlic
1 crushed peppercorn
1 oz chives
2 sprigs thyme
2 sprigs tarragon
1 level tsp salt
4 tbsp cold water
2 tbsp oil

1. Chop the tomatoes and crush the garlic clove. Place all ingredients with the exception of the oil in a skillet over a low heat. After a few minutes, raise to a simmer.

2. When tender, rub the mixture through a sieve before returning it to the pan. Add the oil and simmer for about 3 minutes. Chill before serving.

Appetizers

Sardine Salad

3 cans sardines in oil
1–2 tsp wine vinegar
pepper
6 hard cooked eggs
few sprigs of fresh parsley
3 lemons
French dressing made with 1¼ cups oil

1. Drain 6 sardines, remove the tails and bones and mash the sardines with the wine vinegar and pepper to taste. Arrange near the center of an oval serving dish.

2. Drain the remaining sardines and arrange in a fan shape on the dish. Separate the whites and yolks of the eggs and chop finely, keeping eggs and whites separate.

3. Arrange the whites and yolks in separate sections on the dish around the sardines. Put a border of parsley heads along the outside edge of the whole sardines. Cut the lemons into decorative slices, and use to garnish the dish, adding thin strips of lemon peel around the edge.

4. Serve French dressing separately.

Sardine Salad.

Mayonnaise

Basic Recipe

1 egg yolk
¼ tsp dry mustard
salt and pepper
⅔ cup olive or corn oil
1 tbsp lemon juice or wine vinegar

It is essential to keep mixing bowl and utensils cool when making mayonnaise, and all ingredients should be at room temperature. Be careful to add the oil very slowly at first, or the mayonnaise will curdle.

1. Put the egg yolk, mustard and salt and pepper to taste in a bowl. Beat with a wooden spoon, electric or rotary beater until well mixed. Add the oil a drop at a time, beating well all the time until the mayonnaise begins to thicken.

2. Beat in the oil faster when the mayonnaise thickens, then add the lemon juice or wine vinegar. Beat until well mixed and taste for seasoning. Cover and store in a cool place until required.

Note: if mayonnaise curdles, start again with a fresh egg yolk. Beat the curdled mayonnaise into the egg yolk a drop at a time until the mixture becomes thick and smooth, then add the remaining oil.

Lemon Mayonnaise

Basic Recipe

2 egg yolks
¼ tsp prepared French mustard
salt
¼ tsp finely ground black peppercorns
1¼ cups olive or corn oil
juice of 1 lemon

To finish
1 lemon
1 tbsp light cream

Orange juice and segments can be substituted for the lemon in this recipe. See the basic Mayonnaise for rules on making and how to rescue mayonnaise that has curdled.

1. Put the egg yolks, mustard, salt and pepper in a bowl. Beat with a wooden spoon, electric or rotary beater until well mixed. Add the oil a drop at a time, beating well all the time until the mayonnaise begins to thicken.

2. When half the oil is incorporated, beat in half the lemon juice. Continue adding the oil in a steady stream, then beat in the remaining lemon juice. Taste for seasoning, then cover and store in a cool place until required.

3. Cut the peel, pith and skin away from the lemon by cutting from the top and working in a spiral down to the bottom, using a sawing motion. Cut the lemon into segments, then chop into small pieces. Discard all seeds, pith and central core.

4. Stir lemon pieces into the mayonnaise with the cream just before serving.

MAKING MELBA TOAST

1. Cut off the crusts of thin slices of bread and lightly toast. Using a sharp knife, cut through the middle to make 2 slices.

2. Lightly toast the untoasted sides and serve the hot toast immediately.

French Dressing

½ tsp salt
¼ tsp finely ground black pepper
¼ tsp prepared French mustard
⅔ cup olive or corn oil
4 tbsp wine vinegar

1. Put the salt, pepper and mustard in a salad bowl with a little oil. Beat with a wooden spoon or fork until thick. Add the remaining oil gradually, beating it in alternately with the wine vinegar.

2. Taste for seasoning and add more salt if too oily. Beat again to combine before tossing salad vegetables.

3. The dressing can also be made quickly by putting all ingredients in a screw top jar and shaking vigorously until well mixed. It can be stored in a jar for a few months.

Variation:
For a classic vinaigrette add 2 tsp finely chopped herbs, shallot or onion to the dressing just before serving.

Roquefort Dressing

3 tbsp vinegar
10 tbsp olive oil
salt
black pepper
French mustard
sugar
3 oz Roquefort cheese
lemon juice

1. Pour the vinegar in a small bowl and add the oil, a spoonful at a time, beating with a fork. Add the salt, pepper, mustard and sugar to taste. Beat well.

2. Put the cheese in another bowl and mash to a paste with a fork. Add the oil and vinegar dressing and beat well until blended. Flavor with a little lemon juice and check seasoning.

Melba Toast.

Appetizers

Cheese Soufflés in Pastry

¼ cup butter or margarine
puff pastry made from 1½ cups flour
1 egg
¼ cup plus 1 tbsp flour
1¼ cups hot milk
⅜ cup grated Parmesan cheese
powdered nutmeg
salt and pepper
5 egg whites
powdered mace

1. Set the oven at 425°F.

2. Soften a quarter of the butter or margarine and use to brush the insides of 4 individual soufflé dishes.

3. Roll out the pastry on a floured board and cut into about 4 squares large enough to fit inside the 4 inch diameter individual soufflé dishes. Put the squares in the dishes, pressing them down in the middle so that the 4 corners protrude above the rim of each dish. Beat the whole egg and use to brush the pastry. Stand the soufflé dishes on a cookie sheet and set aside.

4. Melt the remaining butter or margarine in a large pan. Stir in the flour with a wooden spoon and cook gently for 1–2 minutes until the mixture forms a soft ball, stirring constantly.

5. Remove the pan from the heat and gradually stir in the hot milk, beating vigorously all the time to obtain a smooth sauce. When all the milk is incorporated, return the pan to the heat and bring to the boil, stirring constantly.

6. Lower the heat and add a dash of the seasonings. Simmer gently until the sauce thickens, stirring constantly. Remove the pan from the heat and stir in the cheese.

7. Whip the egg whites until stiff. Fold into the sauce until evenly distributed. Divide soufflé mixture between prepared dishes. Bake in pre-set oven on shelf above center for 10–15 minutes until well risen and golden brown. Serve immediately

Caviare Stuffed Tomatoes

12 small tomatoes
1¼ cups heavy cream
1 small jar or can caviare or lumpfish roe
2 tsp lemon juice
browned almonds to garnish
salt
freshly ground black pepper

1. Place the tomatoes in very hot water for a few moments to split the skin and make it easy to remove. Peel the tomatoes and whip cream thoroughly.

2. Slice the tops off the tomatoes from the flower end. Remove and discard seeds, and turn each tomato upside down to drain.

3. Drain and stir the caviare or lumpfish roe into the whipped cream and then, very carefully, add the lemon juice to flavor the cream. Season to taste with salt and black pepper.

4. Place tomatoes upright on a serving dish and, with a pastry bag and plain pipe – or use a small teaspoon – fill each tomato case. Replace tops and garnish with flaked browned almonds, if liked.

Note: Lumpfish roe is often known as poor man's caviare. It is quite delicious, and much cheaper than caviare itself!

Cheese Soufflé in Pastry.

Soufflé Tomatoes.

Soufflé Tomatoes

12 large tomatoes
3 tbsp butter or margarine
¼ cup plus 1 tbsp flour
1¼ cups hot milk
¾ cup grated mature Cheddar type cheese
1 tsp anchovy flavoring
pepper
5 egg whites

To finish
1–2 tbsp chopped chives

1. Set the oven at 400°F.

2. Cut the tops off the tomatoes, scoop out all flesh, seeds and central cores and discard (or use in casseroles, soups, stock, etc). Put the tomato cases on a cookie sheet and set aside.

3. Melt the butter or margarine in a large pan. Stir in the flour with a wooden spoon and cook gently for 1–2 minutes until the mixture forms a soft ball, stirring constantly.

4. Remove pan from heat and gradually stir in the hot milk, beating vigorously all the time to obtain a smooth sauce. When all the milk is incorporated, return the pan to the heat and bring to the boil, stirring constantly.

5. Lower the heat and simmer gently. Add the grated cheese, anchovy flavoring and pepper. Stir constantly until the cheese melts and the sauce is thick and smooth. Remove the pan from the heat.

6. Whip the egg whites until stiff. Fold into the sauce until evenly distributed.

Spoon into prepared tomato cases. Bake in the pre-set oven on shelf above center for 15 minutes until well risen and golden brown. Transfer to a warmed serving dish, sprinkle with snipped chives and serve immediately.

Bean Soup.

Soups

Bean Soup

½ lb dried large white beans
1 large onion
1 clove garlic
¼ lb firm white cabbage
large can tomatoes
¼ cup pork or goose drippings
7½ cups well flavored stock
½ tsp dried oregano
salt and pepper

To finish
4 tbsp freshly chopped parsley

1. Put the beans in a bowl, cover with cold water and leave to soak overnight.

2. The next day, peel the onion and slice into fine rings. Peel and crush the garlic. Chop the cabbage finely. Blend the canned tomatoes in a liquidizer or strain through a sieve.

3. Melt the dripping in a large pan. Add the onion, garlic and cabbage. Cover pan with a lid and cook gently for 5 minutes, shaking the pan occasionally.

4. Drain the beans and add to the pan with the tomatoes, stock, oregano and salt and pepper to taste. Stir well to mix.

5. Bring to the boil, stirring constantly. Lower the heat and cover the pan with a lid. Simmer very gently for 1½–2 hours until the beans are tender, stirring in a little more stock or water if level becomes low during cooking.

6. Remove the soup from the heat. Skim off any fat on the surface of soup. Taste for seasoning. Pour into warmed soup bowls, sprinkle each with 1 tbsp parsley and serve hot.

Soups

Cream of Cauliflower Soup

1 cauliflower
1 small onion
2 large potatoes
¼ cup butter or margarine
2½ cups milk
3 cups well flavored chicken stock
¼ tsp powdered mace
salt and pepper
⅔ cup light cream

To serve
toasted croûtons

1. Divide cauliflower into flowerets, then chop roughly. Peel the onion and chop finely. Peel the potatoes and cut into small dice.

2. Melt the butter or margarine in a large pan. Add the prepared vegetables. Cover pan with a lid and cook gently for 5 minutes, shaking the pan occasionally.

3. Stir in the milk gradually, then add the stock, mace, salt and pepper to taste. Bring to the boil, then lower the heat and cover the pan with a lid. Simmer gently for 25–30 minutes until the cauliflower and potatoes are tender, stirring occasionally.

4. Remove pan from the heat and leave to cool slightly. Blend until smooth in a liquidizer or strain through a sieve.

5. Return soup to rinsed pan and stir in the cream. Reheat gently, but do not allow to boil. Remove pan from the heat and taste for seasoning. Pour into warmed soup bowls and serve hot with toasted croûtons.

Watercress and Potato Soup

1 small onion
2 bunches watercress
¾ lb potatoes
¼ cup butter or margarine
2½ cups milk
2½ cups well flavored chicken stock
salt and pepper

To serve
salted almonds

1. Peel the onion and chop finely. Chop the watercress finely, reserving a few whole leaves for the garnish. Peel the potatoes and cut into dice.

2. Melt the butter or margarine in a pan. Add the onion and watercress. Cover the pan with a lid and cook gently for 5 minutes, shaking the pan occasionally.

3. Stir in the milk, stock and salt and pepper to taste, then add the potatoes. Bring to the boil, stirring constantly. Lower the heat and cover pan with lid. Simmer gently for about 20 minutes, or until the potatoes are tender, stirring occasionally.

4. Remove the pan from the heat and leave to cool slightly. Blend soup until smooth in a liquidizer or strain through a sieve.

5. Return the soup to the rinsed pan and reheat gently. Taste for seasoning and add more milk if the soup is too thick. Pour into warmed soup bowls and garnish with reserved watercress leaves. Serve hot, with a platter of salted almonds served separately, if liked.

Country Beef and Vegetable Soup

1 lb stewing beef
2 tbsp flour
salt and pepper
1 large onion
2 large carrots
4 stalks celery
2 leeks
¼ cup beef drippings or lard
10 cups water
1 bouquet garni
2 large potatoes

Make this soup the day before it is required, as it must be chilled overnight in order to take off the fat.

1. Cut the stewing beef into very thin strips, then coat in the flour seasoned with salt and pepper. Peel the onion and carrots and chop finely with the celery and leeks.

2. Melt the drippings or lard in a large pan. Add the beef and fry briskly until browned on all sides, stirring occasionally. Remove from the pan with a slotted spoon and set aside.

3. Add the prepared vegetables to the pan and cover with a lid. Simmer gently for 5 minutes, shaking the pan occasionally.

4. Return beef to pan. Stir in the water and bring to the boil. Lower the heat, add the bouquet garni and cover the pan with a lid. Simmer very gently for about 2 hours or until the beef is tender. Skim and stir occasionally during cooking and top up with more water if the level becomes rather low.

5. Peel the potatoes and cut into dice. Add to the pan and cook for a further 20 minutes or until tender.

6. Remove pan from the heat. Discard the bouquet garni and taste soup for seasoning. Leave until cold, then chill in the refrigerator overnight.

7. The next day, remove the fat that has risen to the surface of soup. Reheat soup until bubbling, then taste for seasoning. Pour into warmed soup bowls and serve hot with French bread.

Cream of Artichoke Soup

1 lb Jerusalem artichokes
juice of 1 lemon
salt
1 clove garlic
2 tbsp butter or margarine
¼ cup flour
2½ cups hot milk
2½ cups well flavored chicken stock
⅛ tsp powdered mace
pepper
⅜ cup grated Parmesan cheese

1. Peel the artichokes and sprinkle immediately with lemon juice to prevent discoloration. Cut into dice and boil in salted water for about 30 minutes or until tender.

2. Meanwhile, peel and crush the garlic. Melt the butter or margarine in a pan. Add the garlic and fry gently for 1–2 minutes.

3. Stir in the flour and cook gently for a further 1–2 minutes, stirring constantly.

4. Remove pan from the heat and gradually stir in the hot milk, beating vigorously after each addition.

5. When all the milk is incorporated, re-

Cream of Artichoke Soup

turn pan to the heat. Stir in the stock, mace and salt and pepper to taste.

6. Bring to the boil, stirring constantly, then lower the heat and simmer for a few minutes.

7. Drain the artichokes when tender and

stir into the sauce.

8. Remove pan from the heat and leave to cool slightly. Blend soup until smooth in a liquidizer or strain through a sieve.

9. Return the soup to the rinsed out pan. Stir in $\frac{1}{8}$ cup grated Parmesan cheese and

reheat soup without boiling, stirring occasionally. Taste for seasoning and add more milk if the soup is too thick.

10. Pour into warmed soup bowls and serve hot with remaining Parmesan served separately.

Soups

Crab Soup

5 oz packet frozen crabmeat
¼ cup butter or margarine
¼ cup flour
2½ cups fish stock
1¼ cups dry white wine or apple cider
cayenne pepper
salt
1¼ cups creamy milk or light cream

1. Unwrap the frozen crab and leave to thaw.

2. Melt the butter or margarine in a large pan. Stir in the flour and cook gently for 1–2 minutes, stirring constantly.

3. Remove the pan from the heat and gradually stir in the fish stock. Stir in the wine or apple cider with cayenne pepper and salt to taste.

4. Bring to the boil, stirring constantly, then lower the heat and simmer gently until the soup thickens. Beat in the thawed crab until evenly distributed. Stir in the milk or cream and heat through. (Do not allow to boil if using cream.)

5. Remove pan from the heat and taste soup for seasoning. Pour into warmed soup bowls and serve with a sprinkling of cayenne pepper on each serving.

Croûtons

Basic Recipe

Cut some slices from a stale white loaf and chop them into dice. Then shallow fry them in equal quantities of butter and olive oil until golden brown. Leave to drain on absorbent paper.

Croûtes (a large version of croûtons): dip the stale bread pieces in a mixture of beaten egg and milk before frying as above.

Crab Soup.

Minestrone

½ cup dried fava or navy beans
1 large onion
few stalks celery
1 clove garlic
2 carrots
2 zucchini
2 potatoes
2 tbsp olive or vegetable oil
1 large can tomatoes
5 cups chicken stock
1 bouquet garni
salt and pepper
¼ lb frozen green beans
¼ lb frozen peas

To serve
grated Parmesan cheese
bread sticks
small croûtons

1. Put the beans in a bowl and cover with cold water. Leave to soak overnight.

2. The next day, peel the onions and chop finely. Chop the celery. Peel and crush the garlic. Peel and grate the carrots. Slice the zucchini finely. Peel the potatoes and cut into dice. Drain the beans.

3. Heat the oil in a large pan. Add the onion, celery and garlic, and fry gently for about 5 minutes until lightly colored. Add the remaining prepared vegetables, the beans, canned tomatoes and stock. Stir well and bring to the boil.

4. Lower the heat, add the bouquet garni and salt and pepper to taste. Cover pan with a lid and simmer gently for 1½–2 hours until the beans are tender and all the other vegetables are soft and broken down.

5. Discard bouquet garni. Add the frozen beans and peas and cook for a further 5 minutes or until tender.

6. Taste soup for seasoning. Pour into warmed soup bowls and serve hot with grated Parmesan cheese, potato sticks and croûtons served separately.

Egg and Brandy Soup

1½ lb large mild onions
⅓ lb ripe tomatoes
3 tbsp butter or margarine
2 tbsp olive or corn oil
2 tbsp flour
5 cups well flavored beef stock
2½ cups full bodied red wine
salt and pepper
2 egg yolks
6 tbsp brandy

To serve
grated Parmesan cheese

1. Peel the onions and slice very thinly. Skin the tomatoes and chop roughly.

2. Heat the butter or margarine and oil in a large pan. Add the onions and tomatoes and cover pan with a lid. Cook gently for 5 minutes, shaking the pan occasionally.

3. Stir in the flour and cook for a further 2 minutes, stirring constantly. Stir in the red wine gradually, then add the stock. Season to taste with salt and pepper.

4. Bring to the boil, then lower the heat and cover the pan with a lid. Simmer gently for 20–25 minutes or until the onions are soft and broken down.

5. Remove the pan from the heat and leave to cool slightly. Blend until smooth in a liquidizer or strain through a sieve.

6. Return the soup to the rinsed pan and reheat gently. Meanwhile, put the egg yolks and brandy in a bowl or a serving tureen, and whisk together. Pour a little of the hot soup over the egg and brandy mixture. Whisk to combine, then stir gradually into the soup.

7. Taste soup for seasoning. Serve in warmed soup bowls, with grated Parmesan cheese served separately.

1. Fry the onions gently in oil and butter until very soft.

2. Add the tomatoes and cook until soft.

6. Pour into a large pan.

7. Add the remaining stock and stir until well blended.

8. Whip the eggs and brandy together in the serving tureen. Gradually pour in the soup, still whipping.

3. Stir in the flour and seasoning

4. Increase the heat, add the wine and stir until it is absorbed.

5. Add some stock and stir well.

Egg and Brandy Soup.

Soups

Stock

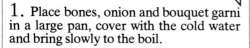

2¼ lb raw beef bones
1 onion studded with 2 cloves
bouquet garni
10–12 cups cold water

1. Place bones, onion and bouquet garni in a large pan, cover with the cold water and bring slowly to the boil.

2. Skim the surface, refresh with a cup of cold water and return to the boil. Leave to simmer gently for about 2 hours.

3. For a stronger stock, continue to simmer with the pan half covered to allow the liquid to reduce. The more it reduces the stronger the stock will be.

4. When the stock has cooled, skim the fat off the surface before using.

Stockpot Soup with Noodles

1 large onion
2 stalks celery
¾ lb carrots
2 tbsp butter or margarine
6¼ cups well flavored beef stock
salt and pepper
2 oz small noodles

1. Peel the onion and chop finely. Chop the celery. Peel and grate the carrots.

2. Melt the butter or margarine in a large pan. Add the onion and celery and fry gently for about 5 minutes until lightly colored. Add the carrots. Cover the pan with a lid and cook gently for a further 5 minutes, shaking the pan occasionally.

3. Stir in the stock and season to taste with salt and pepper. Bring to the boil, stirring occasionally. Lower the heat and cover the pan with a lid. Simmer for about 20–30 minutes or until the carrots are tender.

4. Remove the pan from the heat and leave to cool slightly. Blend until fairly smooth in a liquidizer or strain through a sieve. If the soup is too thick, add a little stock or water.

5. Return soup to rinsed pan, add noodles and simmer until tender. Taste for seasoning. Pour into warmed soup bowls and serve hot with pretzels or crusty French bread.

Note: It is essential to use homemade stock for this soup, or it will lack flavor and texture.

Sweetcorn Soup

1 onion
2 tbsp butter or margarine
1 tbsp flour
2 cups hot milk
2 cups well flavored chicken stock
1 large can creamy style sweetcorn
½ tsp celery salt
pepper
¼ cup light cream

1. Peel the onion and chop finely. Melt the butter or margarine in a pan. Add the onion and fry gently for about 5 minutes until lightly colored.

2. Stir in the flour and cook gently for 1–2 minutes, stirring constantly. Remove the pan from the heat and gradually stir in the hot milk, beating vigorously after each addition.

3. When all the milk is incorporated, return pan to the heat. Stir in the remaining ingredients, except the cream. Bring to the boil, stirring constantly.

4. Lower the heat, stir in the cream and heat through. Taste for seasoning. Pour into warmed soup bowls and serve hot with bread sticks or crusty French bread and butter.

Vichyssoise

1½ lb leeks
1½ lb potatoes
¼ cup butter or margarine
2½ cups well flavored clear chicken stock
2½ cups milk
salt and white pepper

To finish
⅜ cup light cream
chopped chives

1. Slice the leeks finely. Peel the potatoes and cut into small dice.

2. Melt the butter or margarine in a large pan. Add the prepared vegetables. Cover pan with a lid and cook gently for 5 minutes, shaking the pan occasionally.

3. Stir in the stock, milk and salt and pepper to taste. Bring to the boil. Lower the heat and cover the pan with a lid. Simmer gently for 20–25 minutes until the vegetables are tender, stirring occasionally.

4. Remove the pan from the heat and leave to cool slightly. Blend the soup until very smooth in a liquidizer or strain through a sieve.

5. Stir the cream into the soup and chill in the refrigerator for at least 3 hours. Pour into chilled soup bowls and sprinkle with chopped chives just before serving.

French Countrystyle Soup

1½ cups dried fava or navy beans
4 carrots
2 large onions
1 small head of celery
6 oz firm white cabbage
1 lb bacon
bouquet garni
¼–½ tsp powdered turmeric
salt and pepper

1. Put the beans in a bowl, cover with cold water and leave to soak overnight.

2. The next day, peel the carrots and onions and chop very finely with the celery and cabbage.

3. Cut the bacon into very small dice and fry briskly over high heat until crisp and browned on all sides. Remove from the pan with a slotted spoon.

4. Set the oven at 300°F. Drain the beans and put in a large casserole. Add the prepared vegetables fried bacon, bouquet garni, and turmeric and salt and pepper.

5. Cover with cold water and stir well to mix. Cover with a lid and cook in pre-set oven for 4–5 hours until all the ingredients are soft and broken down and the soup is very thick.

6. Discard the bouquet garni. Taste for seasoning. Serve hot with hunks of crusty French bread.

French Countrystyle Soup.

Soups

Spinach Soup

1 lb fresh spinach leaves
½ cup butter or margarine
salt
2½ cups well flavored chicken stock
½ tsp powdered nutmeg
pepper
4 egg yolks
⅔ cup heavy cream

To finish
4 tbsp light cream

1. Put the spinach in a large pan with three quarters of the butter or margarine and salt to taste. Cover the pan with a lid and cook gently for 8–10 minutes until the spinach is tender, stirring occasionally.

2. Remove the pan from the heat and leave to cool slightly. Blend in a liquidizer or strain through a sieve, adding a little chicken stock if the spinach is too dry to work.

3. Heat spinach, stock, nutmeg and pepper to taste in the top of a double boiler or in a large heatproof bowl standing over a pan of gently bubbling water. Stir to combine spinach and stock.

4. Whisk together the egg yolks and cream in a separate bowl. Pour in a little of the hot spinach mixture and stir well to combine. Stir this mixture slowly into the spinach and stock. Add the remaining butter or margarine and heat through until the soup thickens, stirring constantly with a wooden spoon.

5. Taste for seasoning. Pour into warmed soup bowls, swirl each serving with 1 tbsp cream and serve immediately.

Pea and Ham Soup

½ lb dried split peas
5 cups well flavored ham stock
few stalks celery
few sprigs parsley
approx ½ cup diced cooked ham
pepper
a little milk

To garnish
fried bread croûtons

1. Put the split peas in a bowl, cover with cold water and leave to soak overnight.

2. The next day, chop the celery and parsley roughly. Drain the split peas.

3. Put all the ingredients in a large pan and bring to the boil. Lower the heat, cover the pan with a lid and simmer gently for 1½–2 hours, or until the peas are tender, stirring occasionally.

4. Remove the pan from the heat and leave to cool slightly. Blend soup until fairly smooth in a liquidizer or strain through a sieve.

5. Return the soup to the rinsed pan and add enough milk to make a pouring consistency. Reheat gently, then taste for seasoning. Pour into warmed soup bowls and serve hot with fried bread croûtons.

Spinach Soup.

Pot au Feu

2 lb beef soup bone or beef shank
water
1 tsp salt
1 small head of celery
1 lb carrots
½ lb swede or turnip
2 large onions
few whole cloves
6 black peppercorns
bouquet garni

1. Slice the beef and chop the bones. Remove excess fat and discard. Put beef and bones in a large pan, cover with 12½ cups water and add the salt. Bring slowly to the boil, then lower the heat. Simmer gently for 1 hour, skimming regularly to remove all scum that comes to the surface.

2. Meanwhile, chop the celery roughly. Peel the carrots and chop if large, or leave whole if small. Peel the swede or turnip and cut into dice. Peel the onions and chop one finely. Press cloves into remaining whole onion. Crush the peppercorns.

3. Add the prepared vegetables to the pan with the crushed peppercorns and bouquet garni. Bring to the boil again, then lower the heat and cover the pan with a lid. Simmer very gently for a further hour or until all ingredients are tender. Skim and stir occasionally during cooking.

4. Remove the pan from the heat and taste soup for seasoning. Discard the clove studded onion. Leave until cold, then chill in the refrigerator overnight.

5. The next day, remove the fat that has risen to the surface of soup. Reheat the soup, then strain through a fine sieve. Return the broth to the rinsed pan, taste for seasoning and reheat.

6. Select pieces of meat and vegetables from the sieve. Put a few pieces in the bottom of each individual warmed soup bowl and pour over the hot broth. Put any remaining meat and vegetables in a warmed serving bowl. Serve crusty French bread separately.

Pot au Feu.

Soups

French Onion Soup.

French Onion Soup

1½ lb large mild onions
1–2 cloves garlic
3 tbsp butter or margarine
2 tbsp olive or corn oil
1 heaped tbsp flour
5 cups well flavored beef stock
1¼ cups dry white wine
salt and pepper

To finish
4 slices French bread
butter or margarine for spreading
4 slices Gruyère or Emmenthal cheese

1. Peel the onions and slice very thinly. Peel and crush the garlic.

2. Heat the butter or margarine and oil in a large pan. Add the onions and garlic and fry very gently for 10–15 minutes until golden, stirring occasionally.

3. Stir in the flour and cook for a further 1–2 minutes, stirring constantly.

4. Stir in the stock gradually, then add the white wine. Season to taste with salt and pepper.

5. Bring to the boil, then lower the heat and cover the pan with a lid. Simmer gently for 20–25 minutes or until the onions are soft and broken down.

6. During the last 10 minutes of cooking time, spread the French bread with butter or margarine and top each slice with a slice of cheese. Put under a hot broiler until the cheese bubbles and begins to brown.

7. Remove the soup from the heat. Taste for seasoning. Pour into warmed soup bowls, float a slice of toasted cheese in each bowl and serve immediately

Potage Bonne Femme

½ lb carrots
½ lb leeks
2 large potatoes
¼ cup butter or margarine
5 cups well flavored chicken stock
salt and pepper
a little milk

1. Peel and grate the carrots. Slice the leeks finely. Peel the potatoes and cut into small dice.

2. Melt the butter or margarine in a large pan. Add the prepared vegetables. Cover the pan with a lid and cook gently for 5 minutes, shaking the pan occasionally.

3. Stir in the stock and add salt and pepper to taste. Bring to the boil. Lower the heat and cover the pan with a lid. Simmer gently for 20–30 minutes until the vegetables are tender, stirring occasionally.

4. Remove the pan from the heat and leave to cool slightly.

5. Blend soup until smooth in a liquidizer or strain through a sieve.

6. Return the soup to the rinsed pan. Add enough milk to make a pouring consistency. Reheat gently, then taste for seasoning. Pour into warmed soup bowls and serve hot with granary bread.

Potage Bonne Femme.

Red Mullet with Tomatoes.

Fish and shellfish

Red Mullet with Tomatoes

4 small red mullet
6 large ripe tomatoes
1 tsp dried thyme
2 tsp chopped parsley
coriander seeds
1 small bayleaf
saffron
salt and pepper
3 tbsp red wine
3 tbsp olive oil

For garnish
juice of 1 small lemon
anchovies
freshly chopped tarragon

1. Set the oven at 400°F.

2. Scald and skin the tomatoes. Chop them up finely and remove the seeds. Tip into a bowl and mix in the thyme, parsley, a few coriander seeds, bayleaf, a pinch of saffron and seasoning.

3. Pour the olive oil into an ovenproof dish. Arrange the mullet in it, add the wine and then tomato mixture. Cover and bake in the center of the pre-set oven for about 15 minutes.

4. Lift out the fish, arrange on a heated dish and pour the tomato pulp around them. Sprinkle over the lemon juice. Garnish if liked with anchovies and chopped tarragon.

FILLETING A FLOUNDER OR A SOLE

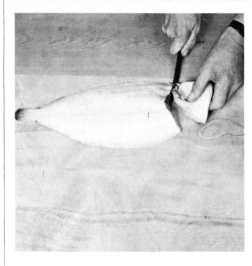

1. Using a sharp knife, remove the head of the fish in one clean movement.

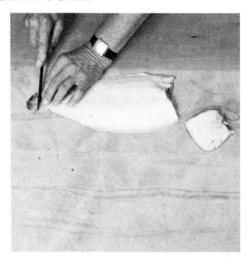

2. Remove the tail tip at the point only halfway down the fish's tail.

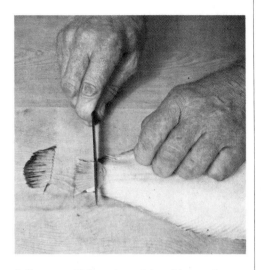

3. Scrape off the edge of the skin on the rest of the tail area.

4. Having loosened the tail skin, ease it away with one hand underneath and the other hand pulling the skin free.

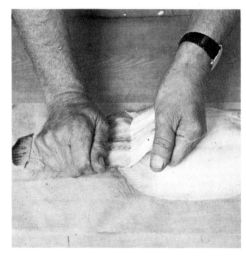

5. When you can get a grip on the tail, hold it firmly and pull the skin steadily away with the other hand.

6. Run the tip of the knife down the fish's spine from head to tail.

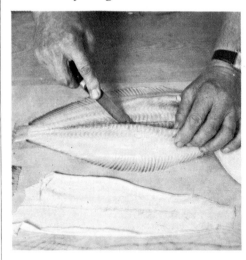

7. Insert the knife and hold it parallel to the fish, flat against the bone. Slowly pare the fillet away.

8. Slip the knife under the free part of the fillet. Cut the remainder away from the fin bones.

9. Having removed one fillet, repeat the process until the whole fish is filleted.

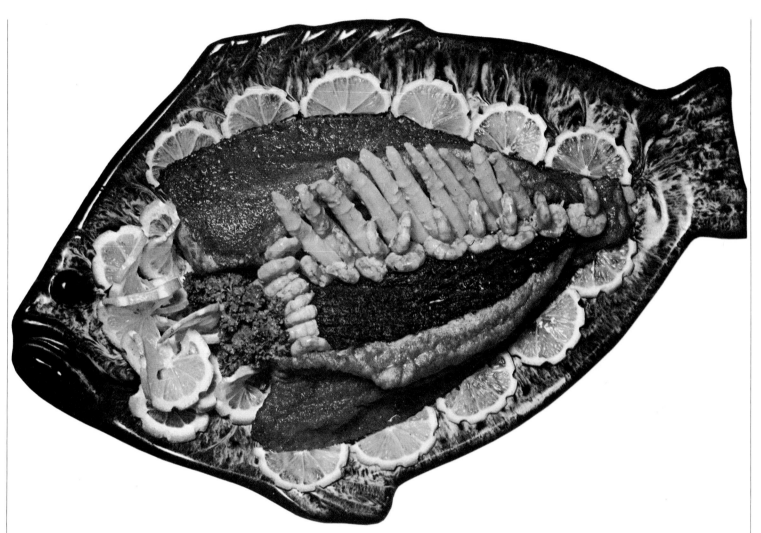

Fried Flounder with Special Garnish.

Fried Flounder with Special Garnish

1 large flounder weighing about 1 lb
seasoned flour
1 beaten egg
fine breadcrumbs
oil for deep frying

For garnish
1 small packet frozen spinach
¼ lb shrimps
1 can asparagus tips
1 lemon
sprigs of parsley

1. First prepare the ingredients for the garnish. Warm the chopped spinach in a pan. Shell the shrimps and drain the asparagus tips. Slice the lemon up thinly.

2. Take a small, sharp knife and make an incision on one side of the fish down each side of the backbone. Then, using the knife, ease the flesh away from the back bone on each side to form 2 flaps. Slices of raw potato can be used to prevent these flaps sealing up again during cooking.

3. Dip the fish in a little flour, then in the beaten egg and breadcrumbs. Place carefully in the deep fryer and fry until golden brown. Drain on absorbent paper and remove potato slices.

4. Arrange the fish on a warmed serving dish. Tip the warmed spinach down one side with the flap turned back, and the asparagus tips along the other side with the shrimps down the middle. Garnish the dish with the thinly sliced lemon and sprigs of parsley before serving.

Fish and shellfish

Sole and Shrimp Tartlets

*savory shortcrust pastry made from 4 cups
 of flour*
1 large fillet of sole or flounder
4 oz shrimps
1 egg
1 egg yolk
4 tbsp light cream
⅔ cup milk
⅛ cup freshly grated Parmesan cheese
salt and pepper
12 thin slices Emmentaler cheese

1. Set the oven at 400°F.

2. Roll out the pastry quite thinly and
line into 12 tartlet shells.

3. Remove any skin from the sole, and
shell the shrimps. Cut the sole into narrow
strips and arrange in the bottom of the
shells with the shrimps on top.

4. Tip the eggs, cream, milk, Parmesan
cheese and seasoning into a bowl together
and beat with a hand whisk. Divide the
mixture between the tartlets and top each
one with a slice of Emmentaler.

5. Bake in the pre-set oven on the shelf
above center for 5 minutes. Then turn the
oven down to 300°F and continue to bake
for about 20 minutes.

Sole Paprika

8 fillets of sole or flounder
1 small onion or shallot
1 tbsp butter
1 tbsp olive oil
1 tsp paprika
2 tomatoes
1 cup fish stock
¼ cup dry white wine
⅔ cup light cream
salt and pepper

To finish
lemon juice
salt and pepper
1 tbsp butter
crescents of puff pastry

1. Peel and chop the onion into small
dice. Heat the butter and oil in a pan and
cook the onion until soft and transparent
taking care not to let it brown. Sprinkle in
the paprika.

2. Scald and skin the tomatoes, roughly
chop and add to the pan. Allow the mixture to simmer for a while. Then add the
fish stock and the wine, followed by the
cream and seasoning.

3. When the contents of the pan have
thoroughly blended, pass through a sieve
and back into the pan. Now add the folded
fish fillets and poach them in the sauce for
about 15 minutes turning once.

4. When they are cooked lift out very
carefully and arrange on a warmed serving
dish.

5. Now finish off the sauce by adding a
few drops of lemon juice, salt and pepper
to taste and the final ½ oz of butter. Reduce
the sauce a little if necessary.

6. Pour the sauce over the sole fillets and
decorate with crescents of puff pastry if
wished.

Sole and Shrimp Tartlets garnished with pastry spoons.

Sole Paprika.

Skate in Black Butter

1–2 wings of skate weighing about 2 lb
court bouillon to cover
salt and pepper
1 tbsp chopped parsley
¼ cup butter
2 tsp wine vinegar
1 tbsp capers

1. Cover the skate pieces well with the court bouillon. Bring to the boil and then allow to simmer for about 15 minutes or until tender. Drain fish on absorbent paper, transfer to a heated serving dish, season with salt and pepper and the chopped parsley and keep warm.

2. Melt butter in a pan and cook until it turns golden brown. Then add the vinegar and capers and quickly pour over the fish. Serve bordered with piped, creamed potatoes if liked.

Jolly Roger Parcel

6 fillets of flounder or sole
12 mussels with their shells
12 shrimps with their shells
4 tbsp dry white wine
4 tbsp light cream
1 tbsp chopped parsley
2 oz shelled shrimps
pepper
oil

1. Set the oven at 350°F.

2. Line a small deep baking pan with foil and brush the base with a little oil.

3. Roll up each fillet from the tail end and stand upright on foil base. Shell shrimps but leave on head and tails and put 2 in the middle of each roll. Clean mussels thoroughly and arrange between rolls.

4. Moisten each roll with the wine and cream. Sprinkle with parsley and shrimps. Season. Fold up the foil to cover the rolls and bake in the pre-set oven for 20–25 minutes.

Fish and shellfish

Fried Dabs with Herb Sauce.

Fried Dabs with Herb Sauce

4 dabs or any small flat fish
a little seasoned flour
1 beaten egg
fine breadcrumbs
oil for deep frying

For herb sauce
⅔ cup heavy cream
1 tsp chopped fennel leaves
1 tsp chopped chives
bouquet garni
salt and pepper
1 heaped tsp grated lemon rind

For garnish
2 hard cooked eggs
1 tbsp chopped parsley

1. Dip the dabs in flour, then the beaten egg and breadcrumbs. Deep fry until crisp and golden. Drain on absorbent paper and keep warm.

2. Tip cream into a heavy based saucepan. Add the chopped fennel, chives, bouquet garni and seasoning. Bring to the boil and simmer until sufficiently thickened. Remove the herb bag and stir in the lemon rind. Pour into a bowl ready to serve.

3. Finely chop the hard cooked eggs. Arrange the dabs on a serving dish, and sprinkle with chopped egg and parsley. Serve with French bread and butter if liked.

Halibut Slices with Seafood Sauce

6 halibut slices
4 oz shrimps
1¼ cups heavy cream
salt and pepper

For garnish
1 lb potatoes
1 large egg yolk
1 tbsp butter
salt and pepper
freshly chopped parsley

1. Peel the potatoes, place them in a pan of cold, salted water and bring to the boil. Simmer until tender. Drain immediately and return to heat to dry off any excess moisture. Rub the potatoes through a sieve and then beat in the egg yolk, butter and seasoning.

2. Season the halibut slices and cook them in a buttered steamer for 10–12 minutes. Take out, remove the skin and keep the slices warm.

3. Peel the shrimps. Reserve about half for decoration and chop the rest up finely. Tip the cream into a heavy based saucepan. Bring to the boil and add the skin from the fish and the shrimp shells. Season with salt and pepper and simmer until the sauce has thickened sufficiently.

4. Pipe a border of creamed potato around the heated serving dish. Arrange the fish slices in the center. Strain the sauce, stir in the chopped shrimps and pour over. Decorate with the reserved shrimps and chopped parsley. Alternatively serve on individual platters.

Court Bouillon

1 carrot
1 onion
1 sprig thyme
¼ bayleaf
2 peppercorns
3 tbsp wine vinegar
5 cups cold water

1. Peel and slice carrot and onion thinly.

2. Place all the ingredients in a saucepan, bring to the boil and simmer for 15–20 minutes. Strain before using.

Halibut Slices with Seafood Sauce.

Fish and shellfish

Cod and Mussel Casserole.

Cod and Mussel Casserole

2 lb cod fillet
1 lb mussels
seasoned flour
¼ cup butter
¼ cup oil
4 shallots or small onions
¼ lb tomatoes
2 lb potatoes
¼ lb Cheddar cheese
1 large clove garlic
1¼ cups dry white wine
7¼ cups fish stock
saffron
salt and black pepper

1. First prepare the mussels. Wash and scrub them well, scraping away any weed. Discard any which are open. Rinse them under running water, then soak in a bowl of fresh water.

2. Set the oven at 325°F.

3. Remove any skin from the cod and cut into rectangular chunks. Dip in seasoned flour and fry in the oil and butter until lightly browned.

4. Peel and finely slice the shallots. Scald and skin the tomatoes. Remove seeds and chop the flesh. Peel the potatoes and slice fairly thinly. Cut the cheese into fine slithers.

5. Now layer these ingredients into a large casserole dish. Begin with the shallots, then cod pieces, tomatoes, cheese and finally the potatoes. Repeat this once, finishing with the potatoes on top.

6. Crush the garlic with a little salt and mix it in with the wine, stock, a pinch of saffron and seasoning. Add this to the casserole and cover.

7. Cook in the center of the pre-set oven for about 45 minutes. At this point add the mussels making sure they are well covered with the liquid. Cook for a further 7 minutes and serve piping hot.

Cod in Spicy Tomato Sauce.

Cod in Spicy Tomato Sauce

2 lb cod
6 tomatoes
1 shallot or small onion
1 tsp dried oregano or thyme
1 tsp dried basil
1 tsp chopped chives
1¼ cups fish stock or equal quantities
  of fish stock and white wine
1 tbsp olive oil
salt and pepper

1. Wrap the cod in foil and steam it over a pan of boiling water for about 20–30 minutes until tender. Strain off the juices and reserve. Place the cod in a dish and keep warm in the oven.

2. Scald, skin and chop up the tomatoes. Peel and chop the shallot.

3. Place the tomatoes, onion, herbs and chosen liquid in a pan and cook slowly until the tomatoes have turned to pulp.

4. Adjust the seasoning to taste, add the olive oil and reserved juices from the fish. Continue to cook until the sauce is thick and well reduced. Then pour over the cod and serve with plainly boiled carrots and potatoes.

Halibut with Shrimp Sauce.

50

Halibut with Shrimp Sauce

1 halibut weighing 2¼–3 lb
butter
salt and pepper
2½ cups mornay sauce
4 oz shelled shrimps
2 tsp tomato paste
knob of butter

For garnish
2 hard cooked eggs
sprigs of parsley

1. Set the oven at 350°F.

2. Place the halibut on a buttered sheet of foil, dot with butter and season with salt and pepper. Seal loosely, put on a cookie sheet and cook in the pre-set oven for 25–35 minutes.

3. Meanwhile prepare the sauce. Make up the mornay sauce and chop the shrimps. Stir the shrimps and tomato paste into the sauce and finish with a knob of butter.

4. Arrange the cooked fish on a warmed dish. Slice up the hard cooked eggs and use to garnish the fish with the sprigs of parsley. If liked one of the eggs can be finely chopped and sprinkled onto the fish. Pour the shrimp sauce around or serve separately.

Fish Croquettes

1 lb cod
1¼ cups thick white sauce made with:
 3 tbsp butter
 ¼ cup plus 1 tbsp flour
 1¼ cups milk
1 egg yolk
salt and pepper
flour
2 beaten eggs
fine breadcrumbs
oil for deep frying

For garnish
wedges of lemon
chopped parsley

1. Place the cod on a buttered dish over a pan of boiling water, season and cover. When cooked, allow to cool a little, then remove any skin and flake fish from the bone.

Fish Croquettes with Butter Sauce.

2. Now prepare the sauce. Melt the butter in a pan over low heat and stir in the flour. Add the milk gradually, stirring all the time. Bring sauce to the boil and allow to simmer for 3–5 minutes.

3. Take off the heat and beat in the egg yolk. Then add the flaked cod and season with salt and pepper. Tip the mixture into a shallow dish and leave in the refrigerator to firm up.

4. Once the mixture has chilled, divide into small portions and roll into fat sausage shapes. Dip in the flour, beaten egg and breadcrumbs and then chill again.

5. Cook the croquettes in the deep fryer, a few at a time, until crisp and golden brown. Drain on absorbent paper, then pile onto a heated serving dish and garnish with lemon and chopped parsley. If liked, serve with sauté potatoes and butter sauce.

Butter Sauce

¼ cup butter
1 shallot or small onion
1¼ tbsp wine vinegar
salt and black pepper
3 tsp boiling water

1. Peel and chop up the shallot very finely. Place in a small pan, add the vinegar and seasoning. Cook until shallot is soft and virtually all the liquid has been absorbed. Pass the mixture through a sieve.

2. Cream the butter until soft. Then start to whip it with an electric or hand beater, adding the shallot purée drop by drop.

3. Now add the first teaspoonful of boiling water. Whip and repeat for the second and third. The mixture should be fluffy and almost white. Pile into a bowl and serve with Fish Croquettes.

Fish and shellfish

White Fish in White Wine Sauce.

White Fish in White Wine Sauce

2 lb white fish
¼ cup butter
⅗ cup dry white wine
1 tbsp freshly chopped parsley
⅗ cup light cream
salt and pepper

For potato border
2 lb potatoes
3 egg yolks
3 tbsp butter
salt and pepper

1. Prepare potato border. Peel and cut potatoes into even size pieces. Place in a pan of cold, salted water, bring to the boil and cook until tender. Drain at once, return to pan and leave over heat for a minute to dry off any excess moisture. Pass through a sieve into a bowl and beat in egg yolks, two-thirds of the butter and seasoning.

2. Turn on the broiler. Tip the potato mixture into a piping bag and pipe a thick border round an oval ovenproof dish. Melt the remaining butter, brush over the potato and leave to brown under the broiler.

3. Meanwhile melt butter in a pan and brown the fish lightly in it. Lift them out and pour in the wine. When this has heated return fish to the pan and simmer gently for about 5 minutes, turning once.

4. Now add the chopped parsley and cream. Season to taste. Take out the fish and arrange on the potato-bordered dish. When sauce has reduced to a creamy consistency pour over and serve.

Baked Stuffed Mackerel

6 filleted mackerel

For stuffing
2 rashers sliced bacon
5 oz fresh white breadcrumbs
2 tbsp chopped chives
2 tbsp freshly chopped parsley
grated rind and juice of 1 lemon
salt and pepper

For lemon sauce
2 lemons
2 cloves garlic
2 tsp dried tarragon
1 tbsp freshly chopped parsley
salt and pepper
1¼ cups olive oil
1 tbsp wine vinegar

For garnish
thin slices of lemon
sprigs of parsley

1. Set the oven at 375°F.

2. Cut the rind off the bacon and cut bacon into thin strips. Then fry until lightly browned.

3. Mix the breadcrumbs, bacon, herbs and seasoning together in a bowl. Then add the rind and juice of the lemon.

4. Place a little of the stuffing mixture in each mackerel, then wrap the fish individually in foil, place on a cookie sheet and bake in the pre-set oven on the shelf above center for 20–25 minutes.

5. Meanwhile prepare the sauce. Peel the lemons, divide into segments and remove all the pips and pith. Crush the garlic with the herbs and seasoning. Then begin to add the olive oil slowly, beating it in drop by drop with intermittent drops of vinegar. Once thoroughly blended, add lemon segments and heat sauce gently.

6. Remove the mackerel from the foil, arrange on a warmed serving dish and pour the sauce over. Serve garnished with thin slices of lemon and sprigs of parsley.

Baked Stuffed Mackerel.

Fish Stock

Basic Recipe

1¼ lb fish trimmings (heads, tails, backbones, skin)
¼ small onion or shallot
1 wedge lemon
2 parsley stalks
1 sprig fennel
3 peppercorns
salt
cold water, or equal quantities of water and white wine, to cover

1. Place the fish trimmings, onion, lemon, herbs and seasoning in a pan. Add enough liquid just to cover and bring to a fast boil.

2. Now skim the surface and refresh with a cup of cold water.

3. Bring the mixture quickly back to the boil and continue to cook briskly for a further 10 minutes. Strain the stock before using.

Mackerel with Gooseberry Sauce

6 mackerel
1⅓ cups raw gooseberries
oil
salt and pepper
fennel or parsley sprigs

For sauce
1 tbsp butter or margarine
1 tbsp flour
1¼ cups plus 2 tbsp water
1 tsp sugar
green vegetable coloring

1. Set the oven at 350°F.

2. Remove the heads and tails of the mackerel and discard. Clean each mackerel thoroughly inside and outside. Top and tail the gooseberries.

3. Stuff each mackerel cavity with an equal quantity of gooseberries and place the fish, split sides upwards, in a lightly greased ovenproof dish.

4. Brush the fish lightly with oil, cover with foil, and bake in the pre-set oven for 20–25 minutes, or until the fish are cooked.

5. Meanwhile make the gooseberry sauce. Cook the gooseberries with the 2 tablespoonfuls of water in a pan over a gentle heat. When soft, rub them through a sieve.

6. In another pan, melt the butter or margarine, stir in the sifted flour, then gradually add 1¼ cups boiling water. Add the strained gooseberries, the sugar and food coloring to enhance the color of the sauce if desired. Bring the sauce to the boil, pour into a sauce boat and keep warm.

7. Take the cooked mackerel from the oven, and season with salt and pepper. Sprinkle a little chopped fennel or parsley over. Serve the sauce separately.

Fish and shellfish

Baked Sea Herrings with Lemon and Caper Sauce

6 filleted sea herrings
1 small shallot
2 bayleaves
a few peppercorns
salt
sprigs of parsley
⅜ cup wine vinegar
⅜ cup water
melted butter

For stuffing
1 cup soft breadcrumbs
1 tbsp chopped chives
1 tbsp chopped parsley
1 soft herring roe
salt and pepper
1 egg

To finish
1 tbsp capers
1 lemon
a little more chopped parsley

1. Peel and slice the shallot finely. Arrange the herrings in a shallow dish and intersperse with the shallot, bayleaves, peppercorns and parsley sprigs. Season with salt and pour over the vinegar and water. Marinate for 24 hours.

2. Set the oven at 375°F.

3. Strain off the marinade and reserve. Mix the herbs, roe and seasoning into the breadcrumbs. Beat the egg and work into the mixture.

4. Fill some stuffing mixture into each herring. Place them in a shallow dish, brush with melted butter and bake in the pre-set oven for about 12 minutes.

5. Now prepare the sauce. Make sure that the capers are well drained and pressed. Peel the lemon, divide into segments and remove all the pith and pips. Pour the strained marinade into a pan and bring to the boil. Remove from heat and add capers, lemon segments and chopped parsley.

6. Arrange the baked herrings on a warmed serving dish, pour the sauce over and serve.

Baked Sea Herrings in Lemon and Caper Sauce.

Whitebait

whitebait
plain flour
oil for deep frying

To serve
slices of lemon
brown bread and butter

1. Sift the flour. Take a few whitebait at a time, toss them in the flour and then shake in a sieve to remove any surplus.

2. Arrange the fish in the bottom of the frying basket so that they do not overlap. Now plunge them into the oil and cook until crisp and golden brown – about 1–2 minutes.

3. Turn onto absorbent paper and keep warm while you cook the rest as above.

4. Serve with thick slices of lemon and thinly cut brown bread and butter.

3. Immerse the frying basket containing the fish in the hot oil for 1 minute.

1. Take a handful of whitebait and turn in flour. Put in a sieve and shake off the surplus flour.

4. Drain on a piece of absorbent paper and keep warm whilst frying rest of fish.

2. Cook only a few fish at a time otherwise they will stick together. Heat the oil in a deep fat frying pan to 390°F keeping the basket out of the oil.

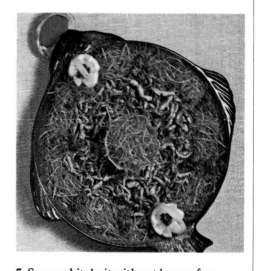

5. Serve whitebait with cut lemon for squeezing over and matchstick potatoes.

Fish and shellfish

Salmon Slices in Red Wine Sauce.

Salmon Slices in Red Wine Sauce

2 lb salmon
2 tbsp butter
1¼ cups red wine
⅔ cup strong fish stock
⅔ cup heavy cream
salt and pepper

For garnish
small packet frozen petits pois
6 mushrooms
⅓ lb creamed potatoes
sprigs of fennel

1. Divide the salmon into 6 slices. Wash and dry them. Butter a flameproof dish, place the slices in it and cover with the red wine. Poach gently until cooked. Then drain them on absorbent paper, arrange on a serving dish and keep warm in the oven.

2. Add the fish stock to the dish with the wine and allow to bubble until liquid has reduced by a third. Add the cream and continue to simmer. Season to taste.

3. Take a small, sharp knife and cut swirls in the caps of the mushrooms. Then poach these mushrooms in a little oil or butter.

4. Strain the sauce and pour over the salmon slices. Garnish the dish with rosettes of creamed potato, twirled mushrooms, petits pois and sprigs of fennel.

Soused Sea Herrings

6 fresh herrings
2 onions
2 tsp black peppercorns
5 small bayleaves
6 thin strips lemon rind
⅔ cup wine vinegar
⅔ cup water
salt and pepper

1. First fillet and clean the herrings. Cut off the heads and tails and slit the fish down the undersides. Flatten out and then, starting from the top, pull the back bone out gently. Now slit down the back as well and wash under cold water, discarding the entrails.

2. Roll up the herring fillets with tail end innermost and secure with a toothpick.

3. Peel and slice the onions into thin rings. Take a large screw top glass jar and arrange the herrings in it, interspersed with the onion, lemon rind, bayleaves and peppercorns.

4. Heat the vinegar, water and seasoning together in a pan. Pour into the jar, seal tightly and keep in the refrigerator for at least 48 hours.

1. Cut off the heads and tails, then carefully split each herring down the underside from top to tail.

2. Open up the herrings so that all the bones are clearly visible.

3. Pull out the spine with one hand, gently pushing from behind with a finger or thumb.

4. Cut the herrings in half and wash thoroughly under running water to clean.

5. Roll each cleaned and wiped fillet, tucking in the tail piece, and impale with a toothpick to secure.

A jar of Soused Herrings with pickles.

Variations:

Soused Herring Salad. Drain the herrings and chop up into neat pieces. Mix with a diced apple, a little grated onion, diced, cooked potato, and chopped hard cooked egg. Blend with soured cream and season to taste. Chill, then serve on a bed of lettuce.

Baked Herring Rolls. Drain and unroll some soused herrings. Make a paste of equal amounts of breadcrumbs and butter, some chopped parsley, lemon juice, seasoning and as little hot water as possible. Spread this paste on the herrings, roll them up again and fasten as before. Place in a greased baking dish, cover with foil and bake in the oven, pre-set at 350°F, for 15 minutes.

Lobster Mornay

2 small lobsters
court bouillon
⅓ cup béchamel sauce
⅓ cup grated Parmesan cheese
salt and pepper
2 level tbsp heavy cream
2 tbsp melted butter ·
⅛ cup fine breadcrumbs

For garnish
watercress
freshly chopped parsley

1. Place lobsters in a pan with lukewarm court bouillon. Cover and bring slowly to the boil. Then simmer for about 15 minutes until they turn bright pink in color. Take out and allow to cool.

2. When cold, place lobsters on a wooden board with the tails tucked underneath. Take a very sharp knife and divide them straight through the middle lengthwise. Remove the poisonous pouches from each side then the coral and the lobster meat. Crack the claws and remove the flesh from these too.

3. Make up the béchamel sauce. Stir in the coral and half the Parmesan cheese. Season as necessary, then whip up the cream and add this to the sauce as well.

4. Tip a little sauce into each shell and cover with the lobster meat. Then pour over remaining sauce. Sprinkle with the rest of the cheese, the melted butter and finally the breadcrumbs.

5. Brown the lobsters under the broiler or in a hot oven. Serve garnished with watercress and chopped parsley.

2. Cut through the top half towards the head in exactly the same manner.

3. Discard the gray-green poisonous pouch and the dark threadlike intestine.

4. Remove body flesh in one piece using a skewer, then scrape out all the remaining meat from the body and claws.

1. Tuck the lobster tail underneath its body. Insert a sharp knife into the center back of the body and cut through towards the tail end.

Lobster Mornay.

DRESSING A CRAB

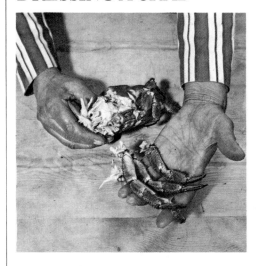

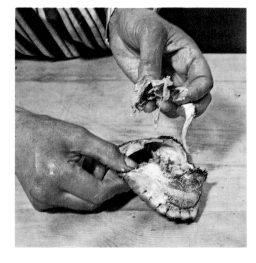

1. Break off the large claws of the crab then the small ones, and set aside.

2. Hold the shell as above and grip the body with the other hand. Pull back until the body comes away from the shell.

3. These gray bits are poisonous and must be discarded.

Dressed Crab.

4. Take out the poisonous pouch: do this by pressing from underneath against the body and it comes away in one piece.

5. Using a skewer, get out all the flesh from the cleaned crab body. Set aside.

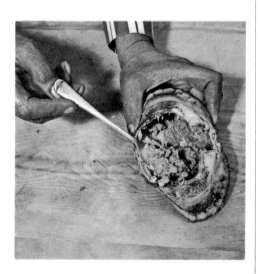

6. Discard the thin membrane on the shell, then remove all the meat.

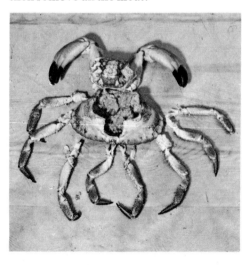

7. Arrange the claws around the empty shell, then fill one side with brown meat and the other with white meat. Decorate with chopped egg yolk, chopped egg white and chopped parsley.

Coquilles St Jacques

6 scallops with their shells
3 tbsp plus ½ oz butter or
  margarine
¼ cup plus 1 tbsp flour
1¼ cups milk
1 tbsp chopped parsley
1 tbsp Parmesan cheese
salt and pepper
creamed potato
1 tbsp bread crumbs
1 tbsp Gruyère cheese

1. Set the oven at 375°F.

2. Cut each scallop from the shell, wash well and remove any black bits. Roughly chop each scallop.

3. Melt 3 tbsp butter or margarine in a small pan. Gradually add the milk, beating well. Stir in the parsley, the grated Parmesan and the seasoning.

4. Put a large spoonful of this mixture on each shell. Add chopped scallop and cover with more sauce.

5. Fill a pastry bag fitted with a rosette nozzle with creamed potato and pipe around each scallop shell. Scatter the tops with the breadcrumbs, then the grated Gruyère cheese, and lastly a few tiny pieces of butter.

6. Place the shells on a cookie sheet and bake in the pre-set oven for 15 minutes or until the potato piping is golden brown.

Boiled Shrimps

1 lb shrimps
1¼ cups water
salt
1 sprig parsley
1 clove
1 tsp vinegar

1. Wash the shrimps, remove the shells and the black vein.

2. Bring the water to the boil with a pinch of salt, the parsley, clove and vinegar. Add the shrimps and cover the pan. Simmer for 5–10 minutes or until tender.

3. Cool in the cooking water, drain and use the liquor for soup.

Roast Rib of Beef.

Meat

Roast Rib of Beef

1. Set the oven at 425°F.

2. Make sure that you have removed the joint from the refrigerator at least 30 minutes before you plan to put it in the oven.

3. Wipe the meat and spread lightly with a little drippings. Put some extra drippings in the roasting pan and place in center of pre-set oven.

4. After 15 minutes reduce the temperature to 375°F and roast at this temperature for the remainder of the cooking time, basting frequently. For a rare roast allow 15 minutes per lb plus an extra 15 minutes. For a well cooked joint allow 20 minutes per lb plus the extra 15 minutes.

5. When the joint is cooked, place on a serving dish and leave to stand in a warming drawer for 10–15 minutes before beginning to carve it. This makes the job of carving much easier.

6. To make the gravy tip the fat off from the roasting pan, leaving the juices and sediment from the meat. Add a little flour (about 2 tsp), allow to color then pour in about $1\frac{1}{2}$ cups of stock or vegetable water. Bring to the boil and simmer until sufficiently reduced. Taste for seasoning and strain into a gravy boat.

Boeuf en Croûte

3 lb tenderloin of beef
puff pastry made from 2 cups flour
butter
salt
black pepper
2 tsp dried mixed herbs
beaten egg

1. Set the oven at 400°F.

2. Trim and tie up the tenderloin. Melt a little butter in a pan, sprinkle the joint with salt and black pepper and seal it in the hot butter. Then roast in the pre-set oven for 15–20 minutes. Take out and allow to cool.

3. Wash and slice the mushrooms very finely. Sauté them in butter for a few minutes, then add the mixed herbs. Draw off the heat and allow to cool.

4. Set the pastry on a lightly floured surface and roll out to a piece large enough to enclose the tenderloin.

5. Lay the pastry in a shallow roasting pan. Remove string from the cooled tenderloin and place meat on the pastry. Pour over the mushroom mixture, then fold over the pastry to cover. Trim and press edges well together. Turn so that joins are on the underneath. make a few slits in the top pastry to allow steam to escape. Brush the pastry all over with beaten egg. Roll out any pastry trimmings and cut out medallions or crescents for decoration.

6. Bake in the pre-set oven for 30–40 minutes until the pastry is well browned.

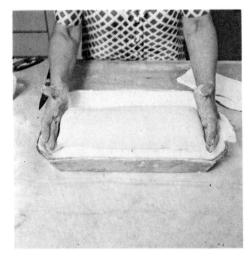

1. After wrapping pastry around the fillet, seal the edges by brushing with cold water and pressing together.

2. Trim the ends neatly with a knife.

3. Brush the pastry case generously with beaten egg.

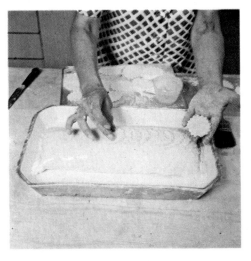

4. Decorate with pastry trimmings.

LARDING

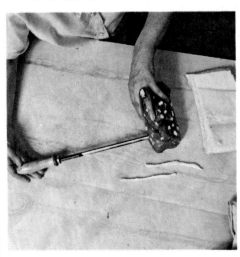

1. Some very lean cuts of meat such as tenderloin of beef or veal have a tendency to dry out when they are roasted. In order to prevent this the meat can be larded – a method by which you actually insert fat into the meat. Take a thin piece of raw, unsalted pork fat which should ideally be cold and firm. Cut off very narrow, long strips and slot these, one by one, into the larding needle.

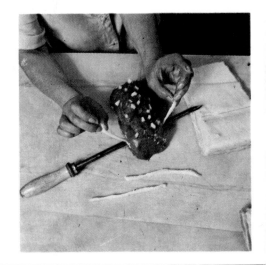

Boeuf en Croûte.

Variations:
For an even more extravagant version of Boeuf en Croûte, try rubbing the beef tenderloin with brandy before seasoning and browning in butter.
Alternatively, omit the mushrooms and mixed herbs, and spread a generous amount of pâté de foie gras or chicken liver pâté over the top and sides of the beef before wrapping in pastry.
The layer of mushrooms or pâté between the meat and the pastry helps to keep the meat juicy and moist.
This dish is also delicious using a veal tenderloin instead of beef.

2. Push the needle through the joint. Then withdraw it again leaving the fat threaded through the meat. Do this at $\frac{1}{2}$ inch intervals starting at the bottom of the joint and working up to the top, and at 2 inch intervals along it.

3. Snip the long ends off with scissors. The joint is now ready for roasting.

PREPARING AND BROILING TOURNEDOS

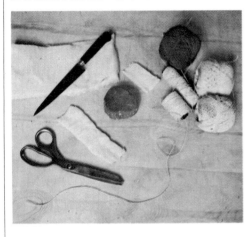

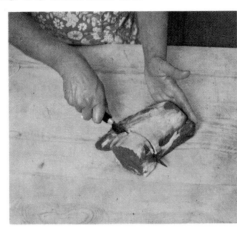

1. You will need a sharp knife, scissors, plenty of string and a thin slice of raw, unsalted pork fat.

2. Place the tenderloin steak on a chopping board and, using a very sharp knife, cut into slices about 1½ inches thick.

3. Trim away any fat or sinuous matter and shape steaks into rounds. Then take a piece of pork fat and cut into strips 1½ inches wide.

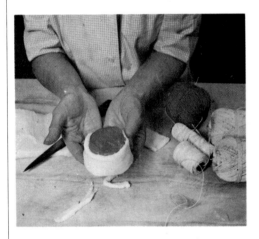

4. Wrap a strip of fat around each steak.

5. Trim the fat off neatly so that the ends just meet around the middle.

6. With fine string tie around the middle. Make a double knot and cut the string. Place under a hot broiler in the highest position for a minute on each side. Continue to cook on a lower level for 3½ minutes on each side for rare steaks, 4½ minutes for medium steaks, and 5 minutes for well done steaks.

Tournedos.

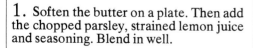

Steak Paprika.

Maître d'Hotel Butter

Basic Recipe

¼ cup sweet butter
1 tbsp finely chopped parsley
juice of ¼ lemon
salt and pepper

1. Soften the butter on a plate. Then add the chopped parsley, strained lemon juice and seasoning. Blend in well.

2. Form into a roll, chill in the refrigerator and serve in pats.

Steak Paprika

6 tenderloin steaks
butter
1¼ cups flat mushrooms
1 onion
¾ cup dry white wine
1¼ cups béchamel sauce
paprika
salt and pepper

1. Chop the mushrooms into very tiny pieces.

2. Finely chop the onion and fry in a little butter until soft. Pour in the wine and béchamel sauce, stirring. Add the mushrooms and enough paprika to color the sauce. Leave to simmer whilst preparing the steaks.

3. Season the steaks and fry them in butter.

4. Season the sauce. Arrange steaks in a serving dish and pour sauce over.

Steak Diane

3 well beaten tenderloin steaks
oil and butter for frying
2 tbsp brandy
2 shallots or small onions
1 tbsp freshly chopped parsley
1 cup jellied stock
1 tbsp tomato paste
salt and pepper
Worcestershire sauce

1. Peel and finely chop the shallots. Heat some butter and oil in a large frying pan and lift the steaks in gently, curling them round a fork if they are very thin.

2. Brown them lightly on each side, then add the brandy, set alight and allow the flames to burn out.

3. Now add the shallots followed by the parsley and, when slightly softened, spoon in the jellied stock. At this point remove the steaks to a heated dish and keep warm.

4. Bring the stock to the boil and cook until well reduced. Stir in the tomato paste and season with salt and pepper and a few drops of Worcestershire sauce. Pour the sauce over the steaks and serve immediately. If liked, garnish with some French fried potatoes and chopped parsley.

1. For clarity a single steak is shown being cooked but you can cook as many as your pan will allow. To lift up each steak after beating, use the prongs of a fork, rolling the steak round it.

2. Carefully unroll the steak into a pan of hot oil and butter.

6. Stir in jellied stock. Remove the steak from the pan and keep warm.

7. Bring the sauce to the boil and cook until well reduced. Season and pour the sauce over the steak.

3. Seal the steak on both sides then reduce the heat and continue cooking.

4. Over a high heat, pour in the brandy and ignite. When flames subside, add the onions and cook gently.

5. Sprinkle chopped parsley over.

Steak Diane.

Meat

Marsala Steak

6 sirloin or top round steaks
butter and oil for frying
2 shallots or 1 onion
1 heaped tbsp flour
2 tbsp Marsala
2 cups stock
2 cups button mushrooms
salt and pepper

For garnish
lemon slices
sprigs of parsley

1. Peel and finely chop the shallots. Wash and slice the mushrooms.

2. Heat enough butter and oil to cover the base of a large pan. Seal the steaks, in the hot fat, then lower the heat and cook to your own taste. Lift out carefully, place on a heated serving dish, season and keep warm.

3. Add the chopped shallot to the pan and cook gently until soft and transparent. Tip in the flour and stir until well blended.

4. Now gradually pour in the stock and Marsala, stirring continually. Allow to bubble up well. Add the chopped mushrooms and continue to cook for a further 3–4 minutes. Season to taste.

5. Pour the sauce over the steaks and garnish with lemon slices and sprigs of parsley before serving.

Rump Steaks à la Maison

2 thick tenderloin steaks
butter for frying
2 tbsp stock
salt and pepper

For garnish
2 tomatoes
watercress
sauté potatoes
¼ cup sweet butter
4 tbsp freshly chopped chives
salt and pepper

1. Trim the steaks of all excess fat and gristle. Melt the butter in a pan, turn up the heat and lay the steaks in. Seal them quickly on each side before turning down the heat to continue cooking.

2. Cook steaks gently for 2½ minutes on each side for rare meat, or for 3 minutes for medium done. Then place them on a heated serving dish, season and keep warm.

3. Add stock to the pan, blend in well with meat juices and bring to the boil. Then pour over the cooked steaks.

4. Serve garnished with lightly broiled tomatoes, watercress, a few sauté potatoes and chive butter. For the chive butter, soften the butter on a plate, mix in the chopped chives and season with salt and pepper. Divide into 4 pats and serve 2 on each steak.

Beef Stroganoff

½ lb tenderloin steak
2 onions
2 cups mushrooms
2 tbsp oil
1 tbsp butter
2 tbsp sherry
¼ cup cultured sour cream
grated nutmeg
salt and pepper

1. Cut the steak into very thin strips with a sharp knife. Chop the onions finely.

2. Heat the oil and butter in a pan and fry the onions gently until soft but not brown.

3. Increase the heat and add steak to the pan. Fry briskly until lightly browned all over. Slice the mushrooms and add to the pan with the sherry. Stir for 2–3 minutes or until the mushrooms are cooked.

4. Stir in the sour cream, a dash of nutmeg and seasoning. Heat through, but do not allow to boil. Serve with boiled rice.

Marsala Steaks.

Rump Steaks à la Maison.

Meat

Beef Beaujolais

3–4 lb topside or similar joint of beef
oil
12 small onions or shallots
1¼ cups red wine
bouquet garni
1 cup water
salt and pepper

1. Set the oven at 350°F.

2. Brown the beef all over in a flame-proof casserole, using the minimum of oil.

3. Place the peeled but whole onions around the meat, pour on the wine and tuck in the bouquet garni. Cover and place in the pre-set oven for 30 minutes.

4. Reduce the heat to 250°F and continue cooking until the onions are tender. If necessary add up to ½ cup water.

5. When the meat is done – test with a skewer – lift out onto a serving dish. Arrange the onions around the joint and keep warm.

6. Make a gravy by adding the remaining water to the cooking pot, season to taste, and take out the bouquet garni. Stir over a high heat to reduce a little, then pour over the meat and onions.

Beef Espagnole

6 thin slices rolled rump or 6 minute steaks
salt and pepper
butter for frying

For mirepoix
2 carrots
2 onions
¼ lb celery
2 tbsp butter
2 tbsp oil
2 sprigs thyme
2 crushed bayleaves
2 tbsp sherry

For espagnole sauce
2 tbsp butter
¼ cup flour
5 cups stock
2 tomatoes
half the given quantity of mirepoix

1. First prepare the mirepoix. Peel and grate the carrots and onions. Wash, trim and chop up the celery very finely. Heat the oil and butter in a heavy based pan. Add the prepared vegetables, herbs and sherry and simmer gently until soft.

2. Now prepare the sauce. Melt the butter in a pan, blend in the flour and allow to cook through. Then add the stock a little at a time, beating well after each addition.

3. Scald, skin and chop up the tomatoes. Add these to the sauce followed, after a few minutes, by half the mirepoix. Allow the sauce to simmer until reduced by half.

4. Set the oven at 350°F.

5. Place the steaks on a board and beat until well flattened. Season and brown lightly in butter.

6. Strain off any excess liquid from the remaining mirepoix and spread a little of the mixture over each steak. Roll up and secure with cocktail picks.

7. Place the meat rolls in an ovenproof dish. Strain the finished sauce over them, cover and cook in the pre-set oven for 30–35 minutes or until tender.

8. Serve with red cabbage and baked potatoes in their jackets if liked.

Beef Espagnole.

Boiled Beef with Vegetables.

74

Boiled Beef with Vegetables

4–5 lb of salted beef, heel of round or
  corned beef brisket
6 onions
8 carrots
2 lb potatoes

1. Place the meat in a large pan, cover with cold water and bring slowly to the boil. Remove any skum which may come to the surface. Cover and simmer gently for 2–2½ hours.

2. Meanwhile, prepare the vegetables. Peel the onions and leave whole. Peel the carrots and half or quarter them if necessary. Peel the potatoes.

3. An hour before the end of cooking, add the onions and carrots and then, half an hour, later the potatoes.

4. Place the beef on a warmed serving dish and surround with the vegetables. Strain off some of the liquor and serve separately in a sauce boat.

Stuffed Beef

1 breast of beef

For stuffing
3 rashers bacon
6 cups breadcrumbs
¼ cup suet
1 tsp oregano
1 egg
salt and pepper

1. Set the oven at 350°F.

2. Chop the bacon finely, and put in a bowl with the breadcrumbs, suet and oregano. Mix well, then beat in the egg. Season to taste.

3. Remove excess fat from the beef. Pack the stuffing tightly into the cavity thus formed. Tie up with string and place in a roasting pan.

4. Roast in the pre-set oven for 1¼–1½ hours or until cooked.

Roast Stuffed Veal

1 small boned and rolled veal shoulder
¼ cup butter
salt and pepper

For stuffing
1 cup fine fresh breadcrumbs
1 onion
butter for frying
1 tbsp freshly chopped parsley
1 tsp dried mixed herbs
juice of ¼ lemon
salt and pepper
beaten egg

1. Set the oven at 400°F.

2. Prepare the stuffing. Peel and chop the onion finely. Sauté in a little butter until soft and transparent.

3. Place the breadcrumbs in a bowl. Add the onion, herbs, seasoning, lemon juice and a little beaten egg to bind. Mix together well.

4. Unroll the veal and spread with the stuffing. Roll up again and tie securely. Spread the joint with the butter, season and wrap loosely in foil. Place in a baking pan and roast in the pre-set oven.

5. When the joint has cooked for 25 minutes for each lb, fold back the foil, baste the joint well and roast for another 20–25 minutes until nicely browned.

6. Suggested vegetable accompaniments are baked parsnips and white cabbage.

Roast Stuffed Veal.

Meat

Garnished Veal Steaks.

Wiener Schnitzel

Wiener Schnitzel

4 thin veal steaks or cutlets
seasoned flour
fine breadcrumbs
beaten egg
3 tbsp butter
3 tbsp oil

For garnish
2 hard cooked eggs
4 anchovy fillets
slices of lemon
sprigs of parsley

1. Roll the steaks or cutlets in seasoned flour, then brush with beaten egg and toss in the breadcrumbs.

2. Peel the hard cooked eggs and separate with whites from the yolks. Then chop each very finely and reserve. Divide the anchovy fillets in half lengthwise. Set aside for garnish.

3. Heat the butter and oil together in a frying pan. Lay the crumbed steaks in carefully and fry over moderate heat for about 10 minutes depending on thickness, turning once only.

4. Arrange the escalopes on a heated serving dish and garnish with the chopped egg white and yolk. Add the strips of anchovy and decorate with slices of lemon and parsley. If liked serve with garden peas or green beans.

PREPARING VEAL STEAKS

The veal steak used for Wiener Schnitzel is correctly called an escalope but is also known variously as a scallop, scaloppine or collop. It must be sliced as thin as possible; no amount of beating will help a slice that is too thick – it will merely revert to size while being cooked. Butchers do not usually prepare this cut so it is a good idea to learn how to do it yourself.

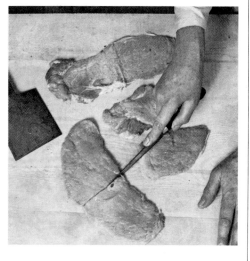

1. Place the meat on a board. Trim off any excess fat and, with a very sharp knife, divide each steak in half.

2. Have a bowl of cold water handy in which to dip your meat batter from time to time. This prevents the meat from tearing. Alternatively lay the veal between pieces of waxed paper before beating.

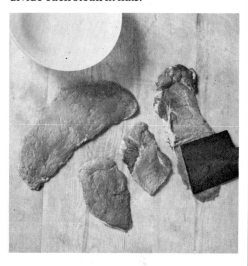

3. Beat out each half the veal into small individual steaks.

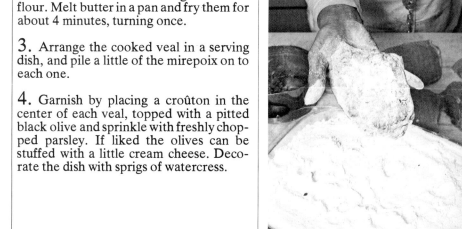

4. Dip in flour before preparing as wished.

Garnished Veal Steaks or Chops

4 veal steaks or chops

For mirepoix
½ lb celery
¾ lb carrots
½ cup diced lean ham
6 tbsp butter
1 bayleaf
2 sprigs thyme
salt and pepper
seasoned flour
butter for frying

For garnish
croûtons
pitted black olives
chopped parsley
cream cheese
watercress

1. First prepare the mirepoix. Wash and trim the celery and chop up into small dice. Peel and grate the carrot. Melt the butter in a heavy based pan. Add the celery, carrot and herbs and allow to cook gently for about 5 minutes. Then add the ham and seasoning. Continue to cook until quite soft.

2. Divide each steak or chop in half and beat out well until you have 8 small pieces of veal. Pass each one through seasoned flour. Melt butter in a pan and fry them for about 4 minutes, turning once.

3. Arrange the cooked veal in a serving dish, and pile a little of the mirepoix on to each one.

4. Garnish by placing a croûton in the center of each veal, topped with a pitted black olive and sprinkle with freshly chopped parsley. If liked the olives can be stuffed with a little cream cheese. Decorate the dish with sprigs of watercress.

Veal Steaks with Cream Sauce

4 veal steaks or cutlets
oil
1 onion
3 cups mushrooms
salt and pepper
dry white wine
scant 1 cup light cream
2 egg yolks

1. Set the oven at 375°F.

2. Tear off 4 generous size strips of foil, brush the center of each piece with oil and lay one steak on each.

3. Peel and grate the onion. Wash and slice the mushrooms finely, including the stalks. Then cover each steak with a layer of onion followed by a layer of chopped mushroom. Season with salt and pepper.

4. Sprinkle a little white wine over each steak – just sufficient to moisten the mushrooms. Pinch the foil together at the top to make loose parcels, taking care to turn up the corners to prevent liquor escaping during baking.

5. Place the foil parcels in a roasting pan and bake in the pre-set oven for 45 minutes or until cooked.

6. Meanwhile prepare liaison for the sauce. Beat the 2 egg yolks together with 1 fl oz of the cream.

7. When the steaks are cooked, strain off the excess liquor from each one into a small pan and arrange them in a heated serving dish. Add the cream to the pan, bring to the boil and simmer for about 5 minutes. Add a little of this sauce to the liaison, blend in well, then return to the pan and reheat, stirring continuously, but do not allow to reboil. Check for seasoning. Now pour this rich creamy sauce around the steaks in their dish and serve if liked with Dauphine potatoes sprinkled with chopped parsley.

1. Place a veal steak in each piece of foil. Sprinkle with grated onion, and salt and pepper to taste.

2. Sprinkle on some of the chopped mushrooms.

3. Flick a little white wine over the veal to moisten it before wrapping up the foil parcels and baking.

Veal Steaks with Cream Sauce.

Bocconcini

3 veal steaks or cutlets
3 thin slices cooked ham
dried sage
Gruyère cheese
¼ cup butter
¼ cup dry white wine
¼ cup good stock
1 tbsp tomato paste
salt and pepper

1. Divide each steak or cutlet in half and beat out well. Divide the cooked ham as well and place a piece of ham on each small steak. Add a dash of sage and a finger of Gruyère cheese. Roll up each one and secure with a cocktail pick.

2. Melt the butter in a heavy based pan, add the veal rolls and brown them on all sides. Add the wine, stock, tomato paste and seasoning. Cover and cook for about 30 minutes.

3. Remove the veal rolls to a heated dish, boil up the sauce until sufficiently reduced and pour over.

Veal with Chestnut Sauce

6 veal cutlets
1 tbsp oil
1 tbsp dry white wine
¼ clove crushed garlic
chopped parsley
salt and pepper
butter
parsley or lemon for garnish
1 can chestnut purée
brown stock

1. Make a marinade with the oil and wine and add the garlic, seasoning and a little chopped parsley. Put in the veal cutlets and leave for a few hours.

2. Set the oven at 350°F.

3. Remove cutlets from marinade and place in an ovenproof dish without draining. Put a little butter on the top of each one, cover with foil and cook in the pre-set oven for about 45 minutes.

4. To make the chestnut sauce: heat the chestnut purée with enough brown stock to give a smooth consistency. Season if required, and serve separately.

Veal Steaks with Mushrooms.

Veal Steaks with Mushrooms

4 veal steaks or cutlets
2 tbsp butter
2 tbsp oil
seasoned flour
1 shallot or small onion
2 cups stock
3 cups mushrooms
¼ cup dry white wine
salt and black pepper

For garnish
¾ cup diced carrot
1 lb creamed potatoes

1. Divide each steak or cutlet in half and beat each piece well so that you have 8 small steaks. Dip them in seasoned flour.

2. Peel and grate the shallot. Wash and slice the mushrooms finely with their stalks. Heat the oil and butter in a skillet and add the shallot. Allow to cook for about a minute before adding the steaks. Brown them lightly on both sides, then lower the heat and add the stock. Leave to simmer for about 5 minutes.

3. Place the mushrooms in a small pan, season with black pepper and add the wine. Cover and simmer gently until soft.

4. Now add mushrooms and their juice to the skillet with the steaks. After 2 minutes remove the veal to a warmed dish and boil the sauce briskly until sufficiently reduced. Pour round the veal, sprinkle with steamed diced carrot and pipe on rosettes of creamed potatoes.

Sauté of Veal

1 lb center cut of leg veal
2 small onions
2 cups mushrooms
¼ cup butter
¼ cup olive oil
seasoned flour
2 cups good white bone stock
⅔ cup light cream
salt and pepper
1 tbsp freshly chopped parsley

1. Peel and slice the onions finely. Wash and slice the mushrooms with their stalks.

2. Cut the meat into narrow strips and toss in seasoned flour. Shake in a sieve to remove any excess flour.

3. Heat the butter and oil together in a skillet. Add the onions and cook gently until soft and transparent. Then add the mushrooms and cook for 3–4 minutes.

4. Now add the floured veal pieces to the pan. Once they have browned, tip in a little of the given stock and blend in well. Add the rest of the stock and bring to the boil.

5. Pour in the cream, a little at a time, stirring continuously. Season with salt and pepper and then add the parsley.

6. Tip into a warmed dish and serve with lima beans and croûtons.

1. Cover the strips of veal with seasoned flour, place in a sieve and shake off the surplus flour.

2. Add veal to the vegetables in the pan and cook, stirring continuously.

3. When the veal is browned, add the wine or stock over a fierce heat.

4. When the sauce has thickened pour in the cream, working it in well.

5. Season with salt and pepper.

6. Stir in the chopped parsley.

Easter Lamb.

Easter Lamb

1 saddle of lamb
1 clove garlic
salt
¼ cup butter

For garnish
6 lambs kidneys
6 rashers back bacon
2 lb spring cabbage
1 white cabbage

1. Set the oven at 375°F.

2. Crush the garlic clove with a little salt. Cream the butter and garlic and blend in.

3. Spread the saddle of lamb with the garlic butter and wrap loosely in foil. Roast in the pre-set oven for 1¼–1½ hours. Fold back the foil for another 30 minutes to allow the joint to brown.

4. Halve the kidneys, remove skin and core. Wash well and dry. Halve the bacon rashers and wrap half a kidney in each piece of bacon. Secure them with toothpicks and roast in the oven round the joint for the last 20 minutes of the cooking time.

5. Wash and shred the spring greens and white cabbage and steam in separate containers until tender.

6. Arrange the cooked cabbage on a warmed serving dish, place the saddle of lamb on it and garnish with the bacon and kidney rolls.

Meat

Carré d'Agneau

1 rib roast of lamb weighing about 2 lb
drippings for roasting
½ cup butter
2 tbsp freshly chopped parsley
1 clove garlic
salt and black pepper
fine fresh white breadcrumbs

1. Set the oven at 375°F.

2. Skin the joint if your butcher has not already done so. Then make a deep incision across the joint about 1–1½ inches from the top ends of the bones. Peel away the fat and meat, then cut down between the bones and remove the meat which joins them. Scrape away any clinging pieces so that the bones are quite clean.

3. Cover the bones with foil, melt a very small amount of drippings in the roasting pan. Season the joint and roast in the pre-set oven for about 45 minutes.

4. Meanwhile prepare the crumb crust. Melt the butter in a pan and crush the garlic with a little salt. Remove butter from heat, add the chopped parsley, garlic and pepper to season. Then start to add the breadcrumbs and blend well together until mixture forms a smooth paste.

5. Remove joint from the oven and increase the heat to 425°F. Once the lamb has cooled sufficiently to handle, spread the paste evenly over the fat side of the joint. Return it to the oven to brown for 10–15 minutes.

6. If this dish is being served for a special occasion top the bones with cutlet frills and serve with colorful vegetable accompaniments.

Carré d'Agneau.

BONING A LEG OF LAMB

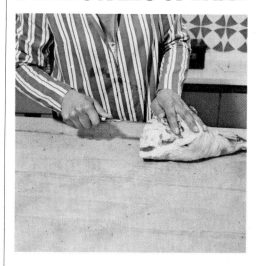

1. Lay the leg of lamb upside down with the broad end facing you. Insert a sharp knife into the joint and ease it round the edge of the bone.

2. Pare away the flesh from the bone until it begins to emerge.

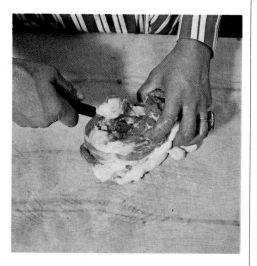

3. Continue to work the knife round the bone, freeing it from gristle.

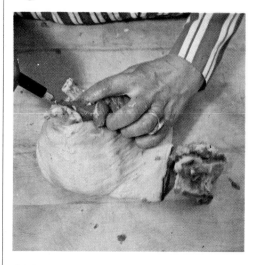

4. Now turn the joint round the other way and approach the bone from this end with the same paring movement until the flesh comes easily away from it.

5. Turn the joint round again. Hold the broad end bone with the left hand and begin to scrape with the knife down towards the tip end.

6. As the bone becomes looser, continue to roll the flesh back from it until you can pull the bone free, either in one piece or 2 pieces.

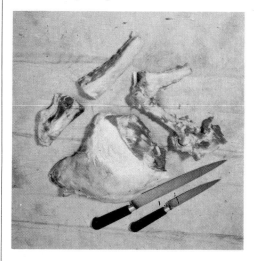

7. Reshape the joint. The bone on the left has been removed whole; the bones on the right show the same bone after it has been cut in half for easier removal.

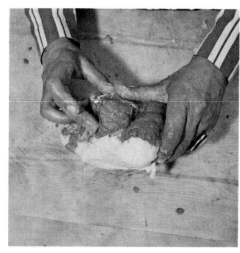

8. Stuff the meat with chosen stuffing and sew up both ends with thread.

9. The finished joint ready for roasting. Remove the thread before serving.

Guard of Honor

2 rib roasts of lamb of equal size
drippings for roasting
salt and pepper

1. Set the oven at 375°F.

2. Place one of the joints on a chopping board with the fat side up. Skin the meat if your butcher has not already done it. Then, with a very sharp knife, cut straight across the joint right through to the bones about 1–1½-inches from the top of the bones. Peel away the meat and fat.

3. Now turn the joint upside down and cut down between the bones to remove the meat which joins them. Scrape any remaining fat or meat from the bones leaving them quite clean. Season the meat.

4. Repeat this process with the second rib roast. Then place the 2 joints facing one another so that the bones interlace. Cover the bones with foil to prevent them charring while roasting.

5. Melt a little drippings in the roasting pan, place the joint in it and roast in the pre-set oven for about an hour depending on the size of the joints. Decorate with cutlet frills and serve with sweetcorn and lima beans if liked.

1. Make an incision through to the bone and pare away the flesh and fat.

2. Cut the meat back from the bones so that the bones are exposed.

3. Scrape the bones really clean.

4. Prepare the second joint as before. Stand the 2 joints face to face and push together so the bones interlace.

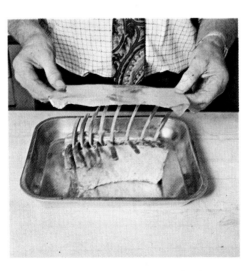

5. Prevent the bones from charring by covering them with a sheet of foil.

Guard of Honor with Sweetcorn and Lima Beans.

Meat

Mutton Soubise

1 shoulder of mutton
stock
4 onions
1 carrot
2 parsley stalks
bouquet garni
onion cream sauce

1. Wipe the meat and trim off the excess fat. Place the joint on a trivet in a large saucepan.

2. Pour on enough boiling stock to cover. Peel and quarter the onions, slice the carrot into rounds.

3. Add the vegetables to the pan with the herbs. Cover and simmer until the meat is tender – the exact time will depend on the size of the joint.

4. Take out the cooked shoulder of mutton and place on a serving dish. Cover with plenty of hot onion cream sauce.

Onion Cream Sauce

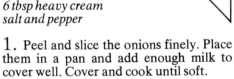

3 onions
milk to cover
6 tbsp heavy cream
salt and pepper

1. Peel and slice the onions finely. Place them in a pan and add enough milk to cover well. Cover and cook until soft.

2. Strain off the milk and reserve. Pass the onions through a nylon sieve.

3. Return the milk to pan and cook gently until reduced to about 4 tbsp. Then add the sieved onions and heavy cream. Season with salt and pepper.

WINGED VICTORY

1. Remove the skin from a saddle of lamb.

2. Using a sharp knife make an incision from left to right through to the bones on both sides of the joint.

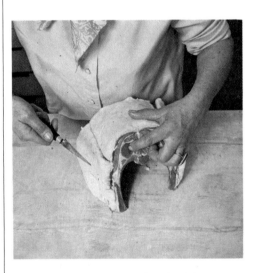

3. Note exact position of the incision.

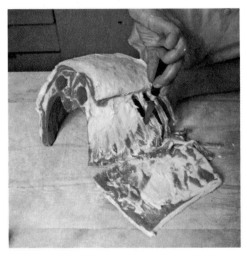

4. Pare away the meat from the bone below the incision line so that the bones are bare on both sides.

5. This is the prepared joint ready for roasting as for Guard of Honor.

French Roast Lamb

1 small Frenched leg of lamb weighing
    about 3 lb
1 eggplant
6 tomatoes
2 zucchini
1 sweet green pepper
3 cups mushrooms
2 onions
salt and pepper
2 cloves garlic
6 tbsp butter
2 tbsp freshly chopped parsley

For garnish
1 lb green beans
4 tomatoes

1. Set oven at 350°F.

2. Prepare the vegetables. Wash and slice the eggplant and chop up the tomatoes. Top and tail the zucchini and cut into rounds. Remove core and seeds from the pepper and chop into dice. Wash and slice the mushrooms. Peel and slice the onions.

3. Peel and chop up the garlic cloves and crush them with a pestle in a mortar with a little salt. Cream the butter, add the crushed garlic and chopped parsley and blend well together.

4. Line the roasting pan with foil. Score the fat surface of the leg of lamb with a sharp knife and chop off the knuckle bone. Spread the joint with the garlic butter.

5. Lay the prepared vegetables in the bottom of the roasting pan and season well with salt and pepper. You can also add the knuckle bone if wished. Then place the joint on top of the vegetables and cover loosely with a piece of foil.

6. Roast on the center shelf of the pre-set oven for about 1 hour and 30 minutes. Remove the foil from the top of the joint for the last 30 minutes of cooking time to allow it to brown well.

7. Serve the cooked joint with the vegetables and garnish with green beans and broiled tomatoes.

1. Score the lamb skin lightly.

2. Cut off the knuckle bone. Spread the joint generously with garlic butter.

3. Arrange the prepared vegetables in a foil lined baking pan and lay the leg of lamb on top of the vegetables.

Lamb Baked in Puff Pastry

1 small to medium Frenched leg of lamb
puff pastry made from 2 cups flour
beaten egg
drippings for roasting

For stuffing
½ lb finely ground lean pork
1 onion
oil for frying
1 tbsp freshly chopped parsley
1 tbsp dried mixed herbs
1 clove garlic
salt and pepper

1. Set the oven at 400°F.

2. Bone out the joint.

3. Now prepare the stuffing. Peel and chop the onion finely. Heat a little oil in a pan and cook onion gently until soft and transparent. Place ground pork in a bowl, add the herbs, cooked onion and the garlic, crushed. Season with salt and pepper and mix together well.

4. Stuff the lamb with this mixture and sew up ready for roasting. Place in a roasting pan with some drippings and partially roast in the pre-set oven for 20 minutes per lb. When time is up, remove joint from the oven, leaving the oven on, and cool joint quickly.

5. Meanwhile roll out the puff pastry into 2 sections, one long and narrow and the other square.

6. Brush the cooled lamb joint with cold water and encase the broad end with the square piece of pastry. Cut the other section into long strips measuring about 1½ inches across and wrap them round the joint gradually working up to the narrow end. Make sure that each piece is sealed well to the last by brushing with beaten egg.

7. Brush the joint all over with beaten egg, place in a baking pan and continue to bake in the moderately hot oven until pastry is crisp and brown – about 35 minutes.

Noisettes of Lamb

2 lb loin or rib roast of lamb
2 tsp chopped mixed herbs
salt and pepper

1. Using a very sharp knife cut the bone from the meat. Sprinkle the underside of the meat with herbs and season with salt and pepper. Then roll the joint up very tightly and use skewers to hold it together.

2. Tie string around the joint at 1¼ inch intervals. Now slice into noisettes.

3. To cook roast in the oven for 15–20 minutes at 375°F, or else fry in butter for 6–7 minutes.

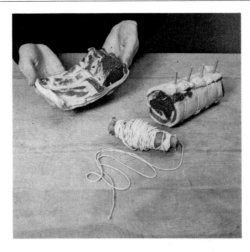

1. You can make noisettes with either a rib roast or a loin of lamb. Whichever joint you use the technique is basically the same. Skin the joint, trim any surplus fat and remove all the bones if the butcher has not already done so.

2. Roll the joint up tightly and use short wooden skewers to hold it in place.

3. Tie up with string in sections of about 1¼ inches.

Noisettes of Lamb.

Lamb Chops à la Nivernaise

6 Frenched rib chops of lamb
salt and pepper
flour
beaten egg
breadcrumbs
1½ lb carrots

1. If the butcher has not done so, remove the meat and fat from the top 1–1½ inches or so, scraping the bone quite clean. Season chops, then coat each one first in flour, then in beaten egg, and lastly in breadcrumbs.

2. Deep fry the chops in hot oil until golden brown. Drain well, arrange on a serving dish, put cutlets frills on and keep warm.

3. Peel and slice carrots into rounds. Steam until tender. Place a carrot slice on each chop and liquidize the remaining carrots. Season the carrot pulp and pipe it round the chops. Serve with green beans and sauté potatoes.

Sweet and Sour Kebabs

2 lb boned lamb, cut from the leg
large can pineapple chunks
2 tbsp lemon juice
2 tbsp soy sauce
1 clove garlic
12 black olives

1. Strain the pineapple chunks and place in a bowl. Add the soy sauce, lemon juice and the crushed clove of garlic.

2. Cube the meat and marinate overnight in the pineapple mixture.

3. Drain the meat. Thread pieces of lamb onto kebab skewers alternately with stoned black olives and drained pineapple chunks.

4. Turn on the broiler to its highest setting. Lay the full kebab skewers in the pan. Baste with marinade and keep turning the skewers, basting well, until the meat is cooked.

Lamb Chops with Garnish.

Lamb Chops with Garnish

2 sirloin lamb chops
1 lb new potatoes
2 large tomatoes
2 tbsp butter
2 tbsp oil
2 tsp freshly chopped parsley or chives
watercress

1. Wash and scrape the new potatoes. Place in a pan of lightly salted water and boil for about 15 minutes, or until just tender.

2. Heat the oil and butter in a skillet. Seal the chops over full heat, then reduce the heat and cook for another 6–7 minutes. Place the chops on a heated serving dish and keep warm.

3. Cut the tomatoes in halves and fry in the skillet. Drain the potatoes and toss in a little butter.

4. Arrange the tomatoes and potatoes on the dish with the chops and garnish with watercress.

Stuffed Blade Roast of Pork

1 blade roast of pork weighing 2 – 3 lb

For stuffing
1⅓ cups fine fresh white breadcrumbs
2 small onions
4 rashers bacon
⅓ cup seedless raisins
1 tbsp chopped chives or parsley
2 tsp paprika
salt and pepper
beaten egg

1. Set the oven at 350°F.

2. Now bone out the joint. Pull away the skin. Then take a very sharp pointed knife and gradually work the meat away from the flat bone in the joint. Do this on both sides of the bone until you can eventually remove the whole bone.

3. Now prepare the stuffing. Peel and chop the onion into small dice. Chop up the bacon and fry lightly. Add the onion and cook gently until soft and transparent. Place the crumbs in a bowl, add the onion, bacon, raisins, herbs and seasoning. Mix together well, then add enough beaten egg to bind.

4. Sew up one side of the joint, add the stuffing from the other side and then sew it together as well. Season the meat. Add a small amount of water to the roasting pan and roast the joint in the center of the pre-set oven for about 2 hours, basting from time to time.

1. Remove skin on the top of the joint.

2. Using a sharp knife, pare away flesh from the flat blade bone.

3. Continue the paring movement until the bone is exposed down to the ridge.

Stuffed Blade Roast of Pork with Savory Crust.

Pork Geneva

1½ lb seedless white grapes
2½ lb boned rolled loin of pork
½ tsp salt
½ tsp black pepper
½ tsp ground coriander
½ garlic clove
1 finely chopped shallot
8 crushed juniper berries
½ tbsp plus ½ tsp Worcestershire sauce
1 tbsp butter
6 tbsp plus ½ tbsp dry white wine
2 tbsp gin
½ tbsp corn starch
cayenne pepper

To garnish
2 tbsp butter
1 lb seedless white grapes

1. Extract the juice from the grapes and discard the pulp. Trim the pork of excess fat and rub with salt and pepper. Place in a shallow dish. Pour over the grape juice. Add the coriander, berries, garlic, half the shallot and ½ tbsp of the Worcestershire sauce. Leave to marinate for 8 hours or overnight.

2. Remove the pork from the marinade and set aside, reserving the marinade. Melt the butter over a moderate heat in a large casserole and add the remaining half shallot. Cook for a few minutes until soft but not brown. Then cook the pork in the casserole for a few minutes, turning occasionally. When lightly browned add the juniper berries, wine, a dash of cayenne pepper, the rest of the Worcestershire sauce and about half of the marinade. Bring the liquid to the boil then cover. Reduce the heat to low and cook until well done. To test: pierce the meat with a knife point. The juices which run out should be clear.

3. To make the garnish, melt the butter in a pan over a low heat. Add the grapes and cook until lightly browned. Remove from the heat and keep warm.

4. Warm the gin; pour over the pork and set alight. When the flames have died down, transfer to a serving dish and arrange the grapes around it. Dissolve the cornstarch in ½ tbsp white wine and stir into the casserole liquid. Increase the heat slightly and cook for 10 minutes stirring frequently. Serve the sauce separately.

4. With the flesh away from the ridge, put the knife right through and sever. Take out the bone and reshape joint.

Variation:
For a blade roast of pork topped with a savory crust, blend 8 cups fresh breadcrumbs with enough melted garlic butter to bind thoroughly. Remove the rind from the roasted joint. Pile the mixture on top of the pork and increase the oven temperature to the highest setting. Return the joint to the oven on a high shelf and brown the crust.

Meat

Sweet and Sour Spare Ribs

2 lb pork spare ribs
3 tbsp soy sauce
salt
2 tsp brown sugar
3 tbsp sherry
2 tbsp pineapple pulp
2 tbsp wine vinegar
1 tbsp arrowroot

1. Cut the meat into individual ribs and place in a pan with a cup of water, the soy sauce and a dash of salt.

2. Bring to the boil, cover and simmer for about an hour, stirring occasionally.

3. Stir in the sugar and increase the heat. Add the sherry, pineapple pulp and vinegar. Keep stirring as the mixture bubbles vigorously.

4. Blend the arrowroot in a little water and stir into the sauce. Stir well until the liquid is reduced and clear.

Apple Sauce

Basic Recipe

1 lb baking apples
1 tbsp sugar
2 tbsp butter

1. Peel and core the apples. Slice them up finely and place them in a pan with 2–3 tbsp water. Cover and cook until soft.

2. Beat with a wooden spoon, add the sugar and butter and serve hot.

Roast Pork with Crackling

1 loin or leg or pork roast
cooking salt
2 lb potatoes
1 large can celery hearts
freshly chopped parsley
1 tbsp flour
2 cups stock

1. Set the oven at 350°F.

2. Place the joint on a board and choose the sharpest knife you can find. The secret of good crackling is very thorough scoring. The rind of the pork should be scored at ¼ inch intervals and the knife cuts deep into the soft fat underneath.

3. Once you have scored the joint, rub cooking salt into it. Then place on a roasting pan without additional fat and roast in the pre-set oven on the middle shelf. Cook for 25 minutes per lb and 25 minutes over.

4. Peel the potatoes and cut into even size pieces. Place them in a pan of cold salted water and bring to the boil. Drain and dry thoroughly. Place them in the fat around the meat 45 minutes before the end of the roasting time. Turn them over halfway through their cooking time.

5. About 30 minutes before the end of the cooking time take joint out of the oven, baste thoroughly and raise the temperature to 450°F. Return joint to oven and baste again 15 minutes later.

6. Tip the celery into a pan and heat in its own juice. Dish the pork up on a warmed serving dish, surround with the roast potatoes and the celery and sprinkle with chopped parsley.

7. To make the gravy, tip off all but about 1 tbsp of fat from the roasting pan. Add the flour and blend well. Then tip in the stock and allow to bubble up well before serving in a sauce boat.

Most butchers do not score pork joints to produce the best crackling. Usually their scoring is too wide and not deep enough. For really crispy crackling, the rind should be scored at ¼ inch intervals and the cuts should be deep. Joints from the hind quarters of the pig give the best crackling.

Roast Pork with Crackling.

Pork Stuffed with Prunes

1 loin roast of pork
18 prunes
strained tea
1 tbsp flour
1¼ cups good stock
2 tbsp sherry
salt and pepper
sprigs of parsley

1. Leave the prunes to soak in strained, freshly brewed tea overnight. Pit them just before using.

2. Set the oven at 375°F.

3. Use a larding needle or a skewer to make a cavity in your rolled joint. Put about half the soaked prunes into the cavity and push well in with the skewer. Reserve remaining prunes and tea marinade. Cover the bottom of the roasting pan with a small amount of water and lace the joint in it. Roast in the center of the pre-set oven for about 2 hours basting occasionally.

4. Poach the reserved prunes in their marinade until tender.

5. Place the cooked joint on a serving dish and keep warm. Add the flour to the meat juices in the roasting pan and blend in well. Then add the stock stirring well followed by the sherry. Bring to the boil and season with salt and pepper. Pour into a sauce boat to serve.

6. Garnish the joint with the poached prunes and sprigs of parsley. Serve with apple sauce, roast potatoes and sautéed mushrooms.

1. Push a larding needle through the rolled boned joint. Pull it out with the meat it contains in the groove.

2. Using a sharp knife make this cavity large enough for you to stuff with prunes.

Pork Stuffed with Prunes.

Meat

Pork Chops with Tortellini

2 lean loin pork chops
olive oil
¼ lb tortellini
¼ cup butter
1 tsp powdered rosemary
2 tsp dried sage
salt and black pepper
sprigs of parsley

1. Trim off any rind on the chops. This can be broiled separately and used for garnish. Brush the chops with olive oil and broil slowly on both sides for 15–20 minutes, making sure that the meat is cooked through without burning the outsides. Season to taste and keep the chops warm until ready to serve.

2. Tip pasta into a large pan of boiling salted water. Bring back to the boil and cook for 12–15 minutes. Strain and return to pan with the butter. Then sprinkle in the dried herbs and season with salt and pepper.

3. Have ready a warmed serving dish. Tip the pasta onto this and lay the pork chops on top. Garnish with sprigs of parsley.

Note: Tortellini is a variety of stuffed pasta. If you are unable to obtain it the dish can be made just as well with tagliatelli (noodles). Tagliatelli needs only 10–12 minutes cooking.

Pork Tenderloins Baked in Puff Pastry

2 small pork tenderloins
basic puff pastry made from 1½ cups flour
beaten egg

For marinade
⅔ cup dry cider
2 tbsp olive oil
1 shallot or small onion
1½ cups mushrooms
1 sprig thyme
1 stalk celery
4 peppercorns
2 parsley stalks
salt and pepper

1. The pork tenderloins should be marinated overnight. To prepare the marinade, peel and chop the shallot very finely. Wash and slice the mushrooms including the stalks. Wash and chop up the celery. Lay the tenderloins in ovenproof dish, pour over the cider and oil and add the shallot, mushrooms, celery, herbs and seasoning.

2. Set the oven at 350°F.

3. Divide the pastry in half and roll into 2 pieces large enough to fold generously over each tenderloin.

4. Remove tenderloins from marinade and drain well. Then lay each one on a piece of pastry. Remove the mushrooms from the marinade, squeeze out any excess liquid and place some on top of each piece of meat.

5. Fold the pastry over the meat and brush the edges with beaten egg to secure them well. Tuck joined edges underneath. Brush pastry with beaten egg, place on a cookie tray and cook on the shelf above center for 30 minutes. If pastry sets too brown, cover with foil.

6. Meanwhile remove celery, parsley, thyme and peppercorns from the marinade leaving just the shallot in the liquid. Tip this into a pan and simmer gently until shallot is cooked. Serve separately with the pork.

Pork Chops with Tortellini.

Pork Tenderloins Baked in Puff Pastry.

Meat

Kidney and Liver Sauté.

Kidney and Liver Sauté

6 lambs' kidneys
¼ lb lambs' liver
1 large onion
3 tbsp butter
3 tbsp oil
⅔ cup stock
1 tbsp tomato paste
salt and pepper

For garnish
¾ lb carrots
1 lb creamed potatoes for piping
croûtons
⅛ cup freshly grated Parmesan cheese

1. Peel and chop the carrots into rounds and simmer in salted water until tender. Prepare the creamed potato for piping.

2. Peel and chop the onion very finely. Heat the butter and oil in a pan, add the onion and cook until soft and transparent.

3. Halve the kidneys, remove skin and core, and cut liver into thin strips. Wash well and dry. Add kidneys to the pan followed by the stock. Then add the liver and simmer gently for a few minutes. Add the tomato paste and season with salt and pepper.

4. Have ready a warmed serving dish. Tip the kidney and liver mixture into the center. Surround with the cooked carrots and then pipe creamed potato round the edge. Garnish with croûtons and sprinkle the finished dish with Parmesan cheese.

Liver Créole

1½ lb calves' liver
4 bananas
3 tbsp fine fresh white breadcrumbs
4 rashers bacon
oil
butter
1 tbsp flour
1 cup stock
salt and pepper to taste

1. Pre-heat the broiler.

2. Halve the bananas lengthwise and brush with a little butter. Coat in bread- crumbs and brown 2 to 3 inches from the heat.

3. Remove the rind from the bacon, roll up the rashers and cook under the broiler. Keep warm.

4. Heat a little oil and butter in a skillet and fry the liver for about 3 minutes on each side. Arrange on a serving dish and keep warm.

5. Add the flour to the skillet and blend with the pan juices. Gradually stir in the stock and season to taste. Simmer 1–2 minutes.

6. Strain the sauce over the liver and garnish with bacon rolls and bananas. Serve with boiled rice.

Kidneys and Mushrooms in White Wine Sauce

8 lambs' kidneys
¼ cup butter
1 onion
2 cups mushrooms
1 tbsp flour
1 cup white wine
⅔ cup good stock
salt and pepper
3 tbsp heavy cream

1. Skin, halve and core the kidneys. Wash well and dry. Peel and chop the onion finely. Wash and slice the mush- rooms.

2. Melt the butter in a pan, add the kid- neys and sauté for about 5 minutes. Take them out and set aside.

3. Now add chopped onion and cook until transparent. Add mushrooms to the pan. After 3 or 4 minutes blend in the flour. Then pour in the wine and stock and bring to the boil. Return the kidneys to the pan and simmer for 10–12 minutes. Final- ly add the cream and season with salt and pepper.

4. Serve with plainly boiled rice and green beans.

Kidneys in Puff Pastry.

Kidneys in Puff Pastry

6 pigs' kidneys
6 rashers sliced bacon
basic puff pastry made from 2 cups flour
prepared English mustard
dried tarragon
beaten egg

For garnish
3 tomatoes
flaked almonds
watercress

1. Set the oven at 375°F.

2. Slit the kidneys down one side, remove skin and core. Wash and dry. De-rind the bacon, fold rashers in half and slip one into each kidney.

3. Roll out the pastry and cut into 6 rectangular pieces – about 6 inches by 8 inches. Spread a little English mustard in the center of each and lay a stuffed kidney on top. Spread the kidney with a little more mustard and add a dash of dried tarragon. Fold over the pastry and brush the edges with beaten egg before sealing. Tuck the edges underneath.

4. Brush the pastry with beaten egg, place on a cookie tray and bake in the pre-set oven on the shelf above the center for about 40 minutes.

5. Serve garnished with flaked almonds, browned under the broiler, watercress and broiled tomatoes.

Roast Stuffed Capon.

Poultry and game

Roast Stuffed Capon

1 capon
butter
salt and pepper

For stuffing
½ cup butter
1⅓ cups fine fresh white breadcrumbs
grated rind of 1 lemon
4 tbsp freshly chopped parsley
marjoram
salt and pepper

1. Set oven at 375°F.

2. Prepare the stuffing. Melt butter in a saucepan. Place breadcrumbs, lemon rind, chopped parsley and a dash of marjoram in a bowl. Pour over the melted butter and season with salt and pepper. Mix together well and spoon into the body of the bird. Skewer the tail end closed and tie the legs firmly in position.

3. Spread the capon with some of the butter and season with salt and pepper. Put the remaining butter in the roasting pan and place the bird in it.

4. Cover loosely with a buttered paper or with foil and roast in the pre-set oven for 20 minutes per lb and 20 minutes over. Towards the end of cooking time remove the paper and baste the bird well.

5. Serve with bread sauce and artichoke bottoms filled with peas.

Poultry and game

Spanish Chicken

6 chicken breasts
2 tbsp flour
1 tsp salt
½ tsp black pepper
¼ cup olive oil
2 cloves garlic
1 onion
1 pimiento
1 green pepper
1¼ cups chicken stock
2 tbsp butter
2½ cups mushrooms
6 tomatoes
10 stuffed green olives
10 pitted black olives

1. Set the oven at 325°F.

2. Mix the flour, salt and pepper and coat the chicken in this seasoned flour. Heat the oil in a large pan and brown the chicken all over then transfer to a casserole.

3. Crush the garlic. Slice the onion, pimiento and green pepper, and fry these for 5 minutes, then transfer to the casserole.

4. Pour hot stock over the chicken and vegetables. Cover the casserole and cook in the pre-set oven for 1–1½ hours or until the chicken is tender.

5. Slice the mushrooms and tomatoes. Halve the stuffed olives. Fry the mushrooms and tomatoes in butter for 5 minutes and add to the casserole with both types of olive. Return to the oven for a further 10 minutes.

CUTTING A CHICKEN INTO PIECES

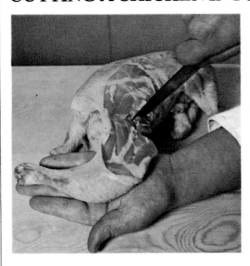

1. Skin the chicken and cut off the legs.

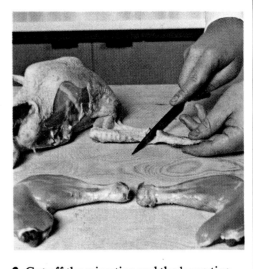

2. Cut off the wing tips and the bone tips of the legs.

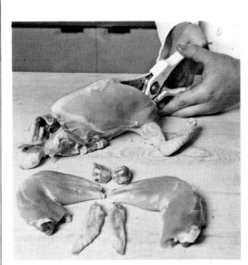

3. Cut right through the center of the bird from head to tail.

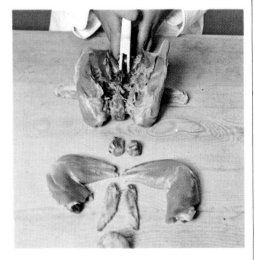

4. Remove the fatty tail and finish separating the 2 halves of the bird.

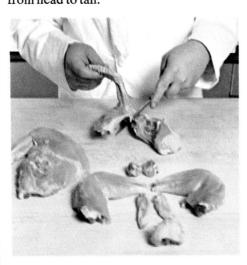

5. Cut the wing from the breast.

TRUSSING POULTRY

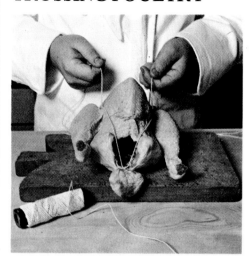

1. Tie string over the fatty tail leaving 2 long ends of string.

2. Wind string around the wings so that the wings are held against the body.

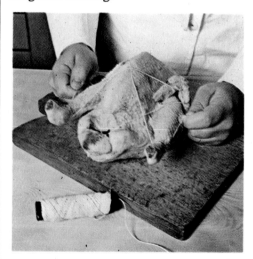

3. Cross the string over the breast then under and over the legs to pull them tight against the body.

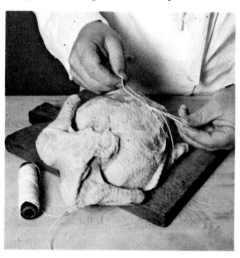

4. Turn the bird over and tie the string in a bow. When the bird is roasted, just pull the string to undo the bow.

If you wish to stuff poultry, do so before you truss it. Wash the inside well, retaining the giblets for gravy. Do not stuff the bird until just before you roast it, although you can make the stuffing in advance and keep in the refrigerator until needed. Spoon the stuffing generously into the bird and sew the opening together with thread and secure it with skewers.

Roast Poussins with Cream Sauce

3 double poussins
12 pistachio nuts
¾ cup finely ground almonds
4 tbsp smooth pâté
1 tbsp dry sherry
2 tbsp heavy cream
salt and black pepper

For the sauce
1¼ cups white stock
2 sprigs thyme
peeled rind of 1 orange
1 tbsp sherry
¼ lb canned or frozen petits pois
⅔ cup light cream
salt and pepper

Double poussins are baby chickens 6–10 weeks old. They are larger than ordinary poussins and one should be sufficient to serve 2 people.

1. Set oven at 400°F.

2. Shell and halve the pistachio nuts. Place them in a bowl with the finely ground almonds, pâté, sherry and cream and season with salt and black pepper. Blend the ingredients well together with a wooden spoon and place a third of the mixture inside each of the birds. Allow the frozen peas to thaw, if using.

3. Spread the poussins with butter and season with salt and pepper. Place them in a roasting pan and cover well with foil.

4. Roast in the pre-set oven on the shelf above center for about half an hour.

5. Meanwhile prepare the sauce. Pour the stock into a pan, add the thyme and the orange rind and simmer until reduced by half.

6. Strain the peas through a sieve and add them to the flavored stock together with the sherry. Simmer the sauce for a few minutes, then add the cream and simmer again. Season to taste with salt and pepper and remove the thyme and the orange rind.

7. Dish the roast poussins up on a warmed serving dish and pour the sauce around them. Serve with new potatoes and string beans.

Poultry and game

Chicken Provençale

3 – 3½ lb ready to cook, broiler/fryer chicken
butter
salt and pepper
½ cup olive oil
1 shallot or small onion
4 pimientos
¼ tsp dried thyme or oregano
¼ tsp dried basil
¼ tsp dried chervil
12 black olives

For garnish
paprika
watercress

1. Set the oven at 375°F.

2. Line the roasting pan with foil. Spread the chicken with butter and season with salt and pepper. Place it in the lined pan and cover loosely with another piece of foil.

3. Roast the chicken in the pre-set oven for about an hour. Cooked in this way it should require no basting and emerge at the end of the cooking time golden brown.

4. While the chicken is roasting prepare the pimiento garnish. Peel and chop the shallot finely. Cut the pimientos in halves and remove the seeds and core. Then cut them in halves again. Cut the olives in halves and remove the pits.

5. Heat the olive oil in a pan and add the chopped shallot and herbs. Cook gently until shallot is soft and transparent, then add the pimientos. When these are tender add the olives.

6. Dish the chicken up on a warmed serving dish and sprinkle with paprika. Spoon the pimiento mixture around it and garnish with watercress.

1. Line a baking pan with foil. Place the chicken in it. Season and brush the chicken with melted butter. Cover the bird with more foil and seal the edges.

2. The cooked chicken will be golden brown without any basting.

Swiss Chicken

3½ lb ready to cook, broiler/fryer chicken
6 tbsp butter
salt and pepper

For sauce
2 tsp potato flour
½ cup dry white wine
1 cup grated Gruyère cheese
1 clove garlic
2 egg yolks
½ cup light cream

croûtons to serve

1. Set the oven at 350°F.

2. Brush the chicken with melted butter and season with salt and pepper. Cover loosely with foil and roast in the pre-set oven for 45 minutes. Keep warm on a serving dish.

3. Blend the potato flour with a little of the wine to make a smooth paste. Pour the wine into a heavy based pan with the grated Gruyère cheese and the crushed garlic. Place over a very low heat and cook until blended, stirring occasionally.

4. Beat the egg yolks with the cream. Add the potato flour paste to the cheese mixture. Stir vigorously to prevent separation. When thick and creamy, stir in the egg and cream mixture. Season.

5. Pour the sauce over the chicken and surround with croûtons to serve.

Chicken Provençale.

Spatchcock Chicken.

Spatchcock Chicken

4 poussins
salt and black pepper
lemon juice
6 tbsp butter

For garnish
watercress
wedges of lemon

1. Cut through the backs of the birds with a pair of scissors. Cut away the backbone, lay the poussins flat on a chopping board and beat well to flatten them.

2. Melt half of the butter. Season the birds with salt and black pepper, squeeze a little lemon juice over and brush with the melted butter. Then leave for 30 minutes before cooking.

3. Heat the broiler and melt the rest of the butter. Place the poussins under the broiler, skin side uppermost, and cook slowly until a good golden brown. Brush with the melted butter when necessary. Turn over and cook on the other side. Allow about 7 minutes per side.

4. Arrange the cooked poussins on a warmed serving dish and pour over juices from the broiler pan. Garnish with wedges of lemon and watercress. Allow one poussin per person.

Chicken Kiev

2 3½ lb ready to cook, broiler/fryer chickens
½ cup butter
salt and black pepper
seasoned flour
beaten egg
dried white breadcrumbs
oil for deep frying

1. Chop off the leg tips and first 2 wing joints from the chickens. Pinch the skin all over and then remove.

2. Pull back each leg and cut away at the point where it joins the body of the chicken.

3. Cut away the breasts. Start by removing the wishbone. Then gently pare the flesh away from the breast bone gradually working right down to the wing.

4. When you have cut around it sufficiently just pull the whole breast away from the carcass.

5. Lay it on a board with the inside facing up to you. You will see a delicate long piece of flesh loosely attached to the rest of the breast. Pull this away gently and reserve. This piece is called the 'filet'.

6. With a very sharp knife make 2 horizontal slits in the thicker end of the breast taking great care not to cut right through the flesh. This will form a pocket to hold the wrapped butter.

7. Now dip the 'filet' in cold water and, using a meat batter, work it into a flat rectangular shape.

8. Place a 1 oz knob of well chilled butter in the center of the 'filet', season with salt and pepper and wrap up into a small parcel.

9. Now tuck this into the pocket in the chicken breast. Re-shape with the fingertips so that butter is well sealed inside.

10. Repeat this process with all 4 breast pieces. Then turn them in seasoned flour and dip in the beaten egg. Roll in breadcrumbs, pressing these on well. They are now ready for deep frying.

11. Place in the hot fat and cook for 6–7 minutes until crisp and golden brown. Drain on absorbent paper and serve garnished with parsley, potato crisps and corn on the cob if liked.

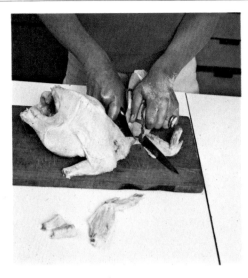

1. Remove the leg bone tips and the first 2 joints of the wing tips.

2. Pinch the skin on the breast and legs to loosen it, then pull the skin off.

6. Cut through the place where the wing bone meets the carcass.

7. Pare away the remaining wing bone piece with the filet attached and pull it out. Detach the filet and set aside.

11. Place a cube of butter in the center of the filet and season.

12. Wrap the butter in the filet so that the butter is quite hidden.

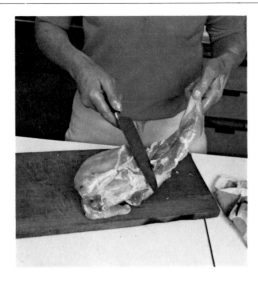

3. Pull the leg out as far as it will go until you see the bone where it joins the carcass. Cut right through this bone.

4. Hold the wishbone and scrape the flesh away right up to the tip. Remove the wishbone.

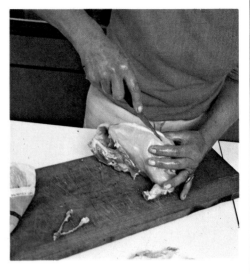

5. Cut along the breast bone on one side to pare away the breast.

8. Lay the breast on a board and make an indentation down the center from the bone tip to within an inch of the other end. Do not cut through.

9. Carefully cut through the fat flesh to make a wide, deep pocket on each side of the central indentation.

10. Dip the filet in cold water and beat into a wide flat piece of meat.

13. Place the butter parcel inside one of the pockets in the breast. Push it right in. Bring the second pocket over the first and press it down.

14. Shape the chicken piece so that one end is fat and the other tapers.

15. This is how the chicken portion should look before cooking.

Poultry and game

Chicken Marengo.

Chicken Marengo

3 lb ready to cook, fryer chicken
¼ cup butter
¼ cup oil
1½ cups small mushrooms
1 tbsp brandy
⅔ cup white wine
1⅓ cups good white stock
8 crayfish (optional)
2 tbsp tomato paste

For garnish
8 heart shaped croûtons
4 fried eggs
chopped parsley

1. Cut the chicken into joints or get your
supplier to do it for you. Heat the butter
and oil in a skillet and lay in the chicken
joints, skin side down. Cook slowly and
turn until golden brown on both sides.
Remove and keep warm.

2. Add the mushrooms, washed but left
whole. Cook until tender, then remove
and keep warm.

3. Return the chicken joints to the pan
and increase the heat. Now add the brandy
and set it alight. Shake the pan and allow it
to burn out. Lower the heat and add the
wine followed by the stock.

4. Wash and clean the crayfish, if using,
and add these to the pan. Allow to simmer

for about 10 minutes, then take them out
and keep warm with the mushrooms.

5. Continue to cook the chicken until
tender, then arrange the joints on a
warmed serving dish and surround with
the mushrooms and crayfish.

6. Bubble up the liquid in the pan, spoon
in the tomato paste and stir in well. Once
the sauce has thickened sufficiently, pour
it over the chicken. Sprinkle with chopped
parsley and garnish with heart shaped
croûtes and a fried egg for each person.

Chicken with Orange Flavored Sauce

1 boiling fowl weighing about 4 lb
3 onions
about 5 cups white stock
bouquet garni
salt and pepper
½ lb mushrooms
⅔ cup white wine
⅔ cup heavy cream
grated rind of ½ orange

For garnish
1½ lb mashed potatoes
2 tbsp flaked almonds

1. Place the bird in a large pan. Peel and
quarter the onions and add to pan. Season
with salt and pepper and pour over stock
to cover. Tuck in the bouquet garni, cover
the pan and simmer very gently on top of
the stove for about 1½–2 hours or until
tender. Skim the fat off from time to time.

2. Wash and roughly chop the mushrooms. Brown the flaked almonds under
the broiler. When the chicken is cooked
removè from pan leaving cooking liquid to
cool for a little. Skin the chicken and cut
away the flesh in large pieces. Pile them
onto a heated dish and keep warm.

3. Skim the fat off the top of the cooking
liquor and then pour about half of it into
another pan with the onions. Boil up
rapidly until reduced to about 1¼ cups.

4. Add the wine and cream and boil
again to reduce further. Finally add the
grated orange rind. Pour the sauce over
the chicken, pipe a border of mashed
potato round the edge of the dish and
sprinkle with the flaked almonds.

Chicken with Orange Flavored Sauce.

Poultry and game

Chicken Sauté with Mushrooms.

Chicken Sauté with Mushrooms

4 lb ready to cook, fryer chicken
¼ cup butter
¼ cup oil
18 small shallots or onions
2 leeks
4 small tomatoes
1 clove garlic
¾ cup white wine
¾ cup white stock
salt and pepper
6–8 flat mushrooms of equal size
butter
⅔ cup heavy cream

1. Cut the chicken up into joints or get your supplier to do it for you. Heat the butter and oil in a skillet and cook the chicken joints gently until golden brown on both sides. Then place them in a flameproof casserole or a pan.

2. Peel the shallots but leave them whole. Wash and chop the leeks, discarding the green part. Scald and skin the tomatoes, remove the seeds and chop roughly. Peel and crush the garlic clove with a little salt.

3. Add the shallots and leeks to the pan and cook gently for a few minutes. Then put them with the chicken, together with the tomatoes and garlic. Pour over the wine and stock and season with salt and pepper. Cover and cook gently for about 45 minutes.

4. Peel and remove stalks from the mushrooms. Cook them in a small pan with some butter.

5. When the chicken is tender, lift out with a draining spoon and arrange on a warmed serving dish together with the leeks and onions. Pour the cream into the cooking liquor and simmer until sauce has reduced sufficiently. Then pour over the chicken.

6. Surround with a border of plainly boiled rice and decorate with the cooked mushrooms.

Chicken Baked with Bacon and Mushrooms

4 lb ready to cook, broiler/fryer chicken
8 rashers bacon
¼ lb mushrooms
¼ cup butter
¼ cup flour
⅔ cup stock
⅔ cup light cream
salt and pepper

1. Set the oven at 400°F.

2. Divide the chicken up into 8 joints if your butcher has not already done it for you. Skin the joints.

3. Wash and slice the mushrooms. Lay a piece of chicken on each bacon rasher. Sprinkle half the given quantity of mushrooms on top, season with pepper and wrap the bacon around tightly.

4. Butter a shallow ovenproof dish with half the butter. Arrange the chicken pieces in it and sprinkle over the remaining mushrooms. Dot with the rest of the butter and season lightly.

5. Cover the dish with foil and bake in the pre-set oven on center shelf for 30–40 minutes.

6. When cooked, arrange the chicken pieces on a heated serving dish and keep warm. Tip the liquor for the dish into a small pan and blend in the flour. Add the stock a little at a time, stirring well after each addition. Then add the cream. When sauce has reached a good consistency pour over the chicken and serve with creamy mashed potatoes.

Chicken Baked with Bacon and Mushrooms.

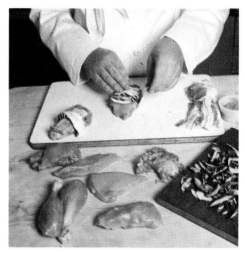

1. Place a portion of chicken on a rasher of bacon. Top with sliced mushrooms and wrap the bacon rasher round.

2. Place all the prepared chicken pieces in the baking dish. Scatter the remaining mushrooms over the top.

Chicken Fricassęe.

Chicken Fricassee

3½ lb ready to cook, broiler/fryer chicken
¼ cup butter
thyme
marjoram
mace
nutmeg
1 onion
3 cloves
¼ lemon
½ cup red wine
1 anchovy
1 tbsp flour
3 egg yolks
½ cup heavy cream

For garnish
triangular croûtes
lemon slices
parsley sprigs

1. Skin and joint the chicken. Cut into small pieces. Place in a pan with 3 tbsp of the butter, a dash of thyme, a dash of marjoram, a blade of mace, a dash of nutmeg, the whole onion stuck with the cloves, the lemon quarter, the wine, the anchovy, salt and pepper and the stock.

2. Bring to the boil, then simmer for 45 minutes, until the chicken is tender.

3. Lift out the chicken pieces and place on a serving dish. Deep warm. Strain the liquor into a clean pan.

4. Work the remaining butter and flour together. Drop small pieces of this into the liquor, stirring over a gentle heat until the sauce has thickened.

5. Remove the pan from the heat. Beat the yolks with the cream, and add slowly to the sauce. Return the pan to a very gentle heat and stir for a few moments. Do not allow the sauce to boil or it will curdle.

6. Pour the sauce over the chicken piece garnish with triangular croûtes, slices of lemon and sprigs of parsley.

Chicken in Lemon Sauce

2½–3 lb ready to cook, broiler/fryer chicken
salt and pepper
1 bayleaf
bouquet garni
2 lemons
¼ cup butter
¼ cup flour
1 cup light cream

1. Place the chicken in a pan with just enough water to cover. Bring to the boil and remove any scum that forms on the top. Add the seasoning and herbs. Slice the lemons and discard the pips. Add to the chicken. Simmer for 1¼ hours or until the chicken is tender.

2. Lift out the chicken and keep hot. Strain off about a cup of stock.

3. Melt the butter in a pan, stir in the flour and cook for a few minutes. Gradually stir in the stock. Bring to the boil, still stirring. Add the cream off the heat. Return to a gentle heat and stir until blended. Season as necessary.

4. Cut the chicken into joints and arrange on a hot serving dish. Pour over the lemon sauce and serve immediately.

Poultry and game

Paprika Chicken.

Paprika Chicken

3 lb ready to cook, fryer chicken
3 tbsp butter
scant ¼ cup oil
1 large onion
1 tbsp paprika
4 tomatoes
1¼ cups chicken stock
salt and pepper
⅔ cup cultured sour cream

1. Divide the chicken into joints. Heat the butter and oil in a skillet, add the chicken and brown evenly on all sides. Remove the joints and place in a flame-proof casserole or a pan.

2. Peel and chop the onion, place in a pan and fry gently until soft. Then work in the paprika with a wooden spoon. Add to the chicken.

3. Pour over the chicken stock, cover and simmer. Meanwhile scald and skin the tomatoes. Remove the seeds and chip roughly. After about 20 minutes, add these to the casserole and continue to cook until chicken is tender.

4. Arrange chicken joints on a warmed serving dish. Allow cooking liquor to bubble up well. Then remove from heat and stir in the sour cream. Pour over the chicken and serve with plainly boiled rice.

Miss Sue's
Southern Fried Chicken

1 chicken cut into serving pieces
milk
1 cup flour
⅟₄ tsp baking powder
salt and pepper
fat for frying

For cream gravy
1 tbsp flour
1 chicken bouillon cube
⅟₄ cup milk
⅟₄ cup light cream
salt and pepper

1. Dip the chicken joints in milk. Mix the flour, baking powder, salt and pepper. Coat the chicken as thickly as possible with this flour.

2. Pour 2 inches of fat into a deep wide pan with a lid. Heat the fat but do not let it smoke. Put in the chicken and fry for 20–30 minutes until tender and golden brown. For a crisp crust, cover the pan and cook half the required time, then remove the lid for the last half of cooking. For a tender crust, cook uncovered for half the time, then cover to finish the cooking.

3. Drain the chicken on absorbent paper and keep warm whilst making the gravy.

4. Pour off all but 2 tbsp fat from the pan. Stir in the flour over a moderate heat until blended and pale brown. Stir in the milk and cream. Heat through, stirring well. Season to taste.

Chicken Lyonnaise

1 boiling fowl weighing about 4–5 lb
½ lb mushrooms
2 lb carrots
2 lb potatoes
20 shallots or small onions
white stock
bouquet garni
salt and pepper

1. Wipe the bird well. Then start to lift skin away from the flesh by pinching with the fingers to create a cavity in which to put the mushrooms.

2. Wash the mushrooms and slice them across the bottom to remove the stalk and some of the base of the mushrooms.

3. Peel the carrots and potatoes and cut into even size pieces if necessary. Peel the shallots and leave whole.

4. Push the mushrooms between the flesh and skin of the bird so that they cover the breast of the bird. Secure the flap of skin underneath with a small skewer.

5. Place the prepared bird in a deep flameproof casserole dish. Surround with the carrots, potatoes and onions and pour over sufficient stock to cover. Tuck in the bouquet garni and season with salt and pepper.

6. Simmer the casserole on top of the stove for about 1½–2 hours, or until the vegetables are tender and the chicken is cooked.

7. Dish up the chicken and vegetables on a heated serving dish. Skim off fat from the cooking liquor, boil to reduce, strain and serve separately.

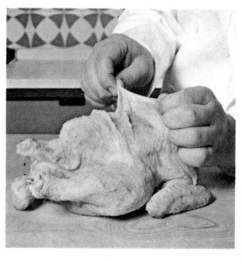

1. Pinch the chicken skin all over to help to loosen it from the flesh.

2. Push whole mushrooms under the skin.

3. Place the chicken and vegetables in a casserole and pour over the stock.

113

Poultry and game

Chicken Curry shown here with plainly boiled rice and chapatis. Other suitable accompaniments for a curry are mango chutney, sliced bananas, shredded coconut, sliced cucumber in plain yoghourt, and curried lentils. Never serve wine with curry – try beer or iced water instead.

Chicken Curry

3 lb ready to cook, fryer chicken
3 cloves garlic
powdered ginger
2 tbsp curry paste
½ tsp crushed cardamoms
⅔ cup wine vinegar
2 large onions
4 tbsp olive oil
salt

1. Divide the chicken into joints. Peel and chop the garlic cloves and crush them with a dash of ginger in a mortar with a pestle.

2. Mix together with the curry paste, crushed cardamoms and vinegar. Place the chicken joints in a bowl and pour over the spicy mixture. Cover and leave to marinate for about 6 hours.

3. Peel and chop the onions. Heat the oil in a skillet and cook the onions gently until soft. Then add the chicken and the marinade. Cover and simmer slowly for about 1½ hours. Serve with plainly boiled Patna rice and chapatis if available.

Chicken with Oregano

3½ lb ready to cook, broiler/fryer chicken
3 tbsp butter
3 tbsp oil
½ cup dry white wine
1 cup white stock
½ tsp oregano
½ cup light cream
salt and pepper

1. Joint the chicken into 4 portions.

2. Fry the joints in butter and oil until lightly browned.

3. Add the wine, stock and oregano. Cover and simmer until the chicken is tender. Take out joints and arrange on a serving dish.

4. Add the cream to the liquor in the pan. Increase the heat and reduce to the consistency of thick cream. Season and strain the sauce over the chicken joints.

Stuffed Roast Turkey

1 turkey
butter
salt and pepper

For pork stuffing
1½ lb ground lean pork
3 tbsp butter
1 large onion
2 tsp dried mixed herbs
1 tbsp freshly chopped parsley
⅔ cup fine fresh breadcrumbs
beaten egg
salt and pepper

For celery, apricot and walnut stuffing
1 small head of celery
½ cup dried apricots
1 cup shelled walnuts
3 tbsp butter
2 onions
1½ cups fine fresh breadcrumbs
1 tbsp freshly chopped parsley
salt and pepper

For garnish
½ lb bacon rashers
watercress

1. Set oven at 325°F.

2. Prepare the pork stuffing. Place the ground lean pork in a bowl. Peel and chop the onion. Melt the butter in a pan and fry the onion gently until soft and transparent.

3. Add the onion to the pork together with the herbs and breadcrumbs and mix well. Add enough beaten egg to bind the mixture thoroughly and season with salt and pepper. Stuff into the carcass of the bird.

4. For the second stuffing the dried apricots should be soaked in water overnight. Peel and chop the onions. Melt the butter in a pan and cook the onions until soft.

5. Drain and cut the apricots into quarters. Wash and thinly slice the celery and chop the walnuts. Add the apricots, celery and walnuts to the pan with the onions and cook for about 4 minutes. Turn into a bowl and allow to cool. Then add the breadcrumbs, parsley and season with salt and pepper. Mix together well and stuff into the breast of the bird.

6. Brush the turkey with melted butter and sprinkle with salt and pepper. Wrap the bird loosely in transparent cooking foil and place in a roasting pan.

7. Roast in the pre-set oven for 20 minutes per lb plus 30 minutes over. For the garnish, remove rind from bacon rashers, roll them up, place on skewers and cook them under the broiler. Serve the turkey with Brussels sprouts and chestnuts, roast potatoes and cranberry sauce.

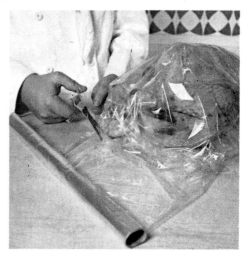

1. Take a large sheet of transparent foil. Brush it with melted butter and season it. Place the turkey on one end of the foil and bring the remaining foil up over the top of the bird.

2. Tuck the ends up under the turkey and place in a baking pan for roasting.

Poultry and game

Roast Stuffed Duck

1 large duck weighing about 5 lb
salt and pepper
clear honey

For stuffing
3 onions
¼ cup butter
2 cups fine fresh breadcrumbs
2 tsp dried sage
1 tsp chopped parsley
salt and pepper
beaten egg

1. Set oven at 400°F

2. Prepare the stuffing. Peel and slice the onions, place in a pan of salted water and boil for about 15 minutes. Drain, place in a bowl, add the butter and then the bread-crumbs, herbs and seasoning. Work in enough beaten egg to bind and then stuff mixture into the duck.

3. Pat the bird completely dry with a clean cloth. Then rub in some salt and pepper. Prick the duck well with a fork and place on a grid which will sit over the top of your roasting pan. Spread the duck with clear honey and work in well with the fingertips. Roast in the pre-set oven for 15 minutes per lb and 15 minutes over. or until cooked and well browned.

4. Serve apple sauce, peas and new potatoes with the roast duck.

ROASTING A DUCK

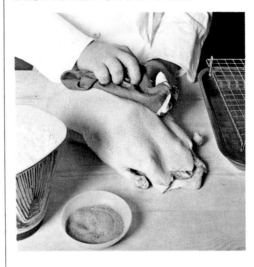

1. Gently pat the skin of the duck dry with a clean cloth.

2. Rub the bird with salt and pepper.

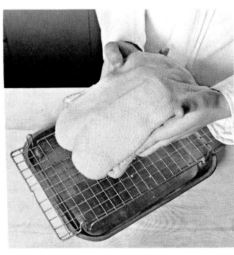

3. Place on a grid over a baking pan.

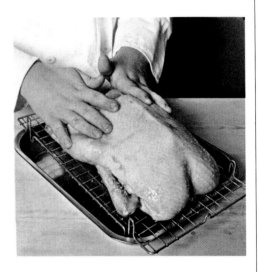

4. Rub honey all over the bird.

5. The cooked duck is a rich brown.

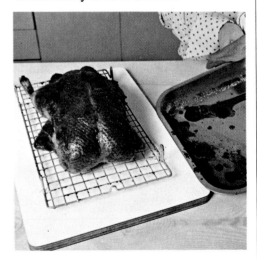

6. The succulent pan juices are used for making the accompanying sauce.

Duck with Grape Sauce.

Duck with Grape Sauce

1 duck weighing about 4 lb
salt and pepper
clear honey
1 tbsp flour
2½ cups stock
¼ lb green grapes

1. Set oven at 375°F.

2. Pat the skin of the duck completely dry with a clean cloth. Then season with salt and pepper, prick the skin, and spread with honey rubbing in well with the fingertips.

3. Place the duck on a grid which will stand in the roasting pan. Pour enough boiling water into the bottom of the pan to cover the base and place the grid on top.

4. Roast the duck in the pre-set oven for 15 minutes per lb and 15 minutes over or until cooked and well browned.

5. Meanwhile peel the grapes and remove the seeds. If the skin is difficult to remove, cover them with very hot water, count to 12 and replace the hot water with cold water before peeling them.

6. When duck is cooked, place on a serving dish and keep warm. Skim the fat off the juices in the pan, then add the flour and blend in well with a wooden spoon.

Stir in the stock and boil up to reduce. Season to taste and add about half the peeled grapes. Heat gently to warm through.

7. Pour the sauce around the duck and garnish with the remaining grapes. If liked the duck can be placed on a large deep-fried croûte.

Poultry and game

Duck Cooked with Onions.

Duck Cooked in Cider

1 duck weighing about 4 lb
seasoned flour
¼ cup butter
1¼ cups dry apple cider
salt and pepper
6 small baking apples
scant 1 cup light cream

1. Set oven at 400°F.

2. Divide the duck into joints and coat with seasoned flour.

3. Melt butter in a skillet and brown the duck pieces on all sides.

4. Place them in a casserole with the pan juices, pour over the cider and season with salt and pepper. Cover and cook in the pre-set oven until tender.

5. Peel and core the apples. When the duck is cooked take out and keep warm in a separate container. Now place the apples in the cooking liquid, turn oven down to 350°F, cover and cook until tender.

6. Arrange the duck pieces on a warmed serving dish with the cooked apples. Strain the cooking liquid into a pan, allow to bubble up well, then stir in the cream. Pour sauce over the duck and serve with creamy mashed potato.

Duck Cooked with Onions

1 duck weighing about 4 lb
2 tbsp butter
16 shallots or small onions
sprigs of fresh rosemary
1 tbsp chopped parsley
2¼ cups stock
salt and pepper

1. Set oven at 375°F.

2. Melt the butter in a large pan, carefully put in the duck and brown it thoroughly on all sides. Remove the duck from pan and place in an ovenproof casserole dish.

3. Peel the shallots and leave whole. Arrange them around the duck, add the herbs and seasoning and pour the stock over.

4. Cook in the pre-set oven for about 1½ hours. When duck is cooked, place on a warmed serving dish with the shallots. Strain the cooking liquid into a pan, remove the fat and boil up to thicken.

5. Pour a little of the sauce over the duck and the rest over the shallots. Serve with lima beans, croûtons and fresh rosemary for garnish.

Duck à l'Orange

1 duck weighing about 4 lb
seasoned flour
juice and rind of 2 oranges
2 tbsp wine vinegar
1 tsp sugar
1 tsp brandy
salt and pepper
watercress for decoration

1. Set the oven at 350°F.

2. Clean and dry the bird thoroughly and prick the skin all over with a fork. Place the bird in a roasting pan and rub all over with seasoned flour. Cook in the pre-set oven for about 1½ hours until browned.

3. Remove the duck from the oven, and keep warm while making the garnish. Cut one of the oranges into slices and grate the rind of the other. To make the sauce, place the vinegar and sugar in a small pan over a low heat and when dissolved simmer for 1 minute. Add the juice of one orange and simmer quickly until it becomes syrupy. Add the grated rind, pour in the brandy and season.

4. Strain the sauce over the finished bird and arrange the orange segments and watercress around it.

1. Cut one of the oranges into slices.

2. Baste the duck frequently with the pan juices during cooking.

Duck à l'Orange.

Poultry and game

Pheasant with Onion Sauce.

Pheasant with Onion Sauce

1 pheasant
1¼ cups mushrooms
¼ cup butter
salt and pepper
3–4 rashers bacon
beef drippings or pork fat
   for roasting
6 shallots or very small onions
milk

For onion sauce
6 onions
¼ cup butter
¼ cup flour
2¼ cups milk
salt and pepper
2 tbsp heavy cream

For garnish
watercress

1. Set oven at 400°F.

2. Wash and remove stalks from the mushrooms. Wipe out the insides of the pheasant, place the mushrooms inside together with the butter and some salt and pepper.

3. Wrap the breasts with the bacon rashers to prevent them drying out. Place them in a roasting pan with some drippings or pork fat, and roast in the pre-set oven for 45–55 minutes, basting frequently.

4. Peel the shallots, place them in a pan with milk to cover and simmer gently until tender.

5. Now prepare the sauce. Peel and slice the onions, place in a pan cover with salted water and cook until tender. Then drain thoroughly and strain through a sieve.

6. Melt the butter in a pan, remove from heat and blend in the flour. Return to heat and pour on the milk stirring continually. Simmer for 2–3 minutes, then add the sieved onions and season. Finally stir in the cream.

7. When pheasant is cooked remove mushrooms from the inside, skin the bird and place in a deep serving dish. Pour over the onion sauce and then decorate with the mushrooms and poached shallots. Garnish with watercress.

Roast Pheasant.

Roast Pheasant

1 brace of pheasant
6–8 rashers bacon
¼ cup butter
salt and pepper
beef drippings or pork fat for roasting
2 tbsp flour

For gravy
stock made from:
   pheasant giblets
   1 carrot
   1 onion
   bouquet garni
1 tsp flour

For garnish
watercress

1. Set oven at 400°F.

2. Wipe the inside of the birds and place a knob of butter, seasoned with salt and pepper in each one.

3. Wrap the breasts of each pheasant with the bacon rashers to prevent them drying out. Place them in a roasting pan with some drippings or pork fat and roast in the pre-set oven for 45–55 minutes, basting frequently.

4. About 10 minutes before the end of the cooking time, remove the bacon rashers and dredge the birds lightly with the flour. Then return them to the oven to brown.

5. While the pheasants are cooking make the stock. Place the giblets from the birds, a carrot, an onion and bouquet garni to flavor in a pan and cover with water. Simmer for 30–40 minutes.

6. When the birds are cooked, dish them up and keep warm. Pour the fat off from the roasting pan leaving sediment behind. Blend in the flour with a wooden spoon. Then add the stock and bring to the boil. Season if necessary, and strain into a sauce boat.

7. Garnish the pheasants with watercress and serve with bread sauce.

Roast Grouse.

Roasted Grouse

1 grouse
2 tbsp butter
salt and pepper
2 rashers bacon
flour

For garnish
1 croûte same size as the grouse
liver from the grouse
butter
watercress

1. Set oven at 400°F.

2. Wipe out the inside of the bird, season and place a nut of butter in it. Wrap the bacon rashers over the breast to keep it moist.

3. Place remaining butter in roasting pan with the grouse and roast in the pre-set oven for about 35 minutes. Ten minutes before the end of cooking time remove bacon from bird, and dredge lightly with flour and baste. Return to oven to brown.

4. While grouse is cooking, sauté the liver lightly in a little butter, then mash with a fork and spread on the croûte. Place the cooked grouse on this and garnish with the bacon rashers and watercress. Other traditional accompaniments for roast grouse are rowan or red currant jelly, browned crumbs and game chips.

Bread Sauce

⅔ cup fine fresh white
*   breadcrumbs*
1 onion
2 or 3 cloves
1 small bayleaf
1¼ cups milk
1 tbsp butter
salt and pepper
1 tbsp light cream

1. Peel the onion and stud with 2 or 3 cloves. Place in a pan with the milk and bayleaf. Bring to the boil, cover and leave to one side for 15 minutes.

2. Remove onion and bayleaf. Add breadcrumbs and bring slowly to the boil stirring continually. Add the butter and seasoning and allow to simmer gently. Finally stir in the cream.

Pigeons en Croûte.

Partridge with Mushrooms

1 partridge
salt and pepper
2 rashers bacon
⅔ cup mushrooms
1 cup stock

For garnish
1 croûte same size as the partridge
watercress
game chips

1. Set the oven at 375°F

2. Season and cover the partridge breast with bacon rashers. Stuff the bird with the unpeeled mushrooms.

3. Place in a baking pan and pour over half the stock. Roast in the pre-set oven for 35–40 minutes.

4. Remove the bacon rashers and set aside. Place the partridge on the croûte on a serving dish and keep warm. Take the mushrooms out of the bird and use 4 large ones as garnish. Chop up the remaining mushrooms and place in the baking pan.

5. Add the remaining stock and place over a fierce heat. Allow to bubble up until thickened, stirring continuously. Chop up the crispy bacon and add to the sauce.

6. Pour sauce over the bird and garnish with watercress and game chips.

Pigeons en Croûte

1 brace of pigeon
puff pastry made from 1 cup flour
salt and pepper
⅔ cup mushrooms
beaten egg

1. Set the oven at 400°F.

2. Remove the breasts from the pigeons. Season the breasts.

3. Divide pastry into quarters and roll out each quarter very thinly.

4. Place each breast on a piece of pastry. Chop the mushrooms and sprinkle over the breasts. Wrap the pastry over each breast, sealing the edges with cold water.

5. Brush with beaten egg and place on a cookie sheet. Bake in the pre-set oven for 30 minutes or until the pastry is golden brown.

Harvest Pie.

Pies and casseroles

Harvest Pie

2 lb rabbit joints
seasoned flour
dripping for frying
1¼ lb raw pork
2 rashers bacon
2 tbsp parsley
2 tsp dried thyme
2 tsp dried sage
1 egg yolk
1 large onion
salt and pepper
cinnamon
1¼ cups stock
1¼ cups red wine
3 hard cooked eggs
savory shortcrust pastry made from 2 cups
*   flour*
beaten egg

1. Soak the rabbit joints overnight in a bowl of cold salted water.

2. Set the oven at 325°F.

3. Drain and dry the rabbit joints and coat them with seasoned flour. Heat the dripping in a pan and fry the joints until evenly browned.

4. Take a fifth of the pork and cut into cubes. Remove rind from bacon chop the bacon. Pass pork and bacon through a grinder with the herbs. Add the egg yolk to bind, divide and shape into sausage shapes.

5. Cut the rest of the pork into cubes, roll in seasoned flour and brown lightly in the dripping. Peel and slice the onion.

6. Arrange rabbit joints, pork and onions in a 2 cup pie dish. Season with salt and pepper and a dash of cinnamon. Lay the sausage on top and then pour over stock and wine. Cover with foil and cook in the pre-set oven for about an hour.

7. When the meat is tender, remove from oven and allow to cool a little. Turn oven up to 375°F.

8. Roll out the pastry to cover the pie dish. Remove shells from hard cooked eggs and tuck them into the cooled casserole. Cover with the pastry lid using trimmings for decoration. Brush the pastry with beaten egg. Bake in the pre-set oven for 30–40 minutes.

MAKING PUFF PASTRY

4 cups flour
1 tsp baking powder
2 tbsp lemon juice plus
    enough ice cold
    water to make 1 cup
2 cups well chilled butter

Basic Recipe

1. Sift flour and baking powder onto a very cold work surface and make a well in the center of the flour. Cut 6 tbsp chilled butter or margarine into tiny pieces (keep remainder chilled) and place in center of the well. With one hand, begin to draw the flour into the center and rub in the butter until it resembles very fine crumbs. Make a well in the center again, then pour in lemon juice and a little of the cold water.

2. Using 2 knives, work the mixture from the sides to the center, adding a little water from time to time, until a firm but smooth dough is formed. Wrap in waxed paper or foil and chill in refrigerator for about 30 minutes.

3. Meanwhile shape remaining butter into a small rectangle and reserve. Lightly flour work surface again, then unwrap chilled dough and roll out to a narrow rectangle. Place the slab of butter in the center of the dough.

4. Make a parcel of the dough by folding nearest pastry edge into the center of the butter. Fold the sides up and over, pressing down gently as you do so. Complete by folding the edge furthest away into the center. Half turn the dough on the work surface, then roll out again to the same sized rectangle. Wrap again and chill in refrigerator for about 30 minutes.

5. Return the dough to the floured work surface again, unwrap and roll out, repeating this once more giving the dough a half turn each time. Rewrap and chill finally before use according to the recipe. Puff pastry can be stored in the refrigerator for up to a week.

1. Place the sifted flour on a cold work surface – preferably marble. Put some of the butter in the center of the flour.

2. Using really cold hands, draw a little flour into the butter and start rubbing in gently with just 2 fingers and thumb.

6. Take the remaining butter from the refrigerator.

7. With a knife, pat the remaining butter into a rectangle on the cold surface.

11. Make an indentation with your finger in the top fold of the pastry. This will help keep your place when rolling out.

12. Wrap in waxed paper and leave in the refrigerator for 30 minutes. Take out and place in the same position as before. Roll,

3. When all the flour is rubbed in and the mixture resembles fine breadcrumbs, shape into a pile with a well in the center.

4. Pour the lemon juice into the well with a little ice cold water. Using 2 knives, work the liquid into the mixture. Gradually add enough water to bind the mixture together into a dough.

5. Work the dough into a smooth ball with your hands. Sift a little flour over the dough, fold it in a clean cloth and leave in the refrigerator to rest.

8. Take the dough from the refrigerator and roll out into a rectangle on the lightly floured work surface. Place the rectangle of butter in the center.

fold and turn, then repeat the process before refrigerating again. This rolling, folding, turning and refrigerating procedure has to be done 5 times before the pastry can be used.

9. Carefully wrap the pastry round the butter to form a neat rectangular parcel.

10. Turn the pastry 90°. Roll out as before and fold up into a parcel.

Pies and casseroles

Cornish Pasties

savory shortcrust pastry, made with 4 cups flour, without the cheese
2 potatoes
1 rutabaga
½ lb finely diced steak
5 tsp suet
salt and pepper
beaten egg

1. Set the oven at 375°F.

2. Roll out the pastry and cut 5 6 inch diameter circles.

3. Peel and finely dice the potatoes and the rutabaga. Place in a bowl with the steak and the suet. Season and mix well.

4. Place a fifth of the meat and potato mixture on each pastry circle, leaving a generous border. Brush the borders with cold water and bring up the sides to meet over the center. Seal the pastry edges together so that the pasties are standing on an oval base with the edges on top. If the edges are not sealed thoroughly the juices will run out during cooking and the filling will be dry when cooked.

5. Brush with beaten egg and place on a cookie sheet. Bake in the pre-set oven on the center shelf for 30 minutes. Lower the temperature to 325°F and cook for a further 30 minutes.

Savory Shortcrust Pastry

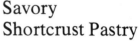

4 cups flour
2 tsp baking powder
1 level tsp salt
½ cup butter
¼ cup lard
¾ cup freshly grated Parmesan cheese
freshly ground black pepper
approx 10 tbsp ice cold water

1. Sift the flour, baking powder and salt together into a bowl. Cut the butter and lard into the flour with a round bladed knife. Once the pieces are evenly coated with flour, rub in lightly with the fingertips until the mixture turns into fine crumbs.

2. Add the grated Parmesan and black pepper and mix in well.

3. Add at least two thirds of the water to the center of the mixture and work in using a fork. Add more of the water if necessary until the mixture forms a firm dough.

4. Turn out onto a floured board and knead lightly until smooth. Wrap the pastry in a polythene bag or a piece of waxed paper and leave in the refrigerator for at least an hour before rolling out.

Veal and Mushroom Flan

savory shortcrust pastry made with 2 cups flour, without the cheese
2 tbsp butter
1 tbsp flour
1 cup stock
1½ cups mushrooms
½ lb diced cooked veal

1. Set the oven at 350°F.

2. Line a flan dish with shortcrust pastry and bake blind.

3. Melt 1 tbsp butter in a pan, stir in the flour and cook for a few minutes, stirring. Gradually stir in the stock and cook gently until thickened. Slice and lightly fry the mushrooms in the remaining butter. Add to the sauce. Fold in the cooked veal and mix well.

4. Spoon the filling into the flan case and place in the pre-set oven for 30 minutes.

Cornish Pasties.

LINING A FLAN AND BAKING IT BLIND

1. Roll out the pastry and lift over the flan ring, using the rolling pin. You can use either a plain or fluted edged ring.

2. Press the pastry against the sides and base with the knuckles.

3. Roll the rolling pin over the flan to cut off the surplus pastry.

4. This provides the flan with a neat edge when it is cooked.

5. Baking blind means cooking the flan without a filling. It is necessary to weight the pastry down with dried beans or rice otherwise the pastry base will be bumpy with air bubbles.

6. Place a circle of waxed paper in the flan ring. Spoon in beans or rice.

7. Fill the pastry case with beans.

8. After baking, lift up the waxed paper and beans. Leave the beans to cool and then store for further use. The flan ring is removed and the case is left to cool before filling according to the recipe.

Pies and casseroles

Beefsteak and Kidney Pudding.

Beefsteak and Kidney Pudding

1¼ lb stewing beef
1 small beef kidney
seasoned flour
½ lb carrots
½ lb onions
Worcestershire sauce
1 tsp tomato paste
good stock

For suet crust
2½ cups flour
salt
1 tsp baking powder
generous 1 cup of shredded suet
⅔ cup cold water

1. Set the oven at 350°F.

2. Trim stewing steak of any excess fat and gristle and cut into cubes. Chop up kidney and turn both in seasoned flour.

3. Peel and chop carrots into dice. Peel and slice the onions finely. Place all these ingredients in a casserole dish. Season with a few drops of Worcestershire sauce and the tomato paste. Pour over enough stock to cover. Cover with lid and cook in the pre-set oven for about 1¼ hours. Then allow to cool.

4. Meanwhile prepare suet crust. Sift the flour with a dash of salt into a bowl. Stir in the suet and then mix to a firm dough with the cold water. Take about two thirds of the pastry and roll out into a circular shape.

5. Grease an ovenproof bowl well. Fold pastry in half and make a dart which tapers to a point where the pastry is folded. Now roll out the dart, open out the pastry and line it into the bowl. Work up the edges of the pastry so it stands ½–1 inch above the rim of bowl.

6. Fill the cooled steak and kidney mixture into the bowl. Roll out the remaining pastry to form the lid. Damp the edges, put on the lid and then pinch edges well together. Cover with foil making a large pleat in the center to allow for expansion.

7. Steam for 2 hours.

Variation:
Beefsteak and Kidney Pie. Use the same steak and kidney mixture and cook in a casserole in the oven as described above. Then using puff pastry made from 2 cups flour, line a pie dish, fill with meat mixture and cover with a pastry lid. Brush with beaten egg and bake in the oven at 400°F for 45 minutes or until golden brown.

Chicken Pie

3 lb cooked chicken
4 leeks
2 cups stock
1 tsp sugar
salt
2 oz cooked ham
1 tbsp chopped parsley
puff pastry made with 1¼ cups flour
beaten egg
4 tbsp heavy cream

1. Wash and slice the leeks, and put in a pan with the stock. Bring to the boil and simmer for 15–20 minutes.

2. Set the oven at 400°F.

3. Cut the chicken into bite size pieces and arrange in a deep pie dish. Pour over the leeks and stock. Sprinkle with the sugar and a dash of salt. Place thin slices of ham over the top.

4. Roll out pastry to 1 inch larger than the pie dish. Cut off a border to fit round the rim of the pie dish. Cover the pie dish, seal the edges to the rim, cut a cross in the center and brush with beaten egg.

5. Place the pie in the pre-set oven and bake for 1 hour.

6. Heat the cream in a pan and pour through the cross in the center.

Shepherd's Pie

1¼ lb cold roast lamb
1 large onion
2 tbsp freshly chopped parsley
¼ lb cooked ham
1¼ cups stock
salt and pepper

For potato topping
2 lb potatoes
3 tbsp butter
warmed milk
salt and pepper
beaten egg

1. Set the oven at 375°F.

2. Peel the potatoes and cut into even size pieces. Place in a pan of cold, salted water, bring to the boil and simmer until cooked.

3. Meanwhile pass the cold lamb, with the onion, peeled and sliced, through the grinder. Place in a bowl, season with salt and pepper and add the parsley.

4. Now grind the cooked ham, place in a pan with the stock and simmer gently for a few minutes. Then add to the minced lamb and mix together well.

5. Place the filling in a pie dish. Drain the potatoes when cooked, return them to the pan and set over the heat briefly to dry off any excess moisture. Season, add butter and a little warmed milk and mash them well until creamy and smooth.

6. Spoon potato over the meat filling and decorate the top with a knife. Then brush with a little beaten egg. Bake in the pre-set oven for about 45 minutes until golden brown.

Shepherd's Pie.

Pies and casseroles

Ham and Vegetable Cream Flan

½ lb cooked ham
puff pastry made from 3 cups flour
beaten egg
1 small cooked cauliflower
¼ lb cooked green beans
¼ lb cooked peas
mornay sauce made from 2 cups milk
1 tbsp grated Parmesan cheese
2 tbsp butter

1. First prepare the pastry case. This can,
of course, be made up the day before. Set
the oven at 425°F.

2. Roll out the pastry to a long rectangular shape ½ inch deep. Trim the rectangle
off neatly. It should measure approximately 5 inches by 15 inches.

3. Place on a well dampened cookie
sheet. Mark an inner rectangle on the
pastry with the back of a knife about ¾ inch
from the outer edge. Take care not to cut
right through the pastry. Decorate the
outer edge with diagonal lines.

4. Chill in the refrigerator for a minimum
10–15 minutes, then brush with beaten
egg and bake in the pre-set oven for
25–30 minutes, or until well risen and
browned.

5. Slide onto a rack to cool. While still
warm go over the marked inner rectangle
with a sharp knife. Then using a metal
spatula, lift out the inner panel and reserve
for a lid. Scoop out some of the soft center.

6. Have ready a freshly made batch of
mornay sauce. Chop ham into dice removing any excess fat. Divide the cauliflower
into florets removing any green leaves.
Chop up the green beans. Mix the ham
and vegetables into the hot sauce folding
over carefully so as not to break up the
vegetables.

7. Pile into the pastry case, sprinkle with
the Parmesan cheese and dot with butter.
Place in the oven for about 10 minutes to
heat through and brown. Place the pastry
lid on a separate cookie sheet in the bottom of the oven to warm.

8. Serve very hot with the lid in position.

Chicken Puff

½ lb cooked chicken
puff pastry made from 3 cups flour
beaten egg
4 oz cream cheese
salt and pepper
2 tsp paprika
4 tbsp light cream
2 eggs
¾ cup milk

1. First prepare the pastry case. This can
of course be made up the day before. Set
the oven at 425°F.

2. Roll the pastry out into a square ½ inch
deep. Trim off the measure approximately
9 inches square. If liked roll out the pastry
trimming into strips 1 inch wide and twist
into straws to use for decoration.

3. Place pastry square on a dampened
cookie sheet. Mark an inner square on it
with the back of a knife about ¾ inch from
the edge. Decorate the outer edge with a
knife.

4. Chill in the refrigerator for 10–15

Ham and Vegetable Cream Flan.

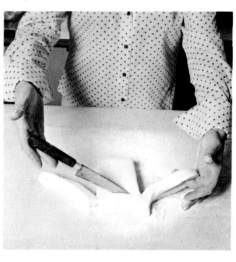

minutes, then brush with beaten egg and bake in the pre-set oven for 25–30 minutes until well risen and a good color. Bake the decorative pastry straws at the same time on a separate cookie sheet.

1. Roll out the pastry to a rectangle measuring 12½ by 7 by ¼ inches.

2. Fold it over so that the cut ends are on top of each other. Make the frame by cutting off a 1 inch border so that the rectangle is smaller but still in the same proportions.

5. Slide onto a rack to cool. While still warm cut around the marked inner square with a knife and then ease out with a metal spatula and reserve for decoration. Scoop out some of the soft center.

6. Reduce oven temperature to 325°F.

7. Cut the chicken into dice removing any skin. Place the cream cheese in a bowl, season with salt and pepper, and half the paprika. Beat well with a wooden spoon, then add the chicken and the cream.

8. Break the eggs into a separate bowl, season with salt and pepper, and whisk in the milk. Add a third of this to the chicken and cheese and mix in well.

9. Pile chicken into the pastry case, then pour the remaining egg mixture on top and cover with a piece of foil.

10. Bake in the pre-set oven for about 10–12 minutes until egg has just set. Then turn up the oven to 400°F and remove foil to allow it to brown. At the same time divide pastry lid into 4 diagonally and place on a separate cookie sheet with the pastry straws to heat.

11. Sprinkle the finished dish with the remaining paprika, garnish with parsley and decorate with the pastry pieces.

3. Roll out the rectangle to its former size and brush with cold water.

4. Open the frame out and lay over the base. Prick the surface of the base.

5. Place the pastry case on a floured cookie sheet and decorate the edges.

Pies and casseroles

Sausage and Potato Pie.

Sausage and Potato Pie

1 lb cooked, brown and serve sausage links
1½ lb waxy potatoes boiled in their skins
puff pastry made from 2 cups flour
2 shallots or small onions
3 tbsp chopped chives
2 rashers bacon
salt and pepper
2 eggs
3 tbsp light cream

1. Set the oven at 375°F.

2. Roll out half the puff pastry quite thinly and line the pie dish or pan.

3. Slice up the sausages diagonally. Skin the cold, cooked potatoes and chop into dice. Peel and chop the shallots finely. Cut the rind off the bacon rashers and chop the bacon.

4. Layer the diced potato and sliced sausages in the pie dish. Sprinkle with the shallots, bacon and chives. Season with salt and pepper.

5. Break the eggs into a bowl and whisk with the cream. Pour this into the pie reserving a little.

6. Roll out the rest of the pastry for the pie lid. Dampen the edges with some of the egg mixture before sealing firmly. Use any trimmings for decoration and brush with the egg mixture.

7. Bake in the pre-set oven for about 45 minutes or until golden brown. This dish can be served hot or cold.

Veal and Ham Pie

1 lb veal stewing meat
1½–2 lb blade steak of pork
salt and pepper
mace
2 onions
2 cooking apples
2 hard cooked eggs
1¼ cups plus 2 tbsp stock
1 envelope gelatin

For raised pie pastry
3½ cups flour
salt and pepper
¾ cup milk and water mixed in equal
   quantities
⅔ cup lard
beaten egg

1. Set the oven at 400°F.

2. Prepare the ingredients for the filling. Remove any excess fat or gristle from pork and veal and chop into dice. Season with salt, pepper and a dash of mace.

3. Peel and chop the onions. Peel and slice the apples removing the cores.

4. Prepare the pastry. Sift the flour with salt and set in a warm place. Measure the lard, milk and water into a pan and bring slowly to the boil so that the fat melts.

5. Pour into the center of the sifted flour and beat well with a wooden spoon. Turn onto a board and knead lightly to a smooth dough. It is important that the pastry should be molded while it is still warm.

6. Roll out the pastry reserving about a quarter for the lid. Line the rest into a well greased pie pan. Layer the meat, onions and apples into the lined pan. When it is half full, halve the eggs and arrange them lengthwise along the pie. Then continue to layer the ingredients to the top. Sprinkle over the 2 tbsp stock.

7. The filling should not quite come up to the top rim of the pastry. These edges should be folded over on top of the meat. Brush pastry edges with beaten egg and then lay the lid on top. Pinch the edges to decorate and brush lid with beaten egg.

8. Roll out the pastry trimmings to a strip about 2 inches wide. With a knife fringe the pastry along one side, brush with beaten egg and roll up to form a tassel. Make a hole in the center of the pie lid and place the pastry tassel over it.

9. Place the pie in the center of the pre-set oven and bake for 20 minutes. Then lower the heat to 350°F and bake for a further 2–2½ hours.

10. When the pie is cooked, heat the remaining stock in a pan and dissolve the gelatin in it. Leave to cool a little until it begins to thicken, then pour through the hole in the center of the lid.

1. Line the baking pan with warm paste.

2. Half fill with meat mixture, then arrange the hard cooked eggs on it.

3. Add the remaining meat. Moisten the pastry rim with a little stock and then push the rim over the meat. Brush the edge with cold water.

4. Put the pastry lid in position and decorate the edges with pastry pincers.

5. Make a fringe out of a 2 inch wide strip of paste.

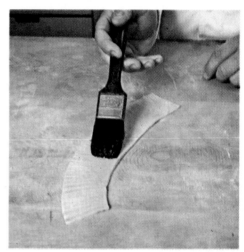

6. Brush with beaten egg.

7. Roll up the fringe to make a tassel.

8. Make a hole in the center of the pastry and place tassel in position. Brush the top of the pastry with beaten egg.

Chicken Waterloo.

Chicken Waterloo

3 lb ready to cook broiler/fryer
  chicken
3 carrots
1 large onion
2 leeks
4 parsley stalks
salt and pepper
2½ cups chicken stock
¼ cup butter

To finish
¼ cup kneaded butter
½ cup heavy cream
freshly chopped parsley

1. Set the oven at 325°F.

2. Peel and slice the carrots into thin rounds. Peel and chop the onion. Wash and trim the leeks removing most of the green leaves. Slice up finely.

3. Melt half the butter in a pan, add the chopped vegetables, parsley stalks and seasoning, cover and cook for about a minute. Then pour over half the stock and simmer until tender.

4. Meanwhile divide the chicken into joints. Melt the remaining butter in another pan and lay the chicken pieces in, skin side downwards, to brown.

5. Strain the cooked vegetables and stock through a sieve to make a paste. Place browned chicken joints in a casserole. Add the paste and the remaining stock. Cover and cook in the pre-set oven for about an hour or until the chicken is tender.

6. Arrange the chicken joints on a warmed dish. Thicken the sauce with the kneaded butter, then stir in the cream. Pour over the chicken and sprinkle with chopped parsley before serving.

Pot Roast of Beef with Prunes.

Pot Roast of Beef with Prunes

3 lb chuck or rump pot roast
dripping for frying
12 prunes soaked in tea
3 onions
1 clove garlic
salt and pepper
⅔ cup red wine
⅔ cup mushrooms
¼ cup pitted black olives
2 tbsp kneaded butter
2 tbsp freshly chopped parsley

1. Soak the prunes overnight in freshly made tea.

2. Set the oven at 325°F.

3. Heat the dripping in a pan, place the joint of beef in it and brown well on all sides. Lift out and place in a deep casserole.

4. Peel and slice the onions. Peel and crush the garlic with a little salt. Fry lightly in the dripping and meat juices and add to the casserole.

5. Pour over the red wine, season with salt and pepper, and cook in the pre-set oven for 2–3 hours, or until meat is really tender.

6. Meanwhile wash the mushrooms and chop roughly. Drain the prunes and remove the stones.

7. During last 30 minutes of cooking time, add the mushrooms, olives and prunes to the casserole.

8. When the meat is cooked, lift it out onto a warmed serving dish, skim any fat from the cooking liquor and thicken it with the kneaded butter. Pour this gravy around the joint and sprinkle with chopped parsley.

Pies and casseroles

Beef Goulash.

Beef Goulash

3 lb stewing beef
oil for frying
1½ lb onions
4 tbsp paprika
2 tbsp flour
1 clove garlic
1 tsp caraway seeds
2 tbsp tomato paste
3 cups stock
bouquet garni
salt and pepper

1. Set the oven at 325°F.

2. Trim the meat of any excess fat and gristle, and cut into cubes. Melt a little oil in a skillet and brown the meat in it quickly. Then place in a large casserole.

3. Peel and slice the onions, place in the pan and fry slowly. After 3 or 4 minutes stir in the paprika, then the flour and blend in well.

4. Peel and crush the garlic clove with the caraway seeds with a pestle and mortar.

Add these to the pan followed by the tomato paste and the stock. Bring to the boil and then pour over the meat in the casserole.

5. Mix ingredients well together, tuck in the bouquet garni and season with salt and pepper. Cook in the pre-set oven for 2½–3 hours until meat is quite tender. Remove bouquet garni and serve with plainly boiled rice.

Braised Oxtail

2 oxtails
seasoned flour
dripping for frying
1 lb onions
1 lb carrots
salt and pepper
stock
2 tbsp tomato paste
Worcestershire sauce
bouquet garni

This is a dish which is inclined to be fatty, so if possible we would recommend that you cook it the day before you plan to serve it. Overnight the fat will rise to the surface and then can be easily skimmed off before reheating.

1. Set the oven at 325°F.

2. Divide the oxtails into joints or get your butcher to do it for you. Coat the pieces with seasoned flour.

3. Heat some dripping in a large skillet and brown them evenly all over. Lift out and place in a deep casserole.

4. Peel and slice the onions. Peel and chop the carrots into rounds. Add these to the casserole dish, season with salt and pepper and pour over enough stock to cover. Stir in the tomato paste and a sprinkling of Worcestershire sauce to flavor. Finally tuck in the bouquet garni.

5. Cook in the pre-set oven for about 3 hours. The meat is cooked when it falls easily away from the bone. Then leave to cool and skim off the fat as described above. Reheat well before serving. Remove bouquet garni before serving.

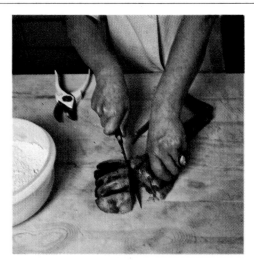

1. Cut through the oxtail joints.

2. Dip the pieces of meat in seasoned flour to coat thoroughly.

3. Shake off the surplus flour.

4. Fry the floured meat pieces in a little fat or oil and butter.

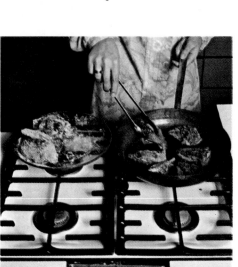

5. Cook over a brisk heat until the meat is evenly browned.

Pies and casseroles

Pork Cooked in Cider

3 lb blade steak of pork
seasoned flour
oil for frying
¼ lb carrots
2–3 leeks
1 tsp powdered rosemary
salt and pepper
2 cups stock
¼ cup dry apple cider

1. Set the oven at 325°F.

2. Trim and chop pork into chunks. Coat in seasoned flour. Heat a little oil in a skillet and brown the meat evenly.

3. Peel the carrots and slice into rounds. Wash and trim the leeks, discarding the green part, and slice into rounds.

4. Place the browned meat in a casserole, add the vegetables, season with the rosemary, salt and pepper. Pour over the stock and cider and cover tightly. Cook in the pre-set oven for 2–2½ hours. Serve if liked with cauliflower.

Pork Cooked in Cider.

Cassoulet

1½ lb small white beans or dried lima beans
¼ lb raw ham
4 cloves garlic
1 small duck
dripping
3 onions
salt and pepper
bouquet garni
¾ lb garlic sausage
½ lb tomatoes
breadcrumbs

1. Soak the beans overnight in a bowl of water. Soak the ham in a separate container. Drain the beans and place in a pan with plenty of fresh warm water. Bring them very slowly to the boil – taking about 30 minutes. Cover and simmer very gently for about an hour.

2. Peel and finely chop the garlic. Place the beans and the ham in a large flame-proof casserole. Add the garlic and enough water to cover well. Cover and simmer gently for 1–1½ hours.

3. Divide the duck into joints. Melt a little dripping in a skillet and brown the duck pieces in it.

4. Drain the ham and beans reserving the cooking liquor. Return the beans and ham to the casserole, and the duck and season with salt and pepper. Peel and slice the onions and add these together with the bouquet garni. Pour over some of the reserved cooking liquor, cover and simmer very slowly for 3–4 hours. Add more cooking liquor and water as necessary.

5. Roughly chop the tomatoes and after 2½ hours of the cooking time add these together with the garlic sausage.

6. Set the oven at 375°F.

7. When the beans are tender take out the ham and garlic sausage, slice up and return to the casserole. Sprinkle the top with the crumbs.

8. Place the casserole in the pre-set oven and cook for a further hour to brown.

Cassoulet.

Pies and casseroles

Chicken Cooked with Tarragon

3 lb ready to cook, broiler/fryer chicken
¼ cup butter
salt and pepper
1 clove garlic
1½ cups mushrooms
6 shallots or small onions
2 tbsp finely chopped tarragon
bouquet garni
2½ cups good stock
2 tbsp kneaded butter

1. Set the oven at 325°F.

2. Melt the butter in a pan and when foaming put in the chicken, breast side downwards. Brown the bird all over on a slow heat for about 15 minutes, turning as necessary.

3. Peel and crush garlic clove with a little salt. Wash and roughly chop the mushrooms. Peel the shallots and leave whole.

4. Place the browned chicken in a deep casserole. Add the tarragon and garlic and season with salt and pepper. Arrange the mushrooms and shallots around it. Pour over the stock and tuck in the bouquet garni.

5. Cook in the pre-set oven for about 1¼ hours. Lift chicken, mushrooms and onions onto a heated serving dish. Remove bouquet garni, thicken the cooking liquor with kneaded butter and pour over.

Kneaded Butter

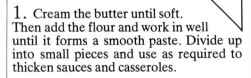

2 tbsp butter
¼ cup flour

1. Cream the butter until soft. Then add the flour and work in well until it forms a smooth paste. Divide up into small pieces and use as required to thicken sauces and casseroles.

2. If liked you can make up kneaded butter in larger quantities and store in the refrigerator for future use.

Chicken Cooked with Tarragon.

Spicy Beef Casserole

5 lb stewing beef
seasoned flour
dripping
3 carrots
3 large onions
2¼ cups stock
4 tbsp molasses
2 bayleaves
allspice
3 tbsp brandy
3 anchovy fillets
1 tbsp wine vinegar
2 tbsp flour
1¼ cups heavy cream

1. Set the oven at 325°F.

2. Trim any excess fat from the meat and cut into cubes. Roll in seasoned flour.

3. Melt some dripping in a skillet pan and brown the meat in it. Then place in a large casserole.

4. Peel and chop the onions and carrots. Add a little more dripping to the pan and lightly fry the vegetables. Add them to the casserole.

5. Pour stock into a pan, bring to the boil and then add molasses, bayleaves, a dash of allspice and the brandy. Pour half of this into the casserole.

6. Chop up the anchovy fillets finely and add these to the rest of the stock in the pan. Blend them in well using a wooden spoon. Then add the vinegar and pour into casserole.

7. Cover and cook in the pre-set oven for about 3 hours or until tender. When the meat is tender lift out into a warmed serving dish. Then blend the flour into the cream and stir into the casserole. Bring back to the boil and simmer gently. Pour over the meat and serve with baked potatoes in their jackets.

Carbonnade of Beef

2½ lb stewing beef
seasoned flour
dripping
2 onions
12 shallots or small onions
2½ cups light ale
1 tbsp light brown sugar
1 tsp wine vinegar
bouquet garni
salt and pepper

1. Set the oven at 325°F.

2. Trim off any excess fat from the meat, cut into cubes, and coat with seasoned flour.

3. Melt a little dripping in a skillet add the meat and brown overall. Put to one side.

4. Peel and slice the onions finely. Peel the shallots but leave whole. Turn the sliced onions in seasoned flour, add a little more dripping to the pan if necessary and fry the onions gently.

5. Have ready a large casserole. Cover the bottom with half the onions, then add half the meat followed by the rest of the onions and the remaining meat. Top with the shallots.

6. Pour over the beer, sprinkle with the sugar and wine vinegar and tuck in the bouquet garni. Season with salt and pepper.

7. Cook in the pre-set oven for about 2½–3 hours. Remove bouquet garni before serving with mashed potatoes.

Irish Stew

2½ lb lamb rib chops
1 lb onions
1½ lb potatoes
3¾ cups stock or water
salt and pepper

1. Set the oven at 325°F.

2. Trim the meat. Peel and thickly slice the onions and potatoes.

3. Layer the meat and vegetables into a casserole starting and finishing with potatoes. Season well with salt and pepper.

4. Pour over the stock or water, cover and cook in the pre-set oven for at least 2 hours. The potatoes will pulp down to thicken the gravy.

Hunter's Hot Pot

½ lb pork loin
2 pork kidneys
3 onions
1¼ cups lager
1¼ cups stock
1 tsp sugar
black pepper
1 bayleaf
1 lb potatoes
1½ tbsp butter
1½ tbsp oil

1. Set the oven at 325°F.

2. Slice the onions thinly and fry gently in oil and butter until soft. Take out and set aside.

3. Skin and slice the kidneys, thinly slice the pork loin. Brown both in the pan in which the onions were fried. Remove the meat and set aside.

4. Still using the same pan, pour in the lager and stock with the sugar. Bring to the boil and then strain off the liquor.

5. Peel and thinly slice the potatoes. Place the kidneys, pork, onions, and potatoes in layers in the casserole. Put the bayleaf on top and pour in the liquor then finish with a thick layer of potato.

6. Cover with a lid and cook in the pre-set oven for 1½ hours. Increase the heat to 425°F. Remove the lid and cook until the potato topping is brown and crisp.

Bouquet Garni

This bunch of herbs traditionally consists of 2–3 parsley stalks, a sprig of thyme and a bayleaf. The herbs can either be tied together with string, or tied up in a piece of muslin. A sprig of marjoram or a few leaves of chives can be added if wished.

Carbonnade of Beef.

143

Special Omelet with Mushrooms.

Eggs and cheese

Special Omelet with Mushrooms

6 eggs
6 tbsp butter
salt and pepper

For filling
2 cups mushrooms
1 shallot
¼ cup white wine
salt and pepper
2 tbsp light cream

To finish
⅔ cup light cream
2 tbsp freshly grated Parmesan cheese
6 very thin slices Emmenthal cheese

1. First prepare the filling. Wash and chop the mushrooms. Peel and grate the shallot. Place both in a pan, season with salt and pepper and pour over the wine and cream. Simmer gently for 5–6 minutes.

2. Break the eggs into a bowl and whisk them with a fork. Cream the butter and drop half of it into the eggs. Season and whisk again.

3. Have the omelet pan heating on a low heat. Also turn on the broiler to heat. Put butter into the pan, turn up heat and when melted and foaming pour in the eggs. Stir briefly with the back of a fork.

4. When eggs have begun to set add half of the prepared filling. Fold over the omelet with a palette knife and turn onto a warmed flameproof dish. Pour over the remaining filling. Add the cream, scatter over the grated Parmesan and cover with the slices of Emmenthal.

5. Place under the hot broiler to brown before serving.

MAKING OMELETS

Basic Recipe

4 eggs
3 tbsp butter
salt and pepper

1. Break the eggs into a bowl and beat them well with a fork.

2. Cream the butter and drop a third of it into the egg. Season with salt and pepper and beat again.

3. While you are doing this have the pan heating over low heat. Now turn up the heat and add remaining butter.

4. When all the butter has melted and is foaming pour in the egg mixture. Leave for a few seconds, then stir slowly with the back of a fork.

5. Cook for another few seconds, then flip over a third of the omelet with a palette knife, away from the handle of the pan.

6. Have ready a warmed plate and turn the omelet onto it making a second fold.

1. Break the eggs into a bowl.

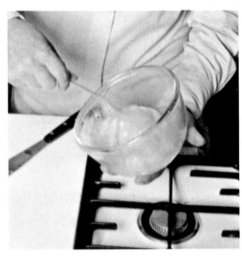
2. Beat the eggs lightly with a fork.

5. Melt some more butter in an omelet pan over a fierce heat.

6. Pour in the egg and butter mixture.

9. You can also use a fork to fold it.

10. Hold the pan at right angles to the serving dish and slide the omelet onto the dish, folding as you slide.

3. Soften some butter with the fingertips and drop pieces into the eggs. Season.

4. Beat in the butter.

7. Work the mixture for a few seconds with the back of a fork.

8. As it sets on the base, but is still moist in the center, shake the pan to partly fold the omelet.

Take care of your omelet pan. Never wash it or use it for cooking anything else. To clean after use, wipe it while it is still hot with a clean cloth or kitchen paper. Prepare an old pan for omelet making by heating the pan and wiping it with raw pork fat immediately before use. To season a brand new pan, place it over a very low heat and half fill with coarse salt. Leave for 2 days then discard the salt. Wipe the pan vigorously with a cloth while it is still very hot. This treatment will prevent your omelets sticking to the pan.

Eggs Benedict

8 thick slices cooked ham
8 English muffins
2 tbsp butter
8 eggs

For hollandaise sauce
3 egg yolks
1 tbsp water
½ cup softened butter
¼ tsp salt
cayenne pepper
1 tsp lemon juice
1 tbsp light cream

1. To make the sauce, beat the yolks and water until pale and thick in a bowl set over a pan of hot water. Beat in the butter in small pieces. Continue beating until the sauce thickens. Add salt, a dash of cayenne pepper and lemon juice. Beat in cream. Keep warm.

2. Broil the ham for 3 minutes on each side. Toast the muffins and spread with butter. Poach the eggs lightly.

3. Arrange a slice of ham on each buttered muffin. Top with a poached egg and spoon a little sauce over.

Florentine Eggs

large packet frozen spinach
¼ cup softened butter
powdered nutmeg
salt and pepper
6 eggs
6 tbsp light cream
¼ cup grated Cheddar cheese

1. Set the oven at 350°F.

2. Thaw and drain the frozen spinach. Brush the insides of 6 individual soufflé dishes with a quarter of the butter. Mix the spinach with nutmeg, salt and pepper. Beat in remaining butter.

3. Divide spinach between the dishes and hollow out the centers. Break an egg into each hollow and pour a spoonful of cream over. Sprinkle the cheese over the top and season.

4. Place in a baking pan half filled with water. Cover with foil. Bake in pre-set oven for 20–25 minutes until eggs are set.

Eggs and cheese

Chicken Liver Omelet

6 eggs
6 tbsp butter
salt and pepper

For filling
6 oz chicken livers
1 small onion
2 tbsp butter
2 tbsp oil
¾ cup good stock
2 tbsp sherry
¼ cup light cream
salt and pepper

1. First prepare the filling. Chop the chicken livers and peel and chop the onion. Heat the butter and oil together in a pan, add the liver and onions and brown well.

2. Pour over the stock and sherry and simmer for a few minutes. Then add the cream and cook briskly to reduce liquid sufficiently and to thicken. Season with salt and pepper.

3. Break the eggs into a bowl, beat them with a fork, add half the butter and season.

4. Put butter into heated omelet pan, and when foaming and melted pour in the egg mixture. Stir with the back of a fork and when it has begun to set add half the prepared filling. Fold over with a palette knife and turn omelet onto a heated serving dish. Cover with the rest of the filling and serve.

Crab Omelet

6 eggs
6 tbsp butter
salt and pepper

For filling
¾ cup mixed white and brown crabmeat
1 tbsp butter
1 tbsp flour
¾ cup white wine
salt and pepper
juice of ¼ lemon
¾ cup cream
chopped parsley

1. First prepare the filling. Melt the butter in a pan, add the flour and blend well together. Pour in the wine stirring continually. Add the crabmeat and the lemon juice and season with salt and pepper.

2. Simmer briefly, then add the cream.

3. Break the eggs into a bowl, beat with a fork, add half the butter and season with salt and pepper.

4. Add remaining butter to the warmed pan and when foaming, add the eggs. When mixture has begun to set add a good spoonful of the prepared filling. Fold the omelet over and turn onto a warmed serving dish. Pour over the rest of the crab sauce sprinkle with chopped parsley and serve immediately.

Eggs Baked with Ham and Tomatoes

5 eggs
¼ cup diced cooked ham
¼ cup diced cooked pork
1 onion
½ lb tomatoes
¼ cup butter
1 tbsp flour
¾ cup stock
salt and pepper
chopped parsley

1. Set the oven at 350°F.

2. Remove any excess fat from ham and pork. Peel and slice the onion. Scald, skin and roughly chop the tomatoes.

3. Melt the butter in a pan and add the diced meat and onion. Cook for a few minutes and then work in the flour.

4. Add the chopped tomatoes and the stock and cook until all ingredients are well blended. Season with salt and pepper.

5. Turn the mixture into a shallow ovenproof dish. Break the eggs on top and cook in the pre-set oven for 8–10 minutes, or until the eggs are cooked.

Chicken Liver Omelet.

Eggs Baked with Ham and Tomatoes.

149

Eggs and cheese

Egg and Onion Flan.

Egg and Onion Flan

*savory shortcrust pastry made
    from 2 cups flour*
3 eggs
1 lb onions
salt and pepper
2 tbsp butter
2 tbsp oil
3 tbsp chopped chives
2 cups milk

1. Set the oven at 400°F.

2. Roll out the pastry and line a 9 inch flan ring. Chill in the refrigerator for about 30 minutes. Now line the pastry with a piece of foil.

3. Bake the flan case in the pre-set oven for about 15 minutes till the pastry is just set but not colored. Remove beans and

waxed paper. Turn oven down to 375°F.

4. Separate 2 of the eggs. Place the 2 yolks in a bowl with the third egg, season with salt and pepper and whisk together. Then add the milk.

5. Peel and chop the onions. Heat the butter and oil together in a pan, add the onions and cook until soft and transparent. Leave to cool and then add to the egg mixture with the chopped chives.

6. Whisk up the egg whites until stiff and fold them into the egg and onions. Pour into the flan case and cook in the pre-set oven for 5 minutes. Then reduce heat to 325°F and continue to cook for a further 30 minutes.

Quiche Lorraine

*savory shortcrust pastry made with 1½ cups
    flour*
1 onion
1 tbsp butter
3 rashers bacon
¾ cup grated Cheddar cheese
2 eggs
¼ cup milk
¼ cup light cream
salt and pepper

1. Set the oven at 400°F.

2. Line a 7 inch flan ring with pastry and bake blind.

3. Chop the onion and fry in butter until soft. Remove the rind from the bacon. Chop the bacon and fry. Arrange bacon and onion in the flan case. Sprinkle with grated cheese.

4. Whip eggs, milk and cream. Season and strain into the flan. Bake in the pre-set oven for 30–35 minutes, covering with foil if necessary to prevent overbrowning.

Cheese and Leek Flan

*savory shortcrust pastry made
    from 1½ cups flour*
2 leeks
1½ cups creamy milk
2 egg yolks
½ cup grated Cheddar cheese or
    ¼ cup grated Parmesan cheese
salt and pepper

1. Set the oven at 375°F.

2. Make up pastry and line a 7 inch diameter flan ring. Prick base and chill. Top and tail leeks, then chop them and cook in boiling salted water until tender.

3. Mix egg yolks into milk, add cheese and season with salt and pepper. Sprinkle a thick layer of chopped, cooked leeks over the base of the flan case, pour over egg mixture and bake flan in the pre-set oven for 30 minutes, until filling is set.

Note: Extra cheese sauce can be served with this flan, which is also good served with small potatoes baked in their jackets.

Cheese and Leek Flan.

Eggs and cheese

Hot Cheese Puffs.

Hot Cheese Puffs

4 eggs
1 cup plus 1 tbsp flour
½ cup cream
¼ cup beer
salt
2 tbsp butter
grated rind of 1 lemon
oil for frying
1 tbsp grated Parmesan cheese

For sauce
3 tbsp butter
¼ cup plus 1 tbsp flour
⅔ cup white wine
⅔ cup good stock
⅔ cup light cream
¼ cup grated Parmesan cheese
¼ cup grated Gruyère or Emmenthal cheese
½ packet cream cheese
salt and pepper

1. Separate the eggs, place the yolks in a bowl and whisk them together.

2. Add the flour, cream and beer a little at a time, beating well. Season with salt.

3. Melt the butter in a pan and blend in the lemon rind. Whisk into the batter.

4. Whip the egg whites until stiff and fold them into the batter.

5. Have ready a heated heavy based skillet. Heat a little olive oil in it and then add about 4 tbsp of the batter. When the bottom has set, turn over with a spatula and cook on the other side. Keep the puffs warm in the oven while cooking the rest and making the sauce.

6. To prepare the sauce, melt the butter in a pan and blend in the flour with a wooden spoon. Pour in the wine, bring to the boil and beat until smooth. Then add the stock in the same manner. Pour in the cream and add the grated Parmesan. Allow sauce to bubble up until thick and creamy. Then add the Gruyère and the cream cheese a little at a time. Season to taste.

7. Spread each puff with a little of the sauce and pile them up on a warmed serving dish, pour over the remaining sauce and sprinkle the top with grated Parmesan. Brown under the broiler and serve piping hot.

Potted Cheese with Herbs.

Potted Cheese with Herbs

2 cups grated Cheddar cheese
6 tbsp butter
1 tsp each of fresh chopped chives,
*   tarragon, chervil, sage, thyme and*
*   parsley*
1 tbsp thick cream
2 tbsp sherry
salt and pepper
clarified butter

1. Place the grated cheese, butter, herbs, cream and sherry in the top of a double saucepan. Set over low heat and stir until all the ingredients melt and turn into a thick cream.

2. Season to taste. Then pour the mixture into small jars and allow to cool. When cold cover each one with ¼ inch layer of clarified butter and seal with lid. Keep in the refrigerator. Serve with fingers of hot buttered toast.

MAKING PANCAKES

Basic Recipe

1 cup flour
salt
1 egg
1¼ cups milk
a little oil or lard
   for greasing the pan

1. Mix the flour and a dash of salt. Make a well in the center of the flour and break in the egg.

2. Add half the milk and gradually work the flour into the milk, beating until the mixture is smooth. Add the remaining liquid gradually and beat until well mixed in and the surface is covered with tiny bubbles.

3. Heat a little oil or lard in a 7 inch, heavy based, flat frying pan until it is really hot, making sure that all the surface of the pan is greased. Pour off any surplus oil and reserve for using before the next pancake is cooked.

4. Pour a little of the batter into the pan, tilting it so that just a thin layer of batter covers the base. Cook over a low heat until the underside of the pancake is golden brown. Turn it over by tossing it or using a palette knife and cook until the second side is golden. Turn out onto waxed paper.

5. Make 7 other pancakes from this amount of batter, greasing the pan each time. If they are to be served immediately keep them warm between 2 plates in a warm oven.

Note: Cooked pancakes may be kept wrapped in waxed paper in an ordinary refrigerator for up to a week. Reheat them both sides in a hot frying pan, without any fat.

1. Take the pan off the heat and pour a little batter in on one side.

2. Tip the pan to spread the batter thinly over the base. Cook on a low heat.

3. When the underside has set, slide a spatula underneath the pancake.

4. Lift carefully and turn the pancake over. Cook the second side for a moment. If the pancake is thick enough to toss, it is too thick.

5. Slide the cooked pancake out onto a piece of oiled waxed paper. Hold the edge of the pancake as it slides out.

6. You can store pancakes stacked on individual squares of oiled waxed paper. Wrap the stack in foil and keep in the refrigerator. Reheat in a low oven.

Cheese Crêpes

For batter
1 cup flour
salt
1 egg
1 egg yolk
1¼ cups milk
1 tbsp salad oil

oil for frying
10–12 strips Emmenthal cheese
1 cup light cream
black pepper
¾ cup freshly grated Parmesan cheese
butter

1. Set the oven at 375°F.

2. First prepare the pancakes. Sift the flour into a bowl with a dash of salt, make a well in the center, add the egg and egg yolk and begin to add the milk slowly, stirring all the time. When half the milk has been added, stir in the oil and beat mixture until smooth.

3. Add the remaining milk and leave to stand for 30 minutes before using.

4. Heat a skillet over low heat, then add a very little oil just to cover pan. Pour off any excess. Add about 2 tbsp of batter to the center of the pan. Tip the pan so that batter covers the base. When lightly browned on the underside flip over and cook the other side. Lay the cooked pancakes on a rack while you cook the remainder.

5. Lay a finger of Emmenthal cheese inside each pancake and roll up. Arrange them in an ovenproof dish.

6. Pour over the cream, sprinkle with Parmesan cheese and season with black pepper. Cook in the pre-set oven for about 15 minutes and serve hot.

Cheese Crêpes.

MAKING CREAM CHEESE

5 cups milk
4 tsp rennet

1. Pour the milk into a saucepan and place over a very low heat until quite hot.

2. Leave to cool down to blood temperature. Then tip it into a bowl and add the rennet. Leave to set in a cool place (not the refrigerator).

3. When the milk has set, take a large piece of muslin, double it over and lay it into a large sieve with the edges hanging well over the rim.

4. Spoon the milk into the muslin. Then tie the 4 corners of the muslin cloth together securely to make a handle.

5. Hang the muslin bag in a convenient place to drip for the next 48 hours. At the end of this time the dripping will have stopped. The cheese should then hang in a draughty place for another 24 hours to let it dry out. It will then be ready to use.

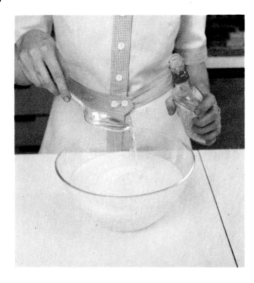

1. Pour the heated milk, or milk and cream, into a large bowl. Add the rennet. Leave to set in a cool place.

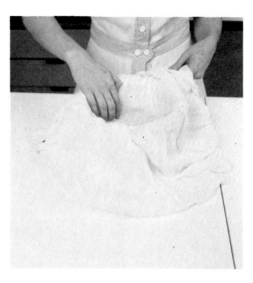

2. Line a sieve with a double layer of clean butter muslin.

4. Tie up the 4 corners of the muslin to make a handle and hang the muslin bag up to drip for 48 hours. It will need another 24 hours hanging in a draughty place before it is ready.

Cream Cheese.

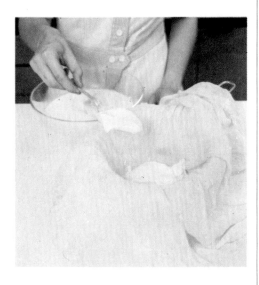

3. Spoon the set milk into the muslin lined sieve set over a bowl.

Swiss Fondue

3 cups Emmenthal cheese
2½ cups Gruyère cheese
1 clove garlic
½ tbsp flour
½ cup dry white wine
1 tsp lemon juice
2 tbsp kirsch
grated nutmeg
black pepper

1. Rub the inside of a fondue pan or any heavy based pan with the halved clove of garlic.

2. Grate the cheese and mix with the flour. Put into the pan with the wine and lemon juice. Slowly bring to the boil, stirring continuously.

3. Add the kirsch and a dash of nutmeg and pepper. Bring back to the boil. When the fondue is thick and creamy, it is ready to serve with cubes of French bread. Keep the fondue simmering during the meal. To eat, dip the bread into the fondue, using long forks.

Cheese Ramekins

2 eggs
¼ cup grated Cheddar cheese
salt and pepper
1¼ cups milk
2 slices bread
butter for frying
8 anchovy fillets
paprika pepper

1. Set the oven at 375°F.

2. Beat the eggs lightly, then add the grated cheese, seasoning and milk.

3. Cut the bread into cubes and fry in butter until crisp. Cut the anchovies in small pieces.

4. Butter 6 individual soufflé dishes. Divide the croûtons and anchovies between the dishes. Pour the egg mixture over. Place in a baking pan half filled with water and bake in the pre-set oven for 15–20 minutes or until firm and golden brown.

5. Dust with paprika pepper and serve.

Cheese Mousse

½ cup cottage cheese
⅜ cup Parmesan cheese
⅔ cup milk
2 eggs
juice and rind of 1 lemon
⅔ cup heavy cream
1 tsp powdered gelatin
cayenne pepper
nutmeg
salt

1. Separate the eggs and whip the cream.

2. Warm the milk to blood temperature. Place the egg yolks in a bowl, pour over the milk and beat gently.

3. Now add the cottage and Parmesan cheese, the lemon juice and rind and the whipped cream. Blend well together.

4. Dissolve the gelatin as directed on the packet. When it begins to thicken, add to the egg and cheese mixture and heat again.

5. Whip the egg whites until stiff and fold them in. Season with a dash of cayenne, a dash of grated nutmeg and salt.

6. Turn into an oiled mold and place in the refrigerator to set. Serve garnished with pretzels if liked.

Cheese Fingers

puff pastry made with 2 cups flour
2½ cups Roquefort cheese
1 beaten egg

1. Set the oven at 425°F.

2. Roll out the pastry to a thin rectangle. Brush half the pastry with water and lay slices of cheese on it. Cover the remaining pastry, pressing down well. Cut out 8 fingers and place on a cookie sheet. Brush with beaten egg.

3. Bake in the pre-set oven for 15–20 minutes.

Farfalle with Bolognese Sauce.

Pasta and rice

Cook pasta in plenty of boiling water. Cover the pan and simmer until barely tender. To test if pasta is cooked try a piece between your teeth; it should be just firm – 'al dente'. Spaghetti takes 12–15 minutes, macaroni 10–12 minutes, tagliatelli 10–12 minutes, conchiglie 12–15 minutes, farfalle 10–12 minutes, fettucine 8–10 minutes, linguine 8–10 minutes, rigatoni 12–15 minutes. Strain off at once and rinse with hot water. Just before serving, drain and toss in butter.

Bolognese Sauce

¼ lb sliced bacon
1 onion
1 carrot
2 stalks celery
2 tbsp butter or margarine
2 tbsp olive oil
½ lb ground lean beef
¼ lb chicken livers
1 tbsp tomato paste
sugar
1¼ cups well flavored beef stock and ¾ cup dry white wine, or 2 cups stock
½ tsp dried oregano
½ tsp dried basil
salt and pepper

1. Cut the rinds off the bacon and discard. Dice bacon finely. Peel the onion and carrot and chop finely with the celery.

2. Heat the butter or margarine and oil in a pan, add the bacon and fry until crisp and brown. Remove from pan with a slotted spoon and set aside.

3. Add vegetables to the pan and fry gently for about 5 minutes until lightly colored. Add the beef and fry for a further 10 minutes until browned, turning and stirring occasionally.

4. Meanwhile, chop the chicken livers and stir into the beef. Return the bacon to the pan and stir in the tomato paste and a dash of sugar. Add remaining ingredients and stir well to mix.

5. Simmer sauce for 25–30 minutes until thick and reduced, stirring occasionally. Taste for seasoning.

6. Serve hot on a bed of freshly cooked spaghetti or pasta bows, with grated Parmesan cheese served separately.

159

Pasta and rice

Spaghetti with Pesto

1 lb spaghetti

For pesto
about 1 cup fresh basil leaves
2 cloves garlic
¾ cup pine nuts
salt
¼ cup freshly grated Parmesan cheese
½ cup olive oil

1. First prepare the pesto. Peel and roughly chop the garlic cloves and place them in a mortar with the basil leaves. Pound well together with the pestle. Then add the pine nuts and a little salt and continue to pound.

2. Now add the grated cheese and work in until the mixture becomes a thick paste.

3. Begin to add the olive oil, a little at a time. Stir continually to make sure that the oil completely amalgamates with the paste.

4. Have ready a very large pan of boiling salted water. Plunge in the pasta and bring back to the boil as quickly as possible giving it a quick stir to make sure none has stuck to the saucepan. Continue to boil steadily for about 12 minutes until pasta is 'al dente' when tested. Drain immediately and turn into a heated serving dish, adding a knob of butter if liked.

5. Serve the pesto with the spaghetti.

Variation:
Pecans may be used instead of pine nuts.

Tagliatelle with Tomato Sauce

½ lb green tagliatelle
1 tsp vegetable oil
grated Parmesan cheese

For sauce
2 lb ripe tomatoes
1 onion
1 clove garlic
salt
4 tbsp olive oil
2 tsp finely chopped fresh oregano or 1 tsp
  dried oregano
sugar
pepper

1. Skin the tomatoes and chop the flesh roughly. Peel the onion and chop finely. Peel the garlic and crush with ½ tsp salt.

2. Heat the oil in a pan, add the onion and garlic and fry gently for about 5 minutes until lightly colored. Add the chopped tomatoes to the pan with the oregano, sugar and pepper to taste. Simmer gently for about 20 minutes until the sauce is thick and reduced, stirring occasionally. For a smooth sauce, you can liquidize it and then reheat, but this is not essential.

3. Meanwhile, put the tagliatelle in a large pan of boiling salted water with the vegetable oil. Cook for 8–10 minutes until tender, then drain and arrange in a warmed serving dish. Taste sauce for seasoning and pour over the tagliatelle. Serve hot with grated Parmesan cheese served separately.

Spaghetti with Pesto.

Veal and Mushroom Sauce

1 onion
1 carrot
2 stalks celery
2 tbsp butter or margarine
2 tbsp olive oil
1 cup mushrooms
$\frac{1}{4}$ lb ground lean veal
2 large tomatoes
1 tbsp flour
1 cup chicken stock
$\frac{2}{3}$ cup dry white wine
1 tsp finely chopped fresh oregano or $\frac{1}{2}$ tsp
   dried oregano
salt and pepper

1. Peel the onion and chop finely. Peel the carrot and dice with the celery. Wipe the mushrooms clean with damp cloth, but do not peel. Chop finely.

2. Heat the butter or margarine and oil in a pan, add the vegetables and fry gently for about 5 minutes until lightly colored. Add the veal and fry for a further 10 minutes until browned, turning and stirring constantly.

3. Meanwhile, skin the tomatoes and chop the flesh roughly. Stir into the veal until evenly mixed. Sprinkle the flour into the pan and cook for 1–2 minutes, stirring constantly. Stir in the stock gradually with a wooden spoon, then add the wine, oregano and salt and pepper to taste.

4. Simmer sauce for 25–30 minutes until thick and reduced, stirring occasionally. Taste for seasoning. Serve hot on a bed of freshly cooked pasta shells, with grated Parmesan cheese served separately.

Conchiglie with Veal and Mushroom Sauce.

Pasta and rice

Cappalletti with Meat Sauce.

MAKING RAVIOLI

2 cups flour
salt
¼ cup butter
¼–⅜ cup cold water
beaten egg

For meat filling
¾ cup cooked ground beef
1 tbsp grated onion
butter
1½ cups cooked, well drained spinach
2 oz cream cheese
¼ cup freshly grated Parmesan cheese
1 beaten egg
nutmeg
salt and pepper

For cheese filling
⅔ cup cottage cheese or cream cheese
1 cup cooked, well drained spinach
⅛ cup freshly grated Parmesan cheese
1 tsp freshly chopped basil or marjoram
nutmeg
salt and pepper

1. First prepare the paste. Sift the flour together with a generous dash of salt into a bowl. Rub in the butter and then work in sufficient water to achieve a firm dough.

2. Place on a floured surface and knead well. Then divide in half.

3. Roll out the first piece very thinly. Dust with flour, set aside and cover with a clean cloth. Roll out the second piece keeping the surface well floured to prevent it from sticking to the rolling pin. If liked, mark out the pastry before you add the filling into 1¼ inch squares.

4. To prepare the meat filling, sauté the grated onion lightly in a little butter. Place the cooked beef in a bowl, add the onion, spinach, cream cheese and grated Parmesan. Mix together well and bind with the beaten egg. Season with salt and pepper and a dash of nutmeg.

5. For the alternative cheese filling, place the cottage cheese or cream cheese, spinach, Parmesan and herbs in a bowl together. Cream well together and season with salt, pepper and a dash of nutmeg.

6. Spoon one of the fillings into a pastry bag fitted with a plain nozzle. Pipe dots of filling onto the paste at regular intervals. Flatten the little piles of filling slightly with a knife dipped in cold water. Brush the paste in between the filling with beaten egg.

7. Lay the other sheet of paste carefully over and press down between the stuffing.

8. Cut the filled ravioli into squares with a knife or pastry wheel. Cover with a floured cloth until ready to cook.

9. Add them into a large pan of boiling salted water and boil for 4–5 minutes.

Meat Sauce

½ lb ground beef
1 onion
1 carrot
1 small stalk celery
1 cup mushrooms
2 tbsp butter
1 tbsp freshly chopped parsley
1 tbsp flour
2 tsp tomato paste
⅜ cup white wine
1¼ cups good stock
salt and pepper

1. Peel and chop onion and carrot. Wash up and chop up celery. Wash and slice the mushrooms including the stalks.

2. Melt the butter in a pan and fry the onion in it. Add the other vegetables and the parsley and lightly brown.

3. Add the ground meat and brown it well. Then sprinkle over the flour and blend in. Stir in the tomato paste followed by the wine and the stock. Season with salt and pepper and simmer gently uncovered for about 30–40 minutes.

Lasagne Verde al Forno

1 lb freshly made lasagne verde
2¼ cups béchamel sauce
nutmeg
Bolognese sauce
butter
freshly grated Parmesan cheese

1. Set the oven at 375°F.

2. Cook the lasagne in pan of boiling salted water for about 5 minutes. Do not overcrowd the pan. Drain and place in a bowl of cold water.

3. Prepare the béchamel sauce and flavor it with a dash of nutmeg. Prepare the Bolognese sauce.

4. Butter a deep ovenproof dish. Now layer in the ingredients beginning with a layer of meat sauce followed by the béchamel sauce and then the pasta. Finish with a layer of béchamel sauce over the meat sauce. Sprinkle generously with the Parmesan cheese. Bake in the pre-set oven for 25–30 minutes until golden brown and bubbling.

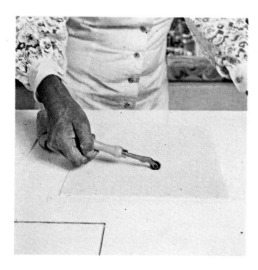

1. Thinly roll out the first piece of paste and mark into squares with a little metal wheel.

2. Fill a pastry bag with the chosen filling and pipe blobs of it in each paste square.

3. Flatten the blobs slightly with a knife which has been dipped in water.

4. Brush the paste with beaten egg.

5. Using a rolling pin, lift the second piece of paste and place over the first.

6. Press into shape with a finger.

7. Using a knife or metal wheel, cut ravioli into squares.

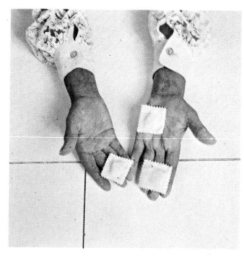

8. Ravioli ready for boiling.

Pasta and rice

Cannelloni with Veal and Mushroom Stuffing

14 cannelloni tubes or pasta squares
salt
water
2 tbsp oil
1 small onion
1 clove garlic
½ lb finely ground lean veal
1½ cups mushrooms
2 tbsp tomato paste
¼ tsp sugar
½ tsp dried oregano
pepper
stock or water
1 small egg
2 tbsp softened butter or margarine

To serve
spinach and cheese sauce
grated Parmesan cheese

1. Set the oven at 350°F.

2. Put the cannelloni or pasta squares in a large pan of boiling salted water with 1 tsp oil. Cook for 8–10 minutes until tender. Lift out with a slotted spoon and leave to drain.

3. Peel the onion and chop finely. Peel the garlic and crush with ½ tsp salt. Heat the remaining oil in a pan, add the onion and garlic and fry gently for about 5 minutes until lightly colored. Add the veal and fry gently for a further 10 minutes until browned, stirring constantly.

4. Meanwhile, wipe the mushrooms clean with a damp cloth, but do not peel. Chop finely. Stir into the pan with the tomato paste, sugar, oregano and pepper to taste. Stir well to combine. Moisten with a little stock or water, cover with a lid and simmer gently for 10 minutes, stirring occasionally. Remove from the heat, taste for seasoning and stir in the egg.

5. Spoon prepared filling into cannelloni tubes or divide equally amongst squares of pasta and roll up. Brush the inside of a shallow ovenproof dish with butter or margarine. Place the cannelloni in the dish in 2 layers, one on top of the other.

6. Spoon over the spinach and cheese sauce and bake in pre-set oven for about 15–20 minutes until the sauce is bubbling. Serve hot straight from the baking dish, with grated Parmesan cheese served separately.

Spinach and Cheese Sauce

¼ lb packet of frozen chopped spinach
¼ cup grated Parmesan cheese
2¼ cups béchamel sauce
salt and pepper
1 tbsp butter or margarine

1. Put the frozen spinach in a colander or sieve and leave to thaw and drain.

2. Stir the spinach into the hot sauce over a gentle heat. Simmer until hot again, stirring constantly. Remove from the heat, stir in the cheese.

3. Add salt and pepper to taste, then beat in the butter or margarine. Use immediately.

Cannelloni with Spinach and Cheese Sauce.

Mushroom Sauce

1 onion
1 clove garlic
salt
¼ cup butter or margarine
1 tbsp olive oil
6 rashers sliced bacon
3 cups button mushrooms
2 tsp flour
4 tbsp stock
½ tsp oregano
pepper

To finish
2 tbsp butter or margarine
1 cup button mushrooms
2 tbsp heavy cream
1–2 tbsp finely chopped fresh parsley
grated Parmesan cheese

1. Peel the onion and chop very finely. Peel the garlic and crush with ¼ tsp salt. Heat the butter or margarine and oil in a pan, add the onion and garlic and fry gently for about 5 minutes until lightly colored.

2. Meanwhile, cut the rinds off the bacon and discard. Dice bacon finely, then add to the pan and fry until browned.

3. Wipe the mushrooms clean with a damp cloth, but do not peel. Slice finely, then add to the pan. Fry until lightly colored and the juices run, turning occasionally.

4. Sprinkle the flour over the mushroom mixture and cook for 1–2 minutes, stirring constantly. Stir in the stock with a wooden spoon, then add the oregano and pepper to taste. Simmer gently.

5. Melt the 2 tbsp butter or margarine in a separate pan. Add cleaned whole mushrooms and fry until lightly colored. Stir in the cream and parsley, then remove from the heat.

6. Serve hot mushroom sauce on a bed of freshly cooked pasta and top with mushrooms, cream and parsley. Serve immediately with grated Parmesan cheese served separately.

FRYING RICE

1⅓ cups long grain rice
1 shallot or small onion
¼ cup butter
2⅓ cups stock

1. Set the oven at 425°F.

2. Peel and chop the shallot. Melt the butter in a frying pan, add the shallot and cook for a few minutes, then add the rice. Cook until all the butter has been absorbed.

3. Transfer to an ovenproof dish, pour over the stock, cover and cook in the pre-set oven for about 20 minutes.

4. The cooked pilaf can be dotted with butter and sprinkled with grated cheese before serving.

1. Fry raw rice in sizzling butter, with a finely chopped onion, until the butter is completely absorbed.

2. If using the oven, turn the mixture into a casserole.

3. Pour on hot stock and cook until the liquid is absorbed.

Pasta and rice

Jambalaya, a traditional Creole dish popular in the Southern States. The name Jambalaya comes from the Spanish 'jamon' meaning ham, one of the basic ingredients. The dish can also contain shrimps, crab or chicken.

Jambalaya

1¼ cups Italian rice
2 large mild onions
1 sweet green pepper
1 clove garlic
salt and pepper
¼ cup butter
¾ cup finely diced cooked ham
6 tomatoes
dried thyme
dried basil
1 tsp paprika
6 drops Tabasco sauce
⅓ cup white wine
2 cups stock
freshly grated Parmesan cheese

1. Peel and chop the onions. Halve the green pepper, remove core and seeds and chop. Peel and crush the garlic clove with a little salt. Scald, skin and roughly chop the tomatoes.

2. Melt the butter in a skillet, add the onion pepper and crushed garlic and cook until tender. Then add the rice and cook until faintly colored.

3. Add the ham, tomatoes a dash each of thyme and basil. Sprinkle over the paprika and Tabasco sauce, and pour in the wine.

4. Simmer until all the wine has evaporated. Pour over half the stock. Cover and cook on top of the stove.

5. Stir the rice from time to time and add more stock as necessary until the rice grains are just tender.

6. Sprinkle with Parmesan cheese before serving.

Risotto with Mushrooms.

Risotto with Mushrooms

2 cups Italian rice
1 shallot or small onion
2 cups mushrooms
3 tbsp butter
¾ cup white wine
4 cups stock
scant ¼ cup freshly grated Parmesan cheese

1. Peel and chop the shallot. Wash and slice the mushrooms.

2. Melt the butter in a large skillet, add the shallot and cook gently until soft and transparent. Then add the sliced mushrooms followed by the rice.

3. Cook until all the butter has been absorbed, then pour over the wine and simmer until evaporated.

4. Now begin to add the stock about 1 cup at a time. As soon as the stock is absorbed by the rice add some more. The rice should take 20–30 minutes to cook. At the end of that time the grains should be just tender and the risotto creamy.

5. Fork in the Parmesan cheese, cover and leave for a few minutes. Then transfer to a heated dish and serve.

Rice with Lentils

2½ cups long grain rice
1¼ cups lentils
1 onion
¼ cup butter
1 tsp turmeric powder
salt
5 cups stock

1. Peel and chop the onion. Melt the butter in a skillet or flameproof casserole, add the onion and cook for a few minutes, then add the rice and lentils and cook for a few minutes.

2. Sprinkle over the turmeric and season well with salt. Pour over the stock, cover and simmer on top of the stove.

3. If all the liquid has been absorbed and rice is still firm, add some more stock. Continue to cook until rice is tender. Serve with mango chutney.

Pasta and rice

Seafood Pilaf

1 onion
1 sweet green pepper
1 pimiento
8 cups mushrooms
¼ cup butter
2½ cups brown rice
saffron
6¼ cups white stock
1 cup flaked, cooked, smoked haddock
2¼ cups unshelled shrimps
¼ cup chopped almonds
4 tomatoes

1. Peel and chop the onion. Cut pepper and pimiento in half, remove core and seeds and cut into strips. Wash and slice the mushrooms.

2. Melt the butter in a skillet. Add the chopped onion and cook until soft and transparent. Then add the rice and cook for a few minutes.

3. Add the chopped pepper, pimiento and mushroom reserving a little of each for decoration.

4. Mix a dash of saffron in some water, pour over and then add the stock. Cover and cook on top of the stove until rice is tender. Add more liquid if necessary.

5. Peel and sever the shrimps leaving the heads on some for decoration. Scald and skin the tomatoes.

6. When rice is cooked (about 45 minutes) fork in the flaked haddock and some of the shrimps. Transfer the rice on to a serving dish and decorate with the reserved mushrooms, peppers, pimientos and shrimps. Sprinkle with the chopped almonds and garnish with the tomatoes.

Kedgeree

1 lb finnan haddie
2 eggs
¾ cup rice
¼ cup butter
black pepper
chopped parsley

1. Cook and flake the finnan haddie. Hard cook the eggs. Boil the rice.

2. Melt the butter and add to the rice. Fork in the finnan haddie. Chop one egg and add to the rice mixture. Mix well and arrange on a hot serving dish.

3. Garnish with the sieved yolk of the second egg and sprinkle with a little chopped parsley.

Paella.

Paella

3 lb ready to cook, broiler/fryer chicken
⅔ cup olive oil
½ lb lean pork shoulder
½ lb thin fresh pork sausages
1 large mild onion
1 pimiento
4 cloves garlic
saffron
¾ lb tomatoes
4 cups long grain rice
8 cups white stock
½ lb mussels
1¼ cups unshelled shrimps
1 cup cooked green beans
1 cup cooked peas

Seafood Pilaf.

6. Decorate the finished dish with the reserved shrimps and arrange some of the mussels around the edge of the dish.

Note: $\frac{1}{2}$ lb of squid and a small lobster may be added to this dish. The squid should be washed and cleaned as usual and added to the pan at the same time as the pork and sausages. The lobster should be cooked as usual and the lobster meat added towards the end of cooking time.

Risotto Milanese

2$\frac{1}{4}$ cups Italian rice
1 small onion
$\frac{1}{4}$ cup butter
1 clove garlic
$\frac{1}{2}$ tsp salt
saffron
salt and pepper
3 cups stock
2 tbsp grated Parmesan cheese

1. Soak a dash of saffron in 2 tbsp hot water for 30 minutes.

2. Chop the onion and fry gently in half the butter for 5 minutes. Add the rice and fry for a further 5 minutes.

3. Add this with a third of the stock. Season and simmer, stirring occasionally until the rice thickens. Add more stock, and continue to cook until all the stock is absorbed.

4. Add the remaining butter and the grated Parmesan cheese. Mix well. Cover the pan, take it off the heat and leave for 5 minutes.

5. Stir with a fork and turn out onto a hot serving dish.

1. Divide the chicken into small joints. Heat approximately half the oil in a large skillet. Add the chicken joints and brown them evenly.

2. Chop pork into dice and add to pan with the sausages. Cook gently until chicken is at least half cooked.

3. Meanwhile peel and chop the onion. Halve the pimiento, remove core and seeds and cut into strips. Crush the garlic with a little salt and blend a generous dash of saffron into it. Scald, skin and roughly chop the tomatoes.

4. Remove chicken, pork and sausages from the pan and set to one side. Add the remaining oil and then the chopped onion. Cook until tender, then add the rice and fry until the grains turn white. Then add the chopped pimiento, the crushed garlic and saffron, chopped tomatoes and some of the stock. Simmer for a few minutes.

5. Have ready the mussels, well scrubbed and washed, and the shrimps peeled and veined. Reserve a few shrimps with their heads on for decoration. Add the shellfish to the casserole together with the peas and beans. Season with salt and pepper and add the rest of the stock. Cover and simmer on top of the stove until rice is tender. Add more liquid if necessary.

Casseroled Onions.

Vegetables and salads

Casseroled Onions

2 lb small onions
stock
⅓ cup seedless raisins
2 tbsp light brown sugar
salt and pepper
arrowroot to thicken

1. Set the oven at 325°F.

2. Peel the onions and leave whole. Place them in a casserole and add sufficient stock to cover. Sprinkle over the seedless raisins and sugar, and season with salt and pepper.

3. Cook in the pre-set oven for about 1¼ hours until onions are tender.

4. Mix some arrowroot with a little water and pour this into the casserole to thicken.

Turnips in Mustard Glaze

2 lb young turnips
2 tbsp butter
⅓ cup stock
1 tsp brown sugar
salt and black pepper
2 tsp Dijon mustard
2 tbsp chopped parsley

1. Peel the turnips and leave whole unless very large. Fry in butter for about 10 minutes, turning frequently, so that they become golden brown all over.

2. Lower the heat and add the stock, sugar and seasoning. Cover the pan and simmer for 20 minutes or until tender.

3. Remove turnips from the pan. Stir mustard into pan juices. Return turnips to pan and coat with the mustard glaze. Sprinkle with parsley and serve.

Vegetables and salads

Vegetable Fritters

1 small cauliflower
1 large eggplant
3 – 4 zucchini
1 onion
oil for deep frying
salt and pepper
freshly chopped parsley

For fritter batter
¾ cup flour
salt
2 tsp salad oil
about ⅓ cup water
1 egg white

1. First prepare the batter. Sift the flour with a dash of salt. Add the oil and water very gradually stirring all the time. Then beat to a smooth consistency. Leave to stand for about 30 minutes.

2. Wash and slice the eggplant thinly. Spread the slices on a plate and sprinkle them with salt. Leave for about 30 minutes to draw out the liquid.

3. Wash and trim the cauliflower. Cut into quarters and place in a pan of cold salted water. Bring to the boil and simmer gently for a few minutes. Then drain well and allow to cool. When cold divide into flowerets.

4. Wash, top and tail the zucchini. Slice into rounds. Peel and slice the onion.

5. Whip the egg white until stiff, then fold it into the batter mixture. Dip the prepared vegetables in the batter and then deep fry in the hot oil, taking care not to add too many to the pan at once. Drain on absorbent paper, sprinkle with salt and pepper, and serve garnished with parsley.

Vegetable Fritters.

MAKING DUCHESS POTATOES

1½ lb potatoes
salt and pepper
¼ cup butter
2 eggs

Basic Recipe ☆

1. Peel the potatoes and cut into even size pieces. Place them in a pan of cold salted water, bring to the boil and cook for about 15–20 minutes, or until tender.

2. Set the oven at 400°F.

3. Drain well, return to the pan and set over the heat for a minute to dry off any excess moisture. Then strain the potatoes through a sieve and season well with salt and pepper.

4. Beat in half the butter and the eggs so that potato is a good piping consistency.

5. Spoon the potato into a pastry bag fitted with a star nozzle. Pipe whirls of potato onto a buttered cookie sheet. Melt the remaining butter and brush each potato pile with this. Bake in the pre-set oven for about 10 minutes until browned.

1. For pyramids, use a fluted nozzle and hold the pastry bag vertically.

2. For rings, use a fluted nozzle and hold the bag at an angle.

4. Use a knife to emphasize the shape.

5. For balls, just use a pastry bag without any nozzle.

7. For galettes, shape little rounds with floured hands.

8. Brush the galettes with beaten egg.

3. For boats, shape the mixture with lightly floured hands.

6. Pipe a large ball and a small ball, indent the top of the larger one and place the smaller one on top.

9. Make a criss cross pattern with a knife on the top.

Stuffed Onions

6 large mild onions

For meat sauce
½ lb ground beef
1 onion
1 carrot
1 cup mushrooms
1 tbsp butter
1 tbsp oil
2 tbsp flour
1 tbsp tomato paste
Worcestershire sauce
2 cups stock
salt and pepper

For meat filling
¼ lb ground beef
oil for frying
1 tsp dried thyme
1 tsp tomato paste
salt and pepper
beaten egg

1. Peel the onions and leave whole. Place in a pan of salted water and simmer until tender.

2. Meanwhile make up the sauce. Peel and chop the onion, carrot and mushrooms. Heat the butter and oil in a pan, add the vegetables and cook for a few minutes. Then add the ground beef and brown thoroughly.

3. Sprinkle over the flour and blend in well. Stir in the tomato paste and a few drops of Worcestershire sauce. Pour in the stock and season with salt and pepper. Simmer for 20–25 minutes.

4. Set the oven at 350°F.

5. Now prepare the meat filling. Heat a little oil in a pan and add the ground beef. Add the thyme, tomato paste, salt and pepper, and cook until tender.

6. Drain the onions and allow to cool a little. Then remove the centers which you can chop up and add to the meat filling. Pile a portion of the filling into each onion, place them in a shallow ovenproof dish and cook in the pre-set oven for about 15 minutes.

7. Pour the hot sauce into a warmed serving dish, arrange the stuffed onions in it and serve piping hot.

Dauphine Potatoes

¾ lb mashed potatoes
salt and pepper
oil for frying

For choux paste
4 tbsp butter or margarine
⅔ cup water
3 tbsp flour
2 eggs plus 1 egg yolk

1. Sieve the mashed potatoes, season and keep warm.

2. Put the butter or margarine in a pan with the water and heat until melted. Sift the flour and stir in over a low heat. Beat the eggs and the extra yolk into the flour paste.

3. Blend the sieved potato with the choux paste.

4. Deep fry small balls of the mixture in hot oil until golden brown. Drain on absorbent paper and serve immediately.

Creamed Carrots

2 lb carrots
2 tbsp butter
salt and pepper
¼ cup light cream
freshly chopped parsley

1. Peel or scrape the carrots, top and tail them and cut into rounds.

2. Place them in a pan of cold, salted water bring to the boil and simmer until tender.

3. Drain and strain through a sieve. Then return to the pan and place over low heat to drive off any excess moisture. Beat in the butter and season well with salt and freshly ground black pepper.

4. Stir in the cream and serve sprinkled with chopped parsley.

MAKING FRENCH FRIED POTATOES

1¼ lb potatoes
oil for deep frying
salt

Basic Recipe ☆

1. Peel and cut potatoes into chips. Dry off thoroughly in a clean cloth before frying.

2. Heat fat to a medium temperature – about 350°F. Lower the raw chips in gently and fry for about 4–5 minutes until just soft but not colored.

3. Lift out, drain well and set aside. The chips do not need to be fried again immediately.

4. Reheat the frying oil to about 390°F. Return the chips to the pan and fry briskly until deep golden brown. Drain them on absorbent paper, turn onto a warmed serving dish and sprinkle with salt.

1. Lower a basket of raw French fries into lightly heated oil.

2. Cook until they are soft and only lightly colored.

3. Heat the oil to smoking hot. Lower the basket again and fry for a few moments until golden.

4. Drain on absorbent paper.

French Fried Potatoes.

Ratatouille

1 large onion
3 pimientos
1 clove garlic
olive oil for frying
4 zucchini
2 eggplants
2 large tomatoes
salt and pepper
parsley for garnish

1. Peel and slice the onion finely. Remove core and seeds from pimientos and cut flesh into strips. Peel and chop garlic clove and crush with a little salt.

2. Take a thick bottomed pan, add sufficient olive oil to cover the base of it and heat gently. Now add the onion, pimiento and garlic and cook over a low heat for about 5 minutes taking care not to let them brown.

3. Meanwhile prepare the zucchini and eggplants. Wash the zucchini, top and tail them and slice into rounds. Wipe the eggplants and chop into rough dice. Add these vegetables to the pan and allow to simmer gently with the lid on for 10–12 minutes.

4. Skin the tomatoes. Place them in a bowl, cover them with boiling water and allow to stand for a minute. Drain and peel away the skins. Remove seeds and chop roughly.

5. Add tomatoes to the pan, cover and continue to cook gently until all the vegetables are soft. Adjust seasoning with salt and pepper. Sprinkle with fresh chopped parsley before serving.

Casserole of Lima Beans

2 lb shelled lima beans
3 small carrots
3 onions
2 cloves garlic
salt and pepper
¼ lb lean pork shoulder
2 tsp light brown sugar
2 cups boiling water
bouquet garni

For garnish
broiled tomatoes
watercress

1. Set the oven at 325°F.

2. Peel and chop the carrots into dice. Cook in boiling salted water for about 10 minutes.

3. Peel and slice the onions. Peel the garlic cloves and crush them with a little salt.

4. Remove rind from pork shoulder and cut into thin strips. Heat a skillet and toss in the pork. Fry gently until nicely browned. Then add the beans, carrots, onions, crushed garlic, sugar and pour over the boiling water.

5. Tuck in the bouquet garni and season with salt and pepper. Cover and cook in the pre-set oven until vegetables are tender.

6. Serve garnished with broiled tomatoes and watercress.

Casserole of Lima Beans.

Vegetables and salads

Savory Zucchini and Tomatoes

4 zucchini
3 tomatoes
1 tbsp grated Parmesan cheese

For zucchini filling
4 tbsp fine fresh white breadcrumbs
2 tbsp grated Gruyère cheese
2 tbsp butter
1 small clove garlic
salt and pepper

For tomato filling
4 tbsp fresh white breadcrumbs
1 tbsp chopped mixed fresh herbs (parsley,
    chives and tarragon)
2 tbsp butter
1 small clove garlic
salt and pepper

1. Wash, top and tail the zucchini and cook in boiling salted water for about 10 minutes. Halve them and scoop out seeds in the center.

2. Mix together the zucchini seeds with the breadcrumbs and grated cheese. Crush the garlic clove with a little salt and blend this into the butter. Then use to bind the stuffing mixture and season with salt and pepper. Fill mixture into the zucchini.

3. Slice tomatoes in halves and scoop out cores and seeds. Mix this into the breadcrumbs and fresh herbs. Peel and crush the garlic clove with a little salt and then cream with the butter. Melt in a small pan and then mix into the crumb mixture. Pile onto the tomatoes.

4. Sprinkle the zucchini and tomatoes with Parmesan cheese and brown them under the broiler before serving.

Red Cabbage

1 red cabbage
2 onions
4 tbsp butter
4 tbsp brown sugar
¼ lb apples
⅓ cup chicken stock
⅓ cup red wine
3 tbsp wine vinegar
salt
black pepper

1. Shred the cabbage finely and blanch in boiling water.

2. Slice the onions and fry in butter until soft and transparent. Stir in the sugar and allow to caramelize but not burn.

3. Add the drained cabbage, chopped apple, stock, wine and vinegar. Mix well and season. Cover and cook gently for 1½ hours or until the cabbage is soft and the liquid absorbed.

Celery with Almonds

1 head celery
4 tbsp butter
2 tbsp blanched, slivered almonds
2 shallots or 1 small onion
salt
black pepper
⅓ cup light cream

1. Cut the celery into 1 inch pieces.

2. Sauté the almonds in butter until crisp and golden. Lift out and set aside.

3. Chop the shallots or onion and fry with the celery and seasoning for 15 minutes in a covered pan. Stir frequently.

4. Stir in the cream and continue to cook for a further 20 minutes or until the celery is tender.

5. Stir in the almonds and cook gently for 5 minutes.

String Beans with Garlic

2 lb green beans
¼ cup butter
1 clove garlic
salt and pepper
freshly chopped parsley

1. Wash the beans well discarding any old ones. You can test these by doubling them over. If they are soft and pliable rather than crisp then they should be discarded.

2. Gather up a handful and top and tail them with a pair of scissors. Continue until all the beans are trimmed.

3. Plunge into a pan of salted boiling water and cook until just tender. If they are very young this should only take 10 minutes but if they are bigger it could take 20–25 minutes.

4. Peel and crush the garlic clove with a little salt. Work it into the butter. When cooked, drain beans immediately and return to the hot pan. Toss in the garlic flavored butter and season.

5. Transfer to a warmed dish and sprinkle with freshly chopped parsley.

1. A bean which does not snap in half when you bend it is too old to eat.

2. Gather up a handful of beans holding them so that the tips are level.

3. Snip off the tips at both ends.

String Beans with Garlic.

Vegetables and salads

Fennel au Gratin. Fennel is a bulbous white root that looks a little like a fat celery heart. It has a pleasant flavor of anise, which is stronger in the raw vegetable. The leaves of the fennel plant can be chopped and used in sauces in place of parsley. Although fennel is considered an unusual vegetable nowadays, it is of ancient origin and was very popular until the last century.

Fennel au Gratin

4 small heads fennel
1 lemon
2 tbsp butter
salt and pepper
1 tbsp grated Parmesan cheese

1. Trim off some of the hard outer leaves. Then peel back some of the leaves and rub fennel all over with cut lemon. Leave to stand for about 10 minutes.

2. Plunge into salted boiling water and cook gently for 30–40 minutes. Drain when tender, return to the warm pan and toss in the butter.

3. Transfer to a warmed serving dish and sprinkle with the Parmesan cheese. Brown under the broiler before serving.

Beans with Peppers

1 green pepper
1 shallot
1 clove garlic
2 tbsp oil
1 tbsp butter
1 lb French beans
2 tsp dried basil
salt
black pepper
4 tbsp grated Parmesan cheese

1. Slice the green pepper, chop the onion and crush the garlic. Fry these gently in oil and butter.

2. Prepare the beans and add to the pan. Sprinkle with basil and seasoning, and mix well.

3. Pour on ⅔ cup boiling water. Cover the pan and cook for 10 minutes, or until the beans are tender and the liquid has evaporated.

4. Stir in the Parmesan cheese, heat through and serve.

Cauliflower au Gratin.

Cauliflower au Gratin

1 large cauliflower
2½ cups mornay sauce
fine fresh breadcrumbs
1 tbsp grated Parmesan cheese

1. Wash cauliflower thoroughly in salted water. Trim stalk and cut off some of the outer green leaves. Divide the cauliflower into flowerets and boil in salted water for about 15 minutes until just tender.

2. Make up the mornay sauce.

3. Drain the cauliflower thoroughly. Have ready a well buttered fireproof dish. Arrange the cauliflower in it and pour over the sauce. Sprinkle with breadcrumbs and grated Parmesan cheese and brown under the broiler before serving.

Sautéed Mushrooms in Cream Sauce

3 cups mushrooms
3 tbsp butter
¼ cup dry white wine
¼ cup stock
⅔ cup light cream
salt and pepper
6 tbsp chopped chives

1. Wash and roughly chop the mushrooms.

2. Melt the butter in a skillet, add the mushrooms and fry gently for 2 or 3 minutes.

3. Stir in the wine and let it bubble up before adding the stock. Simmer for a couple of minutes.

4. Now pour in the cream and simmer until a thick creamy consistency is obtained.

5. Season with salt and pepper and add the chopped chives.

6. This delicious creamy mixture can be served on star shaped croûtes.

1. Add the mushrooms to the pan.

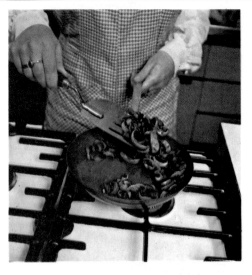

2. Fry gently until butter is absorbed.

Sautéed Mushrooms in Cream Sauce.

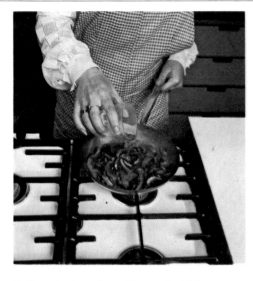

3. Pour in the wine, allow to bubble up. When the liquid is absorbed, add the stock and let it bubble up and become absorbed as before.

4. Add the light cream.

5. Work the mixture together until it is thick and creamy.

6. The mixture is ready when it leaves thick streaks across the pan base when you scrape a spoon across it.

7. Season and add chives.

Deep Fried Eggplant.

Deep Fried Eggplant

3 large eggplant
salt and pepper
4 tbsp flour
cold water
oil for frying
paprika
grated Parmesan cheese

1. Wipe the eggplant and slice up fairly thinly. Lay the pieces on a plate and sprinkle them with salt. Leave for about 30 minutes. The salt removes excess moisture and any bitterness from the eggplant.

2. Meanwhile prepare the batter. Sift the flour into a bowl and fill a jug with cold water. Now begin to add the water to the flour very gradually and beating all the time. The batter is ready when it is the consistency of thin cream.

3. Wipe the water and salt from the eggplant with a clean cloth. Dip the slices in the batter and then deep fry in the hot oil until tender and well browned.

4. Drain on absorbent paper, then arrange in a warmed serving dish. Season each layer lightly with paprika, salt and pepper and sprinkle over a little Parmesan cheese. Brown under the broiler before serving.

1. Slice the eggplant and spread out on a wooden board.

2. Scatter with plenty of salt. Leave for 30 minutes.

3. Wipe each slice with a clean cloth, this removes any bitterness.

Vegetables and salads

1. Trim the asparagus spears to equal lengths. Scrape the lower ends.

Stuffed Cabbage Leaves

1 green cabbage
melted butter

For stuffing
1 cup long grain rice
1 tbsp butter
1 tsp paprika
⅛ cup currants
salt and pepper
1 tbsp freshly chopped parsley

1. First prepare the stuffing. Add the rice to a large pan of boiling salted water and cook for about 12 minutes. Drain and put into a bowl.

2. Chop the currants up finely and add these to the rice with the butter, paprika and parsley. Season with salt and pepper.

3. Wash and trim tough outer leaves from the cabbage. Cut away the stalk. Place in a large pan of boiling salted water and boil gently until just tender. Drain and then begin to peel away the leaves.

4. Spoon some of the stuffing mixture onto each leaf and then roll up like a parcel. When the leaves become too small, use 2 leaves overlapping. Arrange them in an ovenproof serving dish and cover with melted butter.

5. If necessary, reheat in a low oven before serving.

Bean Sprouts with Ginger

2 tsp chopped root ginger
4 sliced spring onions
4 tbsp oil
1 lb bean sprouts
1½ tbsp soy sauce

1. Briskly fry the ginger and spring onions in oil, stirring continuously for 30 seconds.

2. Add the bean sprouts and cook for a minute, stirring.

3. Add the soy sauce, lower the heat and cook, still stirring, for about 4 minutes.

2. Place upright, tips uppermost, in the asparagus container.

Stuffed Cabbage Leaves.

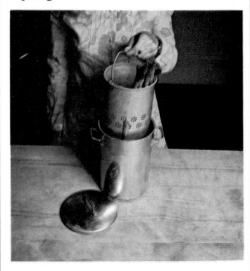

3. Lower the inner pot into the outer pot. Fill the outer pot with boiling salted water. Cover the lid and cook.

Greek Salad

1 crisp lettuce
2 green peppers
6 tomatoes
12 black olives
2 tsp oregano
salt and pepper
¾–1 cup cottage cheese
⅔ cup cultured sour cream

1. Wash and trim the lettuce. Halve the peppers, remove core and seeds and cut into thin strips. Scald, skin and roughly chop the tomatoes. Pit the olives.

2. Arrange the lettuce leaves on a flat serving dish. Place the tomatoes and green peppers on top, sprinkle with oregano and season well with salt and pepper.

3. Place the cottage cheese in spoonfuls over the salad, dot with the sour cream and finally add the olives.

Pepper Salad

¾ lb sweet green peppers
1¼ lb small ripe tomatoes
¼ cup salad oil
1 tbsp wine vinegar
chopped chives and parsley
salt and pepper

1. Cut peppers in half, scoop out seeds and cut flesh into strips. Slice tomatoes, leaving the skins on.

2. Put the peppers and tomatoes in a bowl, sprinkle with salt and pepper, add oil, then vinegar and mix well. Sprinkle chives and parsley over to garnish and adjust seasoning, if necessary.

Note: This simple salad is suitable for serving with a selection of cold meats, or poultry.

Carrot and Walnut Salad, with Beetroot and Onion Salad in the background.

Carrot and Walnut Salad

3–4 carrots
8 walnuts
¼ cup fresh orange juice
¼ cup mayonnaise
salt and pepper

1. Peel carrots and cut into matchstick size julienne strips, using a mandoline grater. Crack walnuts, cut into quarters. Beat orange juice into mayonnaise.

2. Mix walnuts with carrot sticks in a bowl and season. Spoon over dressing and toss salad just before serving.

Note: About ⅔ cup French dressing can be used as an alternative to mayonnaise. Flavor with the grated rind of half an orange, if liked.

Beetroot and Onion Salad

1 large or 4 small cooked beetroots
1 large or 2 medium mild onions
1 tbsp wine vinegar
⅔ cup strong stock

1. Rub skin off the beetroot, if not already peeled. Cut into thin sticks, each about 1½ inches long and put into a bowl with the wine vinegar.

2. Peel onion and cut into thin rings. Add to beetroot and chill while bringing the stock to the boil. Pour over the beetroot and onions and serve.

Variation:
Instead of mild onions, use a bunch of chopped scallions.

Vegetables and salads

Potato Salad with Garlic

3 lb potatoes
1 large clove garlic
1–2 tsp Dijon mustard
⅛ cup white wine vinegar
⅜ cup salad oil
1 large crust of brown or white bread
1 cup stock

1. Boil or steam the potatoes in their skins. Peel the garlic clove and cut in half.

2. Peel the potatoes and cut into dice. Rub the salad bowl thoroughly (preferably a wooden one for this classic salad) with the cut clove of garlic, then add the mustard and some of the vinegar. Adding oil and vinegar alternately, whisk together until a thick French dressing consistency is achieved and the oil is totally absorbed into the mixture.

3. Crush the rubbed garlic and spread it over the crumb side of the bread crust. Cut crust into julienne (matchstick size) strips and place in salad bowl. Stir in the dressing until well coated. Add the potatoes and toss. When coated with the dressing, bring the stock quickly to the boil, and pour over the potatoes. Toss again and serve on a bed of crisp lettuce leaves and garnished with a sprinkling of paprika, a little chopped parsley and a few black olive slices.

Variation:
This salad can be turned into a substantial snack by the addition of matchstick thin strips of continental garlic sausage, salami or Frankfurters. It is good served with watercress or crisp curly endive.

Potato Salad with Garlic.

Salad Marguerite

cooked cauliflower sprigs or carrots
small can French beans
small can asparagus tips
can potatoes
a little French dressing
mayonnaise
1–2 cooked egg whites to decorate

1. Dice French beans, asparagus tips and potatoes. Slice cooked carrots, if using and toss in a little French dressing.

2. Arrange in a bowl, smooth over top and make up just enough mayonnaise to coat the surface. Decorate with strips of egg white and slices of cooked carrot.

American Salad

1 clove garlic
½ pimiento
½ sweet green pepper
6 green olives
6 black olives
2 crisp lettuce hearts from an Iceberg or
    romaine lettuce
5 tomatoes
3 eggs
⅝ cup wine vinegar
paprika
⅞ cup salad oil
1 tbsp sweet pickle
2 bananas
a few flaked almonds to garnish
salt and pepper

1. Crush garlic clove with a little salt. Scoop out seeds and core from the pimiento and the pepper and pit and chop up olives. Wash lettuce leaves and scald, skin and slice tomatoes. Hard cook eggs.

2. In a bowl, pour the vinegar, add the garlic, paprika and oil. Whisk until blended and season with salt and pepper. Cut pimiento and pepper into strips and add, with the olives and sweet pickle. Toss until coated thoroughly with dressing. Leave to chill.

3. On a bed of lettuce leaves, arrange slices of tomato and hard cooked egg. Peel the bananas at the last minute and chop. Add to dish. Garnish with flaked almonds, if liked, and pour over chilled savory dressing. Serve with French bread.

Vegetables and salads

Mimosa Salad.

Mimosa Salad

1 cup peas
1 cup string beans
2–3 sticks celery
6–8 spring onions
½ lb potatoes
mayonnaise

For garnish
6 eggs
1⅓ cups button mushrooms
a little salad oil to moisten
½ tomato

1. Cook peas and drain, if not from a can. Cut string beans into small slices and cook. Wash and chop celery. Wash spring onions and slice, discard tough, dark green stems. Cut potatoes into dice and cook. Make mayonnaise. Chop mushrooms very finely and soak in a little oil.

2. Mix together salad vegetables, adding just enough mayonnaise to bind well. Spoon into a bowl and smooth over top. Mark surface into 6 equal sections, using a knife.

3. Hard cook the eggs and remove the yolks. Push the yolks through a strainer and chop up the whites very finely.

4. Sprinkle the whites, then the yolks, over the top of the salad to decorate, starting from the edge and working to the center. Fill the remaining 2 sections with the drained, oiled mushrooms and place a tomato in the center of the dish to garnish.

Note: the Mimosa of the title refers to the hard cooked egg yolk garnish. This is a special party version of the dish. Usually, the egg yolks are sprinkled liberally over a green salad mixture.

Salade Basquaise

2 pimientos
scant ¾ cup long grain rice
¼ lb green beans
1 shallot or onion
black olives
green olives
¼ lb peas
small can tuna fish or small can shrimps
1 tsp chopped fresh thyme, if available, or
    ½ tsp dried thyme
mayonnaise
salt and pepper

1. Cut pimientos in half lengthwise and remove core and seeds. Cook rice and drain and rinse in cold water. Spread out on a flat dish and leave to dry.

2. Cook green beans – if not from a can – and cut into neat dice. Peel and grate shallot or onion. Pit and chop olives. Cook peas and drain, if not from a can. Drain and flake tuna fish or chop shrimps.

3. Mix together the rice, beans, grated onion, diced olives, peas and fish. When thoroughly mixed, season and bind with mayonnaise and pile into pimiento halves. Sprinkle with thyme and serve.

Note: Extra mayonnaise may be served separately. Alternatively, bind the salad ingredients together with a little French dressing and omit the mayonnaise.

Cauliflower Salad

1 cauliflower
salt
8 anchovy fillets
2 shallots
8 tbsp olive oil
3 tbsp lemon juice
½ tsp French mustard
black pepper

1. Boil the cauliflower in 1 inch of salted water for 8 minutes only. Drain and break into flowerets. Place in a bowl.

2. Finely chop the anchovy fillets and the shallots, and place in a small pan with the olive oil, the lemon juice, the mustard and the black pepper. Bring this mixture slowly to the boil. Pour the hot dressing over the cauliflower. Chill well before serving.

Wilted Salad with Bacon Dressing

½ clove garlic
1 cos lettuce
4 rashers bacon
2 tbsp butter
1 tbsp wine vinegar
1 hard cooked egg
2 tbsp chopped parsley
salt and black pepper

1. Warm the salad bowl and rub the garlic clove around the bowl. Wash and dry the lettuce, tear into small pieces and put in the bowl.

2. Dice the bacon and cook gently in the butter for 10 minutes. Pour the bacon and melted fat over the lettuce.

3. Add the vinegar to the pan in which the bacon was cooked. Heat it through and sprinkle over the lettuce.

4. Chop the hard cooked egg. Toss the salad, add the chopped hard cooked egg, parsley and seasoning, and toss again. Serve immediately.

Coleslaw

1 lb cabbage
2 carrots
1 crisp apple
2 shallots
3 tbsp cider vinegar
1¼ cups mayonnaise
⅔ cup cultured sour cream
1 tbsp sugar
1 tsp celery seed
6 drops Tabasco sauce
salt
pepper

1. Shred the cabbage, grate the carrots and the apple. Finely chop the shallots. Place the prepared vegetables in a large bowl with the cider vinegar.

2. Mix the mayonnaise and sour cream together. Add the remaining ingredients.

3. Pour the dressing over the vegetables and toss thoroughly so that every shred of cabbage is coated. Chill well before serving.

Caesar Salad

6 slices of bread
1 cup salad oil
1 small crisp lettuce
2 cloves garlic
4 anchovy fillets
milk
1 level tsp dry English mustard
scant ¼ cup white wine vinegar
1 egg
1¼ cups grated hard cheese or generous ½ cup
    grated Parmesan cheese
salt and pepper

1. Remove crusts from bread and cut into dice. Wash and tear lettuce leaves into strips. Peel and crush garlic cloves. Soak anchovy fillets in a little milk to remove excess saltiness.

2. Fry the bread croûtons in half the oil until browned and crisp, then drain on absorbent paper. Place lettuce in a salad bowl with the crushed garlic. Drain and chop anchovy fillets and add to salad. Sprinkle over mustard, season with salt and pepper, if needed, and toss salad in the remaining oil. When the ingredients are well coated, add the vinegar and continue tossing the salad.

3. Lightly cook the egg for 1–2 minutes in boiling water, then break it into the salad bowl. Add grated cheese and, finally, the croûtons of bread.

Waldorf Salad

5 apples
4 sticks celery
5 tbsp mayonnaise
salt
pepper
nutmeg
¼ cup chopped pecans

1. Peel the apples and cut into cubes. Slice the celery and mix with the apples and mayonnaise.

2. Season and add a dash of nutmeg. Sprinkle with chopped pecans and serve immediately.

Hamburgers with a choice of barbecue sauces, Chilli Barbecue Sauce (left and in the background) and Apple Barbecue Sauce.

192

Snacks

Hamburgers

1 lb lean ground steak
1 onion
1 tbsp olive oil
1 tbsp butter
3 drops Tabasco sauce
1 tsp Worcestershire sauce
1 level tsp dried mixed herbs
salt and pepper
2 egg yolks
fresh breadcrumbs
seasoned flour
oil

1. Fry grated onion in oil and butter until soft and transparent.

2. Mix the ground steak, sauces, herbs, seasoning and cooked onion in a bowl.

3. Now add the egg yolks and, if the mixture becomes too soft, a few fresh breadcrumbs.

4. Turn the mixture out onto a clean working surface and divide into 6 even-size round flat cakes. Dip each one in seasoned flour and then fry in a little oil.

Chilli Barbecue Sauce

3 onions
½ small dried chilli
6 tbsp olive oil
2 tbsp wine vinegar
1 tsp Tabasco sauce
1 tsp salt
1 tsp dry mustard
1 tbsp brown sugar
½ cup water
½ cup lemon juice
grated rind 1 lemon

1. Chop the onions and pound the chilli.

2. Place all the ingredients in a pan. Bring to the boil and simmer 15 minutes.

Apple Barbecue Sauce

2 cups apple purée
1 tsp brown sugar
1 tsp mixed spice
½ tsp dry mustard
1 tbsp wine vinegar

Simply mix the ingredients and heat.

Snacks

1. Sharpen a very clean garden stake to a point with a scalpel.

2. Thread the sausages onto the stake, brush them with oil and prick with a fork. Lay the stake across the barbecue, turning so that the sausages cook evenly.

Hot Dogs with Fried Onion Rings.

Hot Dogs

1 lb fresh frankfurters or large pork
*   sausages if preferred*
6 – 8 coney buns
butter for spreading
a little made English mustard

For fried onion rings
1 large onion
a little flour mixed with water
oil for frying

1. Broil or fry the frankfurters.

2. Split the buns down the middle, butter them and spread with a little prepared mustard.

3. Peel and slice the onion into thin rings. Mix some flour and water together in a bowl to a creamy consistency. Then dip the onion rings in the mixture and shallow fry until crisp and brown.

4. Fill the prepared buns with the cooked frankfurters and garnish with the onion rings.

Bacon and Mushroom Bread Snack

small round loaf
1 egg
⅓ cup milk
4 or 6 rashers bacon
1 tbsp butter
1 tbsp cooking oil
1 cup mushrooms
1 tbsp flour
English mustard
brown stock
salt and pepper
spring onions

1. Cut base crust off small round loaf and hollow out until a bread 'shell' is left. Invert and cut top into v-shapes to decorate, if liked.

2. Whisk egg with milk and dip bread in the mixture until thoroughly coated. Deep fry in hot fat until browned and crisp. Drain on absorbent paper and keep hot while preparing filling. Wipe and slice mushrooms.

3. De-rind bacon rashers, stretch a little by running the back of a knife along them, and fry in a little extra fat, if necessary. When cooked, roll up each rasher into a 'curl', and keep hot.

4. Add the extra butter and oil to the pan. Add the sliced mushrooms, stalks and all and sauté over low heat until cooked. Sprinkle over flour and stir until absorbed; add a pinch of mustard then gradually add the stock, stirring well between each addition. Season with salt and pepper. If the mixture is too runny, turn up heat and boil to reduce liquid a little.

5. Heap the mixture inside the bread case, top with bacon rolls and serve hot, garnished with spring onions.

Variation:
A sprinkling of dry sherry poured in just before serving gives the sauce a particularly rich flavor.

Scrambled Eggs with Shrimps

2 slices white bread, each ¼ inch thick, cut from the length of a medium size loaf
a little oil or butter for frying
1 tbsp butter or margarine
2 oz peeled shrimps
3 eggs
2–3 tbsp milk
salt and pepper

1. Cut slices of bread with an oval fancy cookie cutter. Fry bread slices in oil or butter until golden brown. Drain on absorbent paper and keep hot.

2. Melt the butter in a pan over low heat, break eggs into a bowl, add milk and whisk briskly. Season with a little white pepper and pour eggs into pan, stirring continuously with a wooden spoon until lightly cooked.

3. As soon as they are lightly set, take pan off heat and stir in half the shrimps. Adjust seasoning and heap onto the fried bread base and decorate with the remaining shrimps.

Variation:
2 oz smoked eel makes a luxury variation of this simple dish. A few snipped chives add a colorful and tasty garnish, too.

Croque Monsieur

For each portion:
2 slices white bread from a standard sandwich loaf
1 tbsp butter
1 slice cooked ham to fit bread slice
2 slices Gruyère or Emmentaler cheese to fit bread slice

1. Trim crusts from bread slices, lightly spread with butter.

2. Lay a slice of cheese on one slice of the buttered bread, place the slice of ham on top, add the second slice of cheese and top with the second slice of buttered bread.

3. Broil on both sides until toasted and golden brown, and the cheese is melted. Eat immediately.

Bacon and Mushroom Bread Snack.

Scrambled Eggs with Shrimps.

Snacks

Block Buster.

Block Buster

1 French stick
butter for spreading

For filling
a selection of cold meats including ham,
*   liver sausage, salami, mortadella*
slices of Cheddar, Dutch Gouda or
*   Emmenthal cheese*
green and black olives
gherkins
pickled onions
sliced tomatoes

For garnish
sprigs of watercress and endive

1. Split the French stick lengthwise and butter on the inside.

2. Fill the loaf generously with all, or a selection of the given ingredients and garnish with watercress and chicory.

Club Sandwiches

18 slices white bread for toasting
butter for spreading

For filling
¼ lb cooked chicken or turkey
¼ lb sliced bacon
3 eggs
3 large tomatoes
¼ cucumber
1 crisp lettuce heart, preferably the Iceberg
*   variety*
¾ cup mayonnaise
salt and pepper

1. Cut the cold chicken or turkey into thin slices. Broil the bacon slowly taking care not to overcook it. Hard cook the eggs.

2. Wash the lettuce heart and divide up. Slice the cucumber and tomatoes.

3. Now toast the bread lightly and butter each slice. Make up 6 3 decker sandwiches dividing the ingredients evenly between each. Season each with salt and pepper and add a dollop of mayonnaise. Serve immediately for a lunch or supper time snack.

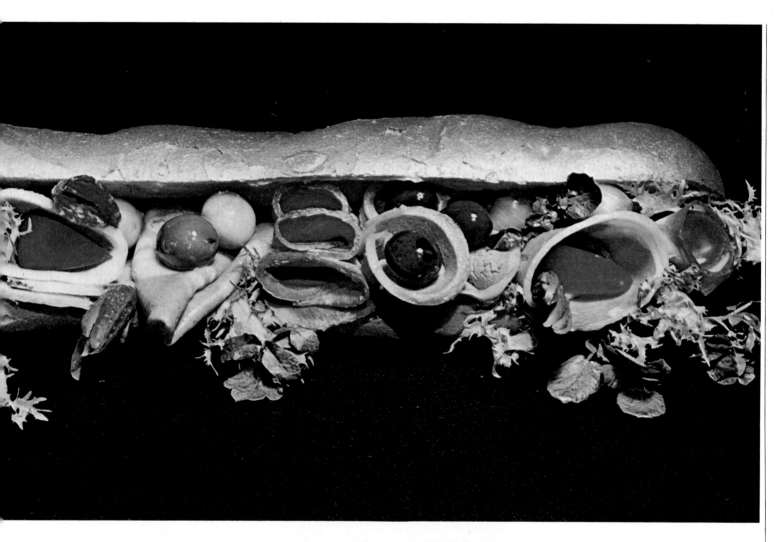

To cut thin slices of bread; spread each slice with soft butter before you cut it, then dip a very sharp knife in hot water, shake off the surplus water, and then with this hot, moist knife you will be able to cut very thin slices of bread. Cut off the crusts if you wish.

Club Sandwiches.

Snacks

Savory Tartlets Provençale

Savory shortcrust pastry made from 2 cups flour
dried rice or beans for baking blind

For filling
1 large onion
3 pimientoes
1 clove garlic
olive oil for frying
2 medium size zucchini
1 medium size eggplant
2 large tomatoes
salt and pepper
freshly grated Parmesan cheese

1. Set the oven at 350°F.

2. Roll the pastry out thinly and line into tartlet shells. Leave to chill in the refrigerator.

3. Now prepare the vegetables for filling. Peel and slice the onion finely. Remove core and seeds from pimientoes and cut flesh into strips. Peel and chop garlic clove and crush with a little salt. Top and tail the zucchini and slice into rounds. Chop the eggplant into rough dice. Scald and skin the tomatoes, chop roughly and remove the seeds.

4. Heat some olive oil in a heavy based pan, add the onion, pimiento and garlic and cook over low heat for about 5 minutes, taking care not to let them brown.

5. Add the zucchini and eggplant to the pan and allow to simmer gently with the lid on for 10–12 minutes.

6. Finally add the chopped tomatoes and continue to cook gently until all the vegetables are soft.

7. Prick small holes with a fork on the base of the tartlets. Put a piece of foil in each and bake in the pre-set oven on the shelf above center for 20 minutes, removing foil after 15 minutes.

8. Spoon some filling into each of the tartlets, sprinkle with Parmesan cheese and brown quickly under the broiler before serving.

Cheese and Potato Croquettes

4 potatoes
2 tbsp butter
1½ cups grated Gruyère or Cheddar cheese
2 egg yolks
2 tbsp flour
⅔ cup fresh white breadcrumbs
1 egg
salt and pepper
oil

1. Peel and boil potatoes. Mash well or push through a sieve. When cool, beat in the butter and chill. Sift flour and beat egg. Put flour, egg and breadcrumbs in separate dishes.

2. Beat cheese and egg yolks into sieved, cooled potato and season with salt and pepper. Chill.

3. Roll out mixture into a long thin strip about 1½ inches in diameter and cut into 4 inch lengths. Dip each croquette into first flour, then beaten egg, then roll thoroughly in breadcrumbs. Chill each coated croquette in the refrigerator until firm. Deep fry in oil until golden brown.

Savory Tartlets Provençale.

Fried Camembert

1 whole Camembert cheese
1 beaten egg
fine breadcrumbs
oil

1. Unwrap the Camembert which should be soft and ready to eat. Carefully scrape away any excess white powdery substance clinging to the rind of the cheese.

2. Cut the cheese in half, then into quarters and then each quarter into 2 so that you have 8 pieces altogether.

3. Dip the pieces in the beaten egg and then turn in the breadcrumbs, making sure that they are completely covered. Then deep fry in oil until golden brown.

Savory Cutlets

6 ¼ inch slices of cold cooked chicken or
*   turkey*
cold creamed potato made with:
*   ¼ lb potatoes*
*   1 small egg yolk*
*   a little butter*
*   salt and pepper*
2 tbsp tomato paste
1 beaten egg
fine breadcrumbs
oil

1. Peel and boil the potatoes until tender. Drain and return to pan over heat to dry off any excess moisture. Press the potatoes through a sieve into a bowl. Beat in the butter and egg yolk and season with salt and pepper. Leave to cool.

2. Using a cookie cutter of your choice, stamp out a cutlet from each slice of meat. Then spread the cutlets with a little tomato paste.

3. Top each with some cold creamed potato, dip in beaten egg and roll in breadcrumbs. Deep fry in oil until crisp and brown.

Fried Camembert.

Savory Cutlets.

Provençale Onion Flan.

Quick Pizza Napolitana.

Provençale Onion Flan

*savory shortcrust pastry made from 1¼ cups
    flour*
2 cloves garlic
16–20 anchovy fillets
32 pitted black olives
3 tbsp oil
3 tbsp butter or margarine
4 large onions

1. Set the oven at 375°F.

2. Make up pastry. Peel and slice onions into very thin rings. Peel and chop garlic finely. Slice anchovy fillets into very thin strips. Soak in a little milk.

3. Roll out pastry very thinly and line into a shallow 10 inch flan ring. Prick the base with a fork and chill. Heat butter and oil in a skillet and fry onion rings with garlic over a low heat until transparent, but not brown. Turn into pastry case and smooth over. Make a neat lattice pattern of drained anchovy strips and place an olive in each square.

4. Bake in the pre-set oven for about 30–35 minutes until pastry is golden brown and topping is cooked.

Note: The mixture of butter and oil – if butter is used – stops the butter from browning too quickly and burning.

Quick Pizza Napolitana

*bread dough or basic puff
    pastry made with 3 cups flour.*
*¼ cup grated Emmentaler or Mozzarella
    cheese*
1 cup pitted green and black olives
8 anchovy fillets
4 tomatoes
dried mixed herbs or dried basil
oil
black pepper

1. Set the oven at 400°F.

2. Roll out the dough to a circle about ¼ inch thick and place on a floured cookie sheet.

3. Slice anchovy fillets in half and soak in a little milk, if liked, to remove excess saltiness. Scald, skin and de-seed tomatoes.

4. Sprinkle the dough round with grated cheese, dot the surface with olives. Drain and arrange anchovy fillets between the olives. Slice the tomatoes and scatter slices over surface. Add a generous pinch or two of dried mixed herbs, or basil, and sprinkle surface with drops of cooking oil. Grind over some black pepper, and place pizza in the pre-set oven, until dough or pastry is golden brown and cooked – about 20–30 minutes.

Note: If dough has not been proved twice, leave pizza for 10–15 minutes in a warm place to rise a little before cooking. A bread mix, ready baked, may be used for this pizza, in which case, bake case before filling, then slide pizza under broiler to cook through the topping until cheese bubbles.

Pineapple Cream.

Desserts and puddings

Pineapple Cream

13 oz can crushed pineapple in syrup
1¾ cup quantity confectioners' custard
⅔ cup heavy cream
1½ packets powdered gelatin
3 tbsp cold water

1. Strain the pineapple, place pulp in a blender and blend thoroughly. Beat in the confectioners' custard.

2. Whip cream until very stiff.

3. Dissolve the gelatin in water and stir into the pineapple mixture. Carefully fold in the whipped cream.

4. Pour into a lightly oiled mold and leave to set.

5. Unmold into the center of a flat oval dish and serve with fresh pineapple if desired.

Vanilla Mold

2½ cups milk
4 tbsp sugar
2 separated eggs
few drops vanilla flavoring
4 tsp powdered gelatin
2 tbsp water

1. Heat together the milk, sugar, egg yolks and vanilla flavoring to make a custard and leave to cool.

2. Dissolve the gelatin in the water and add to the custard.

3. Whip the egg whites stiffly and fold lightly into the cool custard mixture.

4. Pour into a decorative mold or glass dish and leave to set.

5. Turn out onto a decorative plate just before serving. Serve with lemon wedges, stewed fruit or jam.

Note: Do not worry when this mixture separates out. The finished dessert should be in layers with gelatin on the top and the custard underneath.

Desserts and puddings

Cherry Cream.

Cherry Cream

1½ packets powdered gelatin
4 tbsp cold water
16 oz can stoned black cherries or 2 cups
    fresh stoned Bing cherries of which ¾ cup
    have been blended to give approx ¾ cup of
    juice
⅔ cup sweet white wine or water
1¼ cups heavy cream
1 tbsp kirsch
extra heavy cream for decoration

1. Dissolve the gelatin in the cold water. Strain in the juice from the can of cherries or the juice extracted from the fresh cherries. Stir in the wine or water and cool.

2. Whisk the cream lightly and then whisk it quickly into the juice.

3. Pour into a lightly oiled 3¾–4½ cup ring mold and leave to set.

4. Turn out onto a large round flat plate and fill the center with the stoned cherries. Sprinkle kirsch onto the cherries if it is being used. Decorate with piped cream and cherries or serve it plain.

Marie Louise Pudding

¼ lb unsweetened chocolate
2 6 inch rounds of jelly roll sponge
¾ lb unsweetened chocolate
4 egg yolks
1¼ cups loosely whipped heavy cream
1 tbsp rum
2 tbsp orange flower water
1 tsp rose water
⅔ cup heavy cream for decoration

1. First prepare the chocolate case in which the chocolate cream is to be served. Use a loose based cake pan 6 inches in diameter and 3 inches deep. Line it at the bottom and sides with cartridge paper. When it fits exactly with a 1 inch overlap at the sides remove the paper and stick onto it matching shapes in waxed paper. Fit these back into the pan.

2. Melt the ¼ lb unsweetened chocolate in the top of a double saucepan and pour half of it into the pan. Tilt the pan in all directions until the base and sides are well coated. Leave in a refrigerator to set and then repeat the process with the remaining melted chocolate.

3. Leave to set again and then gently ease the case out of the pan by pushing up the base. Carefully remove the paper and place on serving dish.

4. Place the circles of sponge in the chocolate case.

5. Melt the remaining unsweetened chocolate until smooth and thick. Allow to cool.

6. Beat the eggs and cream together well in a large bowl. Add the softened chocolate to the eggs and whip, beating well all the time.

7. Add the rum, orange flower water and rose water and continue whipping until the consistency of stiff whipped cream.

8. Fill the prepared chocolate case, level off the top. Decorate with piped whipped cream and keep refrigerated until served.

Little Pots of Chocolate

¼ lb semi sweet chocolate
2 tbsp light cream
4 separated eggs
heavy cream for decoration
chopped filberts or walnuts for decoration

1. Break up the chocolate and place in the top of a double saucepan over hot water. Add the cream and heat until the

chocolate has melted. Beat well, remove from heat.

2. Add the unbeaten egg yolks one at a time beating well between each addition.

3. Whip the egg whites until very stiff and fold gently and evenly into the mixture.

4. Divide between 6 small glasses and refrigerate until required.

5. Shortly before serving, a spiral of whipped heavy cream can be piped on top of each. Chopped filberts or walnuts may be sprinkled over the top of the cream.

Apricot Cream

2 cups apricot pulp
16 soaked apricot halves, if dried, or 8
    whole, fresh, small apricots, split and
    stoned
1 cup light cream
⅜ cup milk
2 packets powdered gelatin
2 tbsp cold water
4 oz cream cheese
sugar to taste
1 tbsp apricot brandy

1. If using dried apricots for the pulp soak them in cold strained tea for a minimum of 36 hours – then they will not require cooking.

2. Mix the apricot purée with the cream and milk and blend in well. Check for sweetness and add a little castor sugar.

3. Dissolve the gelatin in the water, in a cup placed in a pan of gently boiling water. Add apricot brandy if being used. Beat this into the apricot mixture.

4. Pour into a decorative mold of 4–5 cup capacity and leave to set.

5. Mix the cream cheese with sugar to taste. Put into a pastry bag with a decorative nozzle and pipe it into the reserved whole apricots, sandwiching them together.

6. Unmold the cream onto chosen dish.

7. Place the whole stuffed apricots around the base of the cream.

Apricot Cream.

Desserts and puddings

Crème Caramel

½ cup plus 1 tbsp sugar
⅔ cup water
2½ cups milk
4 lightly whisked eggs

1. Set the oven at 325°F.

2. Put the pans being used – either a 6 inch cake pan or 6×⅔ cup individual pans or molds – in a warm place.

3. Put ½ cup of the sugar and all the water into a small, preferably heavy based, pan and put over a low heat until the sugar has dissolved. Bring to the boil without stirring it until it turns a rich golden brown. Pour the caramel into the large pan or divide it between the individual ones, turning each until the bottom is completely covered. Leave to cool.

4. Warm the milk, add the remaining 1 tbsp sugar and the lightly whisked eggs. Strain this mixture over the caramel.

5. Place in a shallow pan such as a roasting pan with sufficient cold water in it to come half way up the pan containing the crème caramel. This is to prevent the crème caramel boiling during cooking which spoils its smooth texture. Bake for about an hour, or until set. Small pans will need only 45 minutes.

6. Leave in the pans until cold before turning it out onto the serving dish.

Crème Brûlée

1¼ cups heavy cream
1¼ cups light cream
1 vanilla pod
1 tbsp sugar
4 egg yolks

For caramel topping
3 tbsp sugar

1. Put the creams and vanilla pod in the top of a double saucepan.

2. Heat through slowly until the cream reaches scalding point about 125°F. Remove vanilla pod.

3. Cream the sugar with the egg yolks until they look thick and pale.

4. Pour the cream onto the egg yolks, mix together well, and return to the top of the double pan. Continue to heat, but do not boil, until the mixture coats the back of a wooden spoon.

5. Strain the custard into a 3¾ cup shallow ovenproof serving dish. Leave to cool and then refrigerate overnight or for a minimum of 6 hours. This ensures the necessary firm set.

6. Pre-set the broiler to hot.

7. Sprinkle the sifted sugar evenly all over the top of the chilled cream. Place under the broiler for as short a time as possible until the sugar just caramelizes.

8. Remove from the broiler and chill for 2–3 hours before serving.

Mont Blanc

2 egg whites
½ cup sugar
1¼ lb chestnuts or 8 oz can chestnut purée
3 tbsp Marsala
about ¼ cup confectioners' sugar
⅔ cup stiffly whisked heavy cream
coloring

1. Set the oven at 275°F.

2. Whip the egg whites until stiff, add nearly half the sugar and whip again until stiff. Lightly fold in the remaining sugar. At this stage add any coloring you like. Put

Crème Caramel.

the meringue into a pastry bag fitted with a large nozzle.

3. Line a large cookie sheet with lightly oiled waxed paper and mark on it a circle 7 inches in diameter. Pipe a ring of meringue about 2 inches high around the circle and smooth the remainder over the base.

4. Bake the meringue in the pre-set oven for about an hour or until it is crisp and dry. Carefully peel off the paper and leave the meringue case to cool on a wire rack.

5. If using fresh chestnuts place a few at a time into a deep fat fryer basket and lower them into the hot oil until they split. When they are cool remove the shell and inner skin. Place in a pan, cover with boiling water and simmer until they are tender. Drain them and strain through a sieve.

6. Add the Marsala and enough sifted confectioners' sugar to sweeten and bring out the flavor. The mixture should be very stiff and rather dry.

7. Beat in the stiffly whipped cream until thoroughly blended.

8. Place the mixture in a nylon pastry bag with a narrow writing nozzle. Push the mixture through this pipe into the meringue case forming a mound of long, decorative squiggles.

Nesselrode Pudding

18 chestnuts
4 egg yolks
1¼ cups milk
1 vanilla pod
⅔ cup canned pineapple syrup
¼ cup diced citron peel
½ cup crystallized pineapple or fresh
*   pineapple shredded and simmered for 7*
*   minutes in the pineapple syrup*
¼ cup candied cherries or marrons glacés
¼ cup seeded raisins
⅜ cup maraschino
1¼ cups whipped heavy cream

1. Nick the chestnuts and boil them until tender. Peel off and discard the inner and outer skins, and rub them through a sieve to make a purée.

2. Place the pulp in the top of a double saucepan over hot water with the egg

Nesselrode Pudding.

yolks, milk, crushed vanilla pod and pineapple syrup. Stir over heat until the mixture thickens to a thick smooth custard consistency.

3. Turn it into a bowl. If there are any lumps at all in it pass it through a sieve as you turn it into the bowl.

4. In a separate bowl mix together the diced citron peel, the crystallized pineapple roughly cut or the cooled and well drained stewed pineapple, the cherries, raisins and maraschino. Cover the bowl tightly with foil and leave for 4 hours.

5. Place the bowl of custard mixture covered with foil into the freezer or freezing compartment of the refrigerator and freeze until the edges are firm and the center is just beginning to set.

6. Scrape out into a bowl, beat well and fold in the fruit and maraschino.

7. When all ingredients are blended well together, fold in the whipped cream until smoothly blended in.

8. Place in a decorative mold, cover with foil and freeze until required.

9. Just before serving pour hot water over the bottom of the mold for an instant to unmold it.

10. Place on a serving dish and decorate with cherries or marrons glacés as desired.

Desserts and puddings

Lemon Sherbet

1 cup sugar
2½ cups water
rind and juice of 4 lemons
2 stiffly whipped egg whites

1. Dissolve the sugar in the water over a low heat.

2. Add the very thinly pared lemon rind and boil for 10 minutes. Cool and stir in lemon juice.

3. Strain the mixture into ice cube trays and leave in the freezing compartment of the refrigerator until half frozen, ie. edges crystallized but center not set.

4. Turn into a large bowl and fold in the egg whites thoroughly.

5. Turn into a waxed or plastic container with a well fitting lid and freeze until required. Serve scoops of the sherbet directly from the freezer.

Lemon Sherbet.

Floating Island

2 egg whites
¼ cup sugar
2½ cups milk
1 vanilla pod
1 tbsp sugar
1 tbsp cornstarch
⅛ cup sugar

1. Whip egg whites until very stiff, add half the sugar and whip again to its former stiffness. Lightly fold in remaining half of sugar with a metal spoon.

2. Place the milk in a wide shallow pan such as a skillet. Add the vanilla pod and 1 tbsp sugar and heat until very hot but not boiling.

3. Using a tablespoon, scoop up a heaped spoonful of the meringue, slide it into the hot vanilla flavored milk and leave to poach until set – about 4 minutes. Continue to do this until the surface of the pan is covered with half submerged ovals of meringue. Turn them over and poach on the underside. Remove with a slotted spoon onto waxed paper and repeat the process until all the meringue is used up.

4. Blend the cornstarch to a paste with a little cold water. Beat it with the egg yolks and the ⅛ cup sugar until thick and creamy. Slowly beat in the milk the meringues were poached in. Place in the top of a double saucepan and bring to the boil stirring all the time until it has the consistency of fairly thick custard. Turn the mixture into chosen serving dish.

5. Pile the meringues up in the center to make a floating island in the custard.

Red Currant Jelly Glaze

Basic Recipe

12 oz jar red currant jelly
¼ cup water

1. Heat the red currant jelly in the water in a pan over a very low heat until the jelly has completely dissolved.

2. Work the glaze through a sieve and pour into clean dry airtight containers for storage. Reheat the glaze gently before using according to recipe.

Floating Island – a sea of soft, rich vanilla custard, topped with an island of meringues – makes a sumptuous dessert. Serve this classic French pudding with sponge fingers or crisp 'cigarette' cookies, and sprinkle a little chocolate vermicelli over the top. This dish is sometimes known as Snow Eggs.

Desserts and puddings

Peach Melba.

Peach Melba

2 large peaches
juice of 1 lemon
¾ pt vanilla ice cream

For Melba sauce
1½ cups fresh or frozen raspberries
juice of 1 lemon
⅓ cup sugar
2 tbsp kirsch or cold water

1. Plunge the peaches into boiling water for a few seconds so that the skin can be easily removed.

2. Cut them in halves, remove the stones and rub the flesh well with lemon juice to prevent discoloration.

3. Put to one side one raspberry per person for decoration. Simmer together the Melba sauce ingredients for 5 minutes

then strain through a sieve and chill.

4. Assemble the dessert by placing a large scoop of vanilla ice cream in each individual glass sundae dish. Place one peach half on top, rounded side up and coat with the chilled raspberry sauce.

5. Decorate with whipped cream and flaked almonds and raspberries if desired.

Chocolate Ice Cream

¼ lb unsweetened chocolate
⅔ cup water
2½ cups milk
4 egg yolks
½ cup sugar
1¼ cups heavy cream

1. Place the chocolate and water in the top of a double saucepan with the outer pan half full of boiling water. Keep over the heat and stir until the contents are thoroughly blended.

2. Infuse the milk with a vanilla pod by heating the milk slowly to boiling point with the vanilla pod in it.

3. Remove vanilla pod, wipe and store it. Add the milk to the chocolate mixture.

4. Whip the egg yolks and sugar together until pale and very fluffy and add to the rest of the ingredients in the double saucepan.

5. Stir over heat until the mixture is thick and very smooth. Cool until below blood heat.

6. Reserve a little heavy cream for decoration. Whip the remainder into the ice cream and freeze into desired shape.

7. Just before serving turn it out onto chosen dish. Whip the cream for decoration until stiff and pipe small rosettes around the base of the ice cream and around the top. Chocolate shapes may also be used for decoration if desired.

Baked Alaska

1 round sponge cake
2 cups fresh ripe strawberries or 1⅓ cups
*   raspberries or other fruit*
3 egg whites
¾ cup sugar
vanilla ice cream

1. Set the oven at 450°F.

2. Place the sponge cake in a ovenproof dish. Arrange the chosen fruit on top with a little juice to moisten the sponge.

3. Make the meringue and put into a pastry bag with a rose pipe attached. Place the ice cream on top of the fruit. Pipe the meringue mixture all over so that the cake, fruit and ice cream are completely covered, taking the meringue right down to the dish.

4. Place in the pre-set oven for 2–3 minutes or until the outside of the meringue just begins to brown.

5. Decorate with crystallized violets and rose petals and serve immediately.

1. Arrange fruit on the sponge base.

2. Place very firm ice cream on top.

3. Pipe meringue all over so that the Alaska is masked in meringue.

4. Place in a very hot oven to brown.

Baked Alaska.

211

Black Cherries Jubilee.

Black Currant and Raspberry Water Ice.

Black Cherries Jubilee

2 cups stoned Bing cherries
3 tbsp confectioners' sugar
1 cup black currant jelly
2 tbsp kirsch

1. Set the oven at 275°F.

2. Retain any juice resulting from stoning the cherries. Place the stoned cherries and the juice in a covered casserole. Add the sifted confectioners' sugar. Bake in the pre-set oven for about 1 hour until the juices are drawn out of the fruit.

3. Melt the black currant jelly in the top of a double saucepan and add the kirsch. Put to one side off the heat to cool and thicken.

4. Strain the cherries over a bowl and gently stir them into the cooled sauce. Serve the strained cherry juice in a separate jug.

5. Taste and add more sugar if necessary.

Black Currant and Raspberry Water Ice

1 cup black currant pulp made from fresh raw black currants rubbed through a sieve
a few black currants for final decoration
1 cup raspberry pulp made from fresh raspberries rubbed through a sieve
few raspberries and leaves for final decoration
2½ cups stock sugar syrup simmered 5 minutes longer than in usual instructions

1. Mix the 2 fruit pulps together and beat in the syrup.

2. Turn into a wetted 5 cup mold and freeze.

3. Turn out onto a large round flat dish and keep chilled until served.

4. Decorate around the base with the reserved fresh black currants and raspberries and a sprig of fresh raspberry leaves on top.

213

Desserts and puddings

Pineapple Ninon

1 pineapple
sifted confectioners' sugar
¼ lb vanilla ice cream
almond paste made from 1 cup finely
  ground almonds
chantilly cream
2 cups whole strawberries

1. Cut the top off the pineapple. Remove flesh and chop it up. Dust the inside of the pineapple with confectioners' sugar. Put all but 2 tbsp of flesh into the pineapple.

2. Pack vanilla ice cream tightly into the pineapple case. Cover with foil and freeze until just before serving.

3. Roll out the almond paste and line tartlet pans with it. Leave to set for 24 hours.

4. Put a spoonful of pineapple flesh in each tartlet. Fill a pastry bag, fitted with a star nozzle, with chantilly cream and pipe over tarts and pineapple top. Decorate with strawberries. Arrange almond tarts around the pineapple.

Special Fruit Salad

1 medium pineapple
2¾ cups blackberries
2 cups strawberries
¼ cup confectioners' sugar
few drops kirsch

1. Remove green top from pineapple with a straight cut so that the tuft will stand steadily on its own. Place it at the center back of a circular dish for decoration.

2. Cut the pineapple into 3 pieces. First cut right through from top to base ½ inch left of center. Then cut top to base right through ½ inch right of center so that you end up with 1 large wedge of pineapple 1 inch thick, and 2 pineapple 'shells'. Remove all pineapple flesh from shells, dice it and return it to shells. Cut the slice of pineapple from top to base and halve each slice centrally. Place these strips of pineapple across the shells.

3. Fill the spaces in between the strips with strawberries and blackberries and pile blackberries up the center front of the pineapple tuft. Sprinkle the sifted confectioners' sugar all over the fruit and sprinkle on a few drops of kirsch if used. Chill in the refrigerator until required.

Strawberry and Orange Surprise

1 lb strawberries
1 orange
2 tbsp sugar
⅔ cup whipped heavy cream

1. Wash and hull the strawberries and place to one side in a bowl.

2. Grate the orange rind carefully, ensuring none of the pith is removed and squeeze the juice from half the orange into a small bowl. Add the sugar and rind and stir until the sugar melts.

3. Fold the cream into the orange syrup and pour over the strawberries. Cover and chill before serving.

Pineapple Ninon.

Glazed Pears.

Glazed Pears

6 large firm eating pears
juice from 2 lemons
2 cups sugar
⅔ cup water
½ cup red currant jelly
1 tbsp arrowroot
2 tbsp cold water

1. Peel the pears from bottom to tip, leaving them whole and leaving the stalk intact. Rub well with lemon juice so they keep their color. Place pears upright in a saucepan into which they just fit so they will not fall over when cooking.

2. In another pan dissolve the sugar in the water, stir in the red currant jelly and pour over the pears.

3. Simmer the pears in the jelly mixture until they are tender – about 20 minutes. Lift them out into the serving dish keeping them upright and reserving the liquid.

4. While they are cooling blend the arrowroot with the 2 tbsp of cold water and gradually add to the red currant and pear syrup in the pan stirring all the time. Bring to the boil and then simmer until sauce thickens.

5. Pour over the pears and chill well before serving. May be accompanied by unsweetened whipped cream if desired.

Desserts and puddings

Black Mountain Pudding

2 lb black currants
⅔ cup water
approx ½ thinly sliced sandwich loaf
granulated sugar to taste
arrowroot
fruit juice
cream

1. Put the fruit in a pan, add the water and cover the pan. Simmer for 6–7 minutes and strain.

2. Either work the fruit with a little of the juice in a liquidizer or else rub through a sieve. If the liquidizer is used, it is important to remember to strain the pulp to remove any small seeds. Add the rest of the juice.

3. Pour a little of the purée into a bowl. Cut away the bread crusts and place 2 slices on top of this. Then add more purée.

4. Continue this until the dish is full and you have at least ½ cup of the purée remaining. Ensure that each layer is well soaked in the purée.

5. Cover by placing a small plate on top, and pressing it down on the bread. Place a 2 lb weight on top of this. Leave until the following day.

6. To make a sauce: add a little water to the reserved purée. Slake the arrowroot with the fruit juice and add to the purée. Bring to the boil, stirring continuously. Pour off and allow to cool.

7. Turn the pudding out onto a plate or flat dish and spoon the sauce all over it, followed by the cream if desired.

Variations:
This pudding is also delicious if raspberries, loganberries or blackberries are substituted for the black currants, although the initial simmering time should be a few minutes less.

Plum Sponge Flan

1¼ cups flour
½ tsp baking powder
1 tsp cream of tartar
pinch of salt
1½ cups sugar
1 cup water
7 very stiffly whipped egg whites
7 egg yolks
2 tbsp cooking brandy

For filling
3 egg quantity confectioners' custard
1¼ lb cherry plums
¾ cup stock sugar syrup
red currant glaze

1. Set the oven at 350°F.

2. Sift the flour, baking powder, cream of tartar and salt into a large bowl.

3. Place the sugar and water in a thick pan over a low heat for the sugar to dissolve.

4. Bring it to the boil and boil strongly until a big bubble is formed when you dip in a slotted spoon and blow hard through the perforations.

5. Pour the syrup onto the very stiffly whipped egg whites and beat continuously for 5 minutes.

6. Whip the egg yolks and stir in the brandy. Very slowly beat the egg yolk mixture into the meringue mixture. Fold in the flour.

7. Turn into a 10 inch diameter flan case or 2 5 inch flan cases if preferred. Bake in the pre-set oven until the sponge is just springy under very light pressure.

8. Allow it to become completely cold before turning it out onto a serving dish.

9. Cover the base with confectioners' custard.

10. Poach the cherry plums in the stock sugar syrup over a very low heat. Drain over a jug and place them over the custard in the flan. Brush liberally with warm red currant glaze.

11. Serve the strained sugar syrup separately in a jug.

Plum Sponge Flan.

Desserts and puddings

French Apple Flan.

French Apple Flan

*sweet shortcrust pastry made from 2 cups
flour
confectioners' custard made from 3 egg
yolks
6 baking apples
¼ cup sugar
red currant glaze*

1. Set the oven at 375°F.

2. Roll out the pastry thinly and line a 9
inch flan ring.

3. Cover base with confectioners' custard.

4. Peel and thinly slice the apples. Then
cover the flan with overlapping slices of
apple. Dust with sifted sugar.

5. Bake until the pastry edges are lightly
brown and the edges of the apple rings are
quite brown – approximately 15–20
minutes.

6. Remove from oven and immediately
brush the entire surface including edges of
flan case with red currant glaze.

7. When it is cold, transfer to serving dish
using 2 metal slices underneath to prevent
it splitting. Remove flan ring.

Sweet Shortcrust Pastry

*2 cups flour
1 cup sweet butter
½ cup sugar
cinnamon
2 egg yolks
approx 6 tbsp ice cold water*

1. Sift the flour into a bowl. Cut in the
butter with a round bladed knife, and,
once evenly coated with flour, rub in lightly with the fingertips until mixture has
turned into fine crumbs.

2. Add the sugar and a dash of cinnamon
(if wished) and mix in well.

3. Make a well in the center of the mixture, add egg yolks and at least two thirds
of the water and work in using a fork. Add
more of the water if necessary until the
mixture forms a firm dough.

4. Turn out onto a floured board and
knead lightly until smooth. Wrap the
pastry in a polythene bag or a piece of
waxed paper and leave in the refrigerator
for at least one hour before rolling out.

Cherry Pie

*sweet shortcrust pastry made from 1 cup
flour
2 cups cooked, pitted red cherries
2 tbsp sugar
1 tbsp melted butter
1 tbsp tapioca
almond flavoring
1 egg white
extra sugar for dusting*

1. Set the oven at 400°F.

2. Make the sweet shortcrust pastry and
line a 7–8 inch diameter, deep pie dish
with half of it.

3. Strain the cherries and place in a bowl
with 1 cup cherry juice. Add the sugar,
melted butter, tapioca and a few drops of
almond flavoring. Mix the ingredients together and leave to stand for about 15
minutes.

4. Pour the cherry filling into the pie dish
and cover with the remaining pastry, sealing the edges well.

5. Bake in the pre-set oven for 30–40 minutes.

6. Take the pie out of the oven, brush with lightly whipped egg white and sprinkle with a little sugar. Return the pie to the oven and bake for a further 5 minutes or until glazed.

7. Serve hot or cold with cream.

Upside Down Apple Flan

2 tbsp sweet butter
sugar for dredging
4 large or 5 medium baking apples
sweet shortcrust pastry made from 2 cups
*   flour*
confectioners' sugar for decoration

1. Set the oven at 350°F.

2. Grease the base of a 7 inch layer pan with butter. Line it with a fitting circle of waxed paper and butter the paper well. Dredge the buttered paper with a liberal layer of sifted sugar.

3. Peel and core the apples and slice into very thin rounds. Working from the center of the pan outward overlap the apple rings with about $\frac{1}{4}$ inch between each overlap until the pan is filled to within $\frac{1}{2}$ inch of the top. Press down firmly.

4. Roll out shortcrust pastry to about $\frac{1}{2}$ inch thick and cut a round from it by lightly resting the clean based layer pan on it and cutting around neatly with a sharp knife. Using a rolling pin to lift it, transfer the pastry to cover the apple slices and press down lightly.

5. Bake in the pre-set oven until the top of the pastry is golden brown.

6. Refrigerate until cold. Invert over a serving dish and carefully remove the waxed paper. Dust with sifted confectioners' sugar.

Upside Down Apple Flan.

219

Desserts and puddings

Crumb Crust Fruit Flan.

Crumb Crust Fruit Flan

1 cup butter or margarine
8 cups Graham cracker crumbs
3 egg yolk quantity of
*   confectioners' custard*
soft fruit as desired
red currant glaze

1. Melt the butter or margarine in a saucepan and stir in the crumbs until the fat is absorbed.

2. Press the mixture evenly into the base and sides of a 9 inch flan ring standing on a lightly greased cookie sheet. When cool and firm, carefully remove flan ring and place on serving dish.

3. Put the confectioners' custard in the base of the flan.

4. Cover with raspberries or other soft fruit, arranging the fruit either in circles or triangular sections.

5. Brush the top with red currant glaze.

Note: Flan rings are plain metal circles about 1 inch deep in varying diameters. A European type pie pan with a loose base can be used instead; these usually have a fluted edge.

Lemon Meringue Pie

sweet shortcrust pastry made from approx 1 cup flour

For filling
1 tbsp cornstarch
1¼ cups milk
1 tbsp sugar
2 egg yolks
grated rind and juice of 1 lemon

For meringue
2 egg whites
½ cup sugar

1. Set the oven at 375°F.

2. Line a 7 inch diameter flan ring with pastry and bake blind until golden brown.

3. Reduce oven temperature to 325°F.

4. Mix the cornstarch with a little of the milk in a bowl. Heat the remaining milk and pour onto the cornstarch paste, stirring well.

5. Return the mixture to the pan and bring to the boil, stirring continuously. Boil for 3–4 minutes, still stirring, until smooth and thickened.

6. Add the sugar and allow to cool.

7. Beat in the egg yolks and the grated lemon rind and juice. Pour the lemon mixture into the baked pastry case.

8. Bake in the pre-set oven for about 10 minutes or until lightly set. Remove.

9. Reduce the oven temperature to 275°F.

10. Pile the meringue on top of the lemon filling, covering completely.

11. Sprinkle with sugar and place in the pre-set oven for 10–15 minutes. The meringue should be crisp on the outside and soft inside. Serve hot.

Fruit Slice

1 rectangular case of puff pastry
3 egg quantity of confectioners' custard
a mixture of all or some of the following fruits:–
  peeled, halved, or sliced and stoned peaches, apricots, pears, black and red cherries, raspberries, strawberries and apricot glaze plums.
angelica and cherry for decoration

1. Cover the base of the pastry case with the confectioners' custard.

2. Pile the fruits on top, arranging them in a colorful way and taking them above the top of the pastry case.

3. Warm the apricot glaze and pour between the spaces of the fruit until it comes to just below the rim of the pastry. Brush the top surfaces of the fruit with this glaze.

4. Decorate with angelica and cherry if desired.

Chantilly Cream

1⅓ cups heavy cream
2 tsp sugar
¼ tsp vanilla flavoring
1 egg white

1. Whisk the chilled cream until just thick – don't overwhip or it will become too firm to use properly. Stir in the sugar and vanilla flavoring.

2. In another bowl, stiffly whip the egg white and lightly fold into the whipped cream mixture. Use immediately according to recipe.

Fruit Slice.

Desserts and puddings

Apricot Flan

1 cooked flan case made of sweet shortcrust
* pastry 9 inches diameter*
3 egg yolk quantity confectioners' custard
1 lb fresh apricots or 1 large can apricot
* halves*
red currant glaze
chantilly cream
sugar syrup
vanilla pod

1. Half fill flan case with the confection-

ers' custard and level off evenly.

2. Poach apricots if fresh ones are being used. Slice fruit in halves and remove stone. Place the halved fruits in a single layer over the base of a wide shallow pan. Cover with sugar syrup, add a vanilla pod, and poach very gently over a low heat. Remove vanilla pod wipe and store. Remove apricots carefully so that they retain a dome shape.

3. Put apricot cups as closely together as

possible over the custard, placing them dome side uppermost.

4. Brush the apricots with red currant glaze making sure that the glaze fills the empty spaces between the fruit. Leave until cold.

5. Pipe cream around the edge of the flan using a decorative nozzle.

Confectioners' Custard

1¼ cups milk
1 vanilla pod
1 tbsp flour
3 egg yolks
½ cup sugar

1. Gently heat the milk with the vanilla pod in a pan over a very low heat, until tiny bubbles just start to rise to the surface. Do not allow to boil. Immediately take the pan off the heat, remove the pod, and reserve for future use. Then set milk aside.

2. Sift the flour. Whisk together the egg yolks, flour and sugar. Stir in the vanilla flavored milk. Pour the mixture into a double boiler or into a bowl and stand in a pan of hot water over a gentle heat. Using a wooden spoon, stir custard until it becomes thick and creamy and evenly coats the back of the spoon. Remove from the heat at once and use hot or cold according to recipe.

Almond Paste

½ cup ground almonds
1 cup sifted confectioners'
* sugar*
1 lightly whipped egg white
½ tsp each orange flower water and
* rose water*
cornstarch for dusting

1. Knead together the ground almonds and sugar. Make a well in the center and pour in half the egg white and the flavored waters. Knead to smooth paste.

2. Turn paste onto work surface, dusting with cornstarch, and knead until it resembles a soft pastry dough. Only add more egg white if the paste is still crumbly. Wrap in foil and store in refrigerator.

Apricot Flan.

Crêpes Suzette.

Crêpes Suzette

butter for frying
¼ cup sugar
¼ cup butter
juice of 2 mandarins, tangerines or small
  oranges and grated rind of 1 lemon
1 tbsp brandy
2 tbsp Cointreau

For rich pancake batter
1 cup flour
salt
2 eggs
1 tbsp butter
1¾ cups milk

1. Mix the batter in the same way as the basic pancake batter, adding the batter at the same time as the eggs.

2. Heat a little butter in a 7 inch thick based skillet, pour off the excess and cook the pancakes in the same way as ordinary pancakes. When all 8 are made keep them warm between 2 plates in a warm oven.

3. Wipe around the skillet, put in the sugar and heat until the sugar has melted and turned golden brown.

4. Remove the skillet from the heat, add the butter, orange juice, lemon rind and Cointreau. Mix well together and replace over a low heat.

5. Fold each pancake in half and then in half again to form a quarter circle.

6. Place all the pancakes in the skillet and when they are reheated and soaked in the sauce, pour the brandy over them and ignite it.

7. Serve at once by transferring the pancakes to a large flat oval dish, pour the sauce over them and dust them with sifted confectioners' sugar.

Orange and Lemon Curd Pudding

suet crust pastry made from 2 cups flour
segments from 4 skinned oranges
6 tbsp lemon curd
confectioners' sugar for dusting

1. Half fill a steamer or large saucepan with water and put it on to boil.

2. Cut a quarter from the prepared suet pastry and leave to one side for the lid. Roll out the remainder until about ¼ inch thick and 2 inches wider than the top of an ovenproof bowl. Grease the bowl and line it with the pastry.

3. Fill the bowl with alternate layers of the orange segments and lemon curd. Turn in the pastry overhanging the rim of the bowl over the filling. Roll out the pastry for the lid, damp the edges of the pastry in the bowl and cover with the lid, pressing the edges together well to seal.

4. Fold a pleat in a square of kitchen foil or buttered waxed paper – the pleat allows the pudding to rise during cooking. Place the paper or foil over the bowl and twist it under the rim to secure it.

5. Steam for 2½ hours taking care not to let the steamer boil dry. Add boiling water when the water level gets low.

6. Turn pudding out onto a dish. Dust with sifted confectioners' sugar and serve with custard if desired.

Lemon Curd

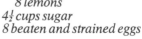

1 cup butter
juice and finely grated rind of
  8 lemons
4½ cups sugar
8 beaten and strained eggs

1. Place the butter, sugar and lemon juice and rind in the top of a double saucepan or in a bowl standing in a pan of simmering water. Stir over heat until the sugar has dissolved.

2. Add eggs and continue stirring over heat until mixture turns thick and creamy.

3. Strain into small pots, cover, and store in a cool place for up to 1 month.

Desserts and puddings

Coconut and Maple Syrup Pudding.

Suet Crust Pastry

Basic Recipe ☆

2 cups flour
1 tsp baking powder
¼ tsp salt
1 cup finely shredded suet
⅔ cup water
These quantities are sufficient for a 3¾ cup ovenproof bowl

Sift flour and salt into a bowl. Add the suet and stir. Add water gradually to form a dough and knead lightly until smooth.

Coconut and Maple Syrup Pudding

basic suet crust pastry made from 2 cups flour
1 cup maple syrup
1 cup shredded coconut

1. Roll out three quarters of the pastry to a circle approx 2 inches bigger than the top of the bowl and line a greased 3¾ cup ovenproof bowl with it. Roll out the remaining pastry and cut 3 circles, one larger one to fit as a lid, and 2 smaller circles.

2. Mix the maple syrup and coconut together to a paste. Place a third of this in the lined bowl and cover with one of the small circles of pastry. Add another third of the filling, then the second small circle, then the rest of filling and seal the lid on the top by damping the edges with water and pressing well together.

3. Cover and steam for 2½ hours as for Orange and Lemon Curd Pudding.

Steamed Chocolate Pudding

½ cup butter
½ cup sugar
1 cup flour
1 tsp baking powder
¼ cup sweetened drinking chocolate powder
2 beaten eggs
approx 4 tbsp milk

1. Half fill a steamer or large saucepan with water and heat to boiling point, keep at this temperature.

2. Cream the butter and sugar together thoroughly. Sieve the flour, baking powder and chocolate powder together and add to the creamed mixture a little at a time alternately with each egg.

3. Add the milk to give a soft dropping consistency, put the mixture in a greased 3¾ cup ovenproof bowl and cover lightly with a circle of buttered paper. Cover the top of the bowl with foil and steam for 1½ hours. Care must be taken not to let the steamer boil dry. Add boiling water from a kettle when the water level gets low.

4. Invert over a serving dish and dredge with sifted confectioners' sugar. Serve hot with hot chocolate sauce and cream if desired.

Hot Chocolate Sauce

5 oz unsweetened chocolate
2 tbsp light brown sugar
2 tbsp water
¼ cup butter
1 tsp rum

1. Put the chocolate, sugar and water in the top of a double saucepan over gently boiling water. Blend ingredients together.

2. Add the butter gradually, beating well all the time, then add the rum.

3. Serve immediately or to keep it hot cover the pan with a tight fitting lid to prevent a skin forming on the surface and keep the pan on the heat, watching that it does not boil dry.

4. Any remaining sauce may be reheated. Beat until smooth and follow directions for stage 3 above.

Light Corn Syrup Pudding

½ cup butter
½ cup sugar
2 beaten eggs
1½ cups flour
1 tsp baking powder
milk to mix
2 tbsp light corn syrup

1. Half fill a steamer or large saucepan with water and put it on to boil.

2. Cream the butter and sugar together until pale and fluffy. Sift the flour. Add the beaten eggs a little at a time alternating with a spoonful of the flour. Beat well. Fold in the rest of the sifted flour. Add a little milk if necessary to make a soft dropping consistency.

3. Grease a 3¾ cup ovenproof bowl. Place the syrup in the bottom and the pudding mixture on top.

4. Cover with greased waxed paper or foil in which a pleat has been made to allow for rising. Tie firmly around the rim of the bowl with string.

5. Steam for 1½ hours. Keep the water in the steamer boiling rapidly and have a kettle of boiling water nearby to top it up regularly or it may boil dry.

6. Turn out onto chosen dish and serve hot with extra syrup if desired.

Steamed Chocolate Pudding with Hot Chocolate Sauce.

Sponge Buns.

Cakes and bread

Sponge Buns

½ cup melted butter or margarine
½ cup sugar
2 cups flour
2 eggs
1 tbsp milk
⅓ cup fruit (white raisins, seedless raisins, currants, chopped candied cherries) or ¼ cup shredded coconut, or flavoring (finely chopped orange or lemon rind, cocoa or coffee powder)

1. Set the oven at 375°F.

2. Cream together the fat and sugar until light and pale colored. Fold in ½ cup flour and 1 egg, then beat well. Do the same with another 1 cup flour and remaining egg. Then beat in remaining flour a little at a time until a stiff mixture is formed. Stir in fruit, coconut or flavoring and milk.

3. Fill mixture into greased bun pans and bake just above the center of the pre-set oven for 15 minutes or until golden and just firm to the touch. Cool on a wire rack.

Raspberry Buns

2 cups flour
salt
½ cup butter or margarine
½ cup sugar
1 lightly beaten egg
1 tbsp milk
¼ cup raspberry jam

1. Set the oven at 425°F.

2. Sift the flour and a dash of salt into a bowl, then rub in the fat until the mixture resembles fine crumbs. Stir in the sugar. Make a well in the center, then stir in the egg, followed by the milk, and blend to form a smooth dough.

3. Turn the dough onto a floured work surface and knead for a few seconds. Then press out a little with your hand and cut dough into 12 pieces. Shape each piece into a round bun and place on a greased, floured cookie sheet.

4. Using the handle of a wooden spoon, make a small hole in the top of each bun and spoon in a little of the jam. Put the buns into the pre-set oven and bake for about 10 minutes or until well risen.

Cakes and bread

Featherweight Jam Sponge

2 eggs plus 1 egg yolk
scant ¼ cup confectioners' sugar
½ cup flour
raspberry, strawberry or black currant jam
*   for filling*
confectioners' sugar for sprinkling

1. Set the oven at 375°F.

2. Beat the eggs, egg yolk and sugar together in a mixing bowl until thick and creamy. Sift the flour and fold into the egg mixture, using a metal spoon.

3. Grease and flour an 8 inch diameter deep cake pan, then line with greased waxed paper cut to fit. Turn the mixture into the prepared cake pan and bake in the pre-set oven for 30 minutes or until pale gold and the top of cake springs back when gently pressed with a finger.

4. Cool on a wire rack, then turn out of pan and cut in half; sandwich with chosen jam and sprinkle the top generously with confectioners' sugar.

Coffee Gâteau

1 cup softened butter or margarine
1 cup plus 2 tbsp sugar
4 eggs
1¾ cups flour
¼ cup cornstarch
2 tbsp coffee syrup
coffee butter cream made from ¾ cup butter

1. Set the oven at 350°F.

2. Cream the fat and sugar in a mixing bowl until pale colored and fluffy. Using a metal spoon fold in a quarter of the flour, then carefully beat in 1 egg, a little at a time to avoid curdling the cake batter. Continue folding in portions of flour, followed by an egg each time, until all are incorporated. Beat in the coffee syrup.

3. Well grease the sides of 12 inch diameter, 1 inch deep cake pan and line with greased and floured waxed paper cut to fit. Pour the cake batter into the prepared pan.

4. Bake the cake in the pre-set oven for 30 minutes or until it is golden, well risen, firm to the touch and just pulls away from the sides of the pan. Take out and cool on a wire rack.

5. With the bottom side up (this always has the smoothest and best looking surface) completely cover the sponge with a good half of the coffee butter cream, chill in the refrigerator, then smooth the top with a knife. Fill remaining butter cream into a pastry bag fitted with a plain nozzle and pipe a trellis pattern on top of the cake. Change the nozzle to a small rosette nozzle and pipe rosettes all round the sides of the cake. Pipe a single rosette at each point on the trellis where the lines cross each other.

Featherweight Jam Sponge.

Sand Cake

1 cup unsalted, softened butter
finely grated rind of 1 small lemon
 (optional)
¾ cup flour
¾ cup potato flour
1½ cups sifted confectioners' sugar plus a
 little extra for sprinkling
6 separated eggs

1. Set the oven at 350°F.

2. Cream the butter in a mixing bowl, with the lemon rind if using, until pale and fluffy. Sift the 2 flours together and then gradually beat in the confectioners' sugar and about a quarter of the flours. Next beat in 2 egg yolks until well combined. Beat in another quarter of the flours and 2 more egg yolks, and repeat this process until all the flour and egg yolks are incorporated and you have a smooth batter. Stiffly whip the egg whites and fold into the batter. Then beat until combined and no streaks of egg white remain.

3. Grease and flour a rectangular cake pan measuring 9 by 5 by 3 inches. Turn cake mixture into the prepared pan and smooth the surface, flattening the center slightly, so it remains flat during baking. Bake in the pre-set oven for 40 minutes. Take out and cool cake in the pan until only just warm. Turn out and sprinkle thickly with confectioners' sugar.

Orange or Lemon Gâteau

1 cup softened butter or margarine
finely grated rind of ½ orange or ½ lemon
1 cup plus 2 tbsp sugar
4 eggs
1¾ cups flour
¼ cup cornstarch
juice of 1 orange or lemon

For vanilla frosting
1½ cups sifted confectioners' sugar
1½ tbsp vegetable oil
1–1½ tbsp milk
2–3 drops vanilla flavoring
crystallized orange or lemon slices for
 decoration

1. Set the oven at 350°F.

2. Put the softened fat in a mixing bowl together with the orange or lemon rind.

Madeira Cake.

Add the sugar and cream with the fat until pale colored and fluffy. Using a metal spoon fold in a quarter of the flour, then carefully beat in 1 egg, a little at a time to avoid curdling the cake batter. Continue folding in portions of flour, followed by an egg each time, until all are incorporated. Beat in the orange or lemon juice.

3. Well grease 2 8 inch diameter cake pans and line with greased and floured waxed paper cut to fit. Pour cake batter into the prepared pans.

4. Bake the cakes in the pre-set oven for 20 minutes or until golden, well risen, firm to the touch and they just pull away from the sides of the pan. Take out and cool on a wire rack.

5. Make vanilla frosting by beating together in a bowl the confectioners' sugar, oil, milk and vanilla flavoring until very smooth. Sandwich the sponge rounds with vanilla frosting and decorate the top of the gâteau with crystallized orange or lemon slices.

Madeira Cake

7 separated eggs
2 tbsp sugar
1 cup flour
confectioners' sugar for sprinkling

1. Set the oven at 350°F.

2. Stiffly whip the egg whites in a large bowl until they hold a peak. Beat the egg yolks in another mixing bowl until they are doubled in volume and foamy. Add the sugar and whip the eggs again. Sift the flour and beat into the sugar mixture. Using a metal spoon, fold in the egg whites, a third at a time. Grease and flour a loaf pan measuring 9 by 5 by 3 inches.

3. Make a domed 'cap' of foil to fit over cake pan. Turn the cake batter into the prepared pan and three quarters fill. Not all of the batter is required so either bake a second smaller cake in a greased and floured 8 inch deep cake pan or fill into greased and floured muffin pans for miniature Madeira cakes.

4. Bake the cake in the pre-set oven for about 15 minutes. Then take out and cover pan with prepared 'cap' of foil. Return cake to oven and bake for 35 minutes longer or until well risen and golden. (Reduce overall baking time by 5 minutes for smaller cake, and by 15 minutes for Madeira buns.) Cool on a wire rack, then sprinkle with sugar.

Cakes and bread

Angel Cake.

Angel Cake

5 egg whites
1 tsp cream of tartar
⅔ cup sugar
salt
½ cup flour
¼ cup cornstarch

To decorate
1 cup flaked blanched almonds
confectioners' sugar for sprinkling

1. Set the oven at 325°F.

2. Stiffly whip the egg whites in a large bowl until they stand in a firm peak; there should be no liquid egg white at all.

Sprinkle over the cream of tartar, then gently draw them to the sides of the bowl to make a well in the center.

3. Pour the sugar and a dash of salt into the well, then fold in carefully with a metal spoon or spatula to retain as much beaten in air as possible. When the sugar is completely combined, make a well again. Sift the flour and cornstarch together and repeat the folding in process with the flours.

4. When combined turn at once into an ungreased, 6 inch, loose bottomed cake pan. Cut through the mixture a few times with a knife to break up any air bubbles present, then cover the top thickly with flaked almonds.

5. Bake in the pre-set oven for 45 minutes or until light and fluffy. Do not be tempted to open the oven during the cooking period because the mixture is very delicate and cannot survive sudden changes of temperature or knocks caused by opening and shutting the oven door or moving the pan. Cool in the pan until cold, then turn out onto a wire rack. Sprinkle with confectioners' sugar.

Confectioners' Sugar Icing

Basic Recipe

1 cup confectioners' sugar
2 tbsp warm milk, cream or water or
    flavored liquid such as fresh orange or
    lemon juice or other fruit juice or black
    coffee

1. Sift the confectioners' sugar into a mixing bowl. Gradually add the water or other preferred liquid and mix until the icing is smooth but fairly stiff. If too much liquid is added, the icing will become too runny and more sieved confectioners' sugar will have to be added until it returns to the required stiffness.

2. If not using the icing immediately, cover the bowl with foil or a damp cloth, or stir in a little lemon juice if not already used to prevent the icing hardening.

Variation:
Use a few drops of edible food coloring to give pink, blue, mauve etc. colored icing. Add colorings sparingly to avoid the result being too garish or dark.

Special Iced Cake

1 cup softened butter or margarine
1 cup plus 2 tbsp sugar
4 eggs
2 cups flour
2 tbsp milk
brandy flavored butter cream made from $\frac{3}{4}$
    cup butter
confectioners' sugar icing
food coloring of choice

1. Set the oven at 350°F.

2. Cream the fat and sugar until pale colored and fluffy. Using a metal spoon fold in a quarter of the flour, then carefully beat in 1 egg, a little at a time, to avoid curdling the cake batter. Continue folding in portions of flour, followed by an egg each time, until all are incorporated.

3. Well grease the sides of a 12 inch diameter, 1 inch deep cake pan and line with greased and floured waxed paper cut to fit. Pour the cake batter into the prepared pan.

4. Bake the cake in the pre-set oven for 30 minutes or until it is golden, well risen, firm to touch and just pulls away from the sides of the pan. Take out and cool on a wire rack.

5. With the bottom side up to give the smoothest possible surface for icing, cover with flavored butter cream, and work it down the sides. Put the sponge into the refrigerator to chill until the butter cream is hard. Take out and smooth off the surface for icing by drawing a palette knife dipped in hot water over the butter cream; shake off drops of water each time before applying the knife. Return the sponge to the refrigerator and chill again until the butter cream is hard.

6. Meanwhile tint the confectioners' sugar icing to desired shade, then spread over the butter cream covered sponge cake. Decorate the iced cake according to personal preference with crystallized fruit, sugar roses, finely chopped nuts etc.

Butter Cream

Basic Recipe ☆

$\frac{3}{4}$ cup softened sweet butter
3 cups confectioners' sugar
$\frac{1}{4}$ tsp vanilla flavoring
3–4 tbsp milk or warm water

Cream the butter until it is soft and fluffy and pale colored, then gradually beat in the confectioners' sugar together with the vanilla flavoring and enough milk or water to blend to a smooth mixture. Use according to recipe.

Variations:

Orange, lime or lemon butter cream: omit vanilla flavoring and add a little grated orange, lime or lemon rind plus about $\frac{1}{2}$ tbsp juice. Beat well to prevent mixture from curdling.
Coffee butter cream: omit vanilla flavoring and add 1–2 tbsp instant coffee powder, according to taste.
Chocolate butter cream: omit vanilla flavoring. Add 1–1$\frac{1}{2}$ tbsp cocoa flavoring dissolved in a little hot water; cool before beating into butter mixture, or melt 1 oz chocolate until just liquid and blend into confectioners' sugar.

Special Iced Cake.

1. Using a pastry bag fitted with a small writing nozzle, practise drawing a series of straight lines in icing. Try it out on a sheet of cardboard first before you decorate the cake.

2. Note the correct position of hands for piping. The second hand steadies the first.

3. Pipe another series of lines across the first set. Try to keep the hands clear of the work surface so that the second line of piping does not pull the first line out of shape.

Cakes and bread

Cream Horns

puff pastry made from 4 cups flour
1 beaten egg
⅔ cup cold water
2–3 tbsp raspberry or other chosen jam
3 tbsp confectioners' custard
⅔ cup whipped heavy cream
few finely chopped pistachio nuts (optional)

1. Set the oven at 400°F.

2. Lightly flour work surface and roll out the pastry very thinly to a square large enough to give a trimmed square measuring 24 inches. Cut this into 1¼ inch strips.

3. Grease and flour the outside of metal cream horn molds. Take one strip of pastry per mold and carefully wind it around the mold, starting from the point and overlapping the pastry as you wind. Moisten the overlapping edges with a little cold water to help them stick together. Trim excess pastry from the top.

4. Place molds, flat side down, on a floured cookie sheet. Brush with beaten egg and bake just above the center shelf in the pre-set oven for about 15 minutes or until the pastry is golden. Take out and transfer to a wire rack; holding a cloth in both hands, immediately begin to ease the pastry off the molds. This is best done before the pastry cools.

5. Mix together the jam, confectioners' custard and about 3 tbsp whipped cream. Spoon this into each horn, then fill remaining cream into a pastry bag fitted with a star nozzle and pipe a large swirl of cream over the end of each pastry horn. Sprinkle with a little of the chopped pistachio nuts if liked.

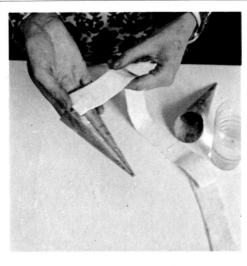

1. The traditional method of winding the pastry round cream horn molds is to start at the top, leaving some surplus pastry over the edge, and wind downwards overlapping generously.

5. When you reach the top of the mold, trim away the surplus pastry making a sloping edge. Stick the top under edge to the upper edge with a little water, and dip the pointed end in cold water and pinch firmly together. This seals the pastry and holds the shape.

Meringue Pavé

2 cups browned flaked almonds
confectioners' sugar for sprinkling

For Swiss meringue
10 egg whites
2¼ cups sugar

For coffee butter cream
¾ cup softened sweet butter
3 cups sifted confectioners' sugar
3–4 tbsp syrup

1. Set the oven at 275°F.

2. Make the meringue in 2 batches (halve the ingredients given above). In a mixing bowl stiffly whip the egg whites until they stand in a peak. Sprinkle over ¼ cup of the sugar and whip again for about 3 minutes. Sprinkle over remaining sugar and fold in lightly with a spatula.

3. Line 2 cookie sheets with a piece of well greased waxed paper cut to fit. Drop spoonfuls of meringue onto the prepared cookie sheets, spacing them fairly wide apart, and bake in the pre-set oven for about 55 minutes or until pale brown and crisp. Take out and cool on a wire rack.

4. Make the coffee butter cream. In a mixing bowl cream the butter until pale and soft, then gradually beat in the confectioners' sugar, and enough coffee syrup to blend to a smooth mixture.

5. Crumble the cold meringue into a mixing bowl and blend in just enough of the butter cream to form a smooth ball of paste, working the mixture in your hands. Divide the paste in half, then place each one on a piece of waxed paper and roll out into 2 equal narrow strips. Cover one strip with butter cream. Top with the remaining strip, using 2 palette knives to lift it, then cover the top and sides with butter cream. Sprinkle thickly with browned almonds, then confectioners' sugar. Pipe rosettes with the remaining coffee butter cream around the base.

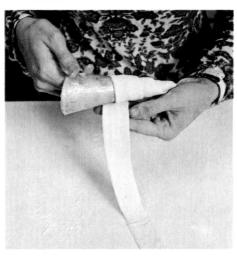

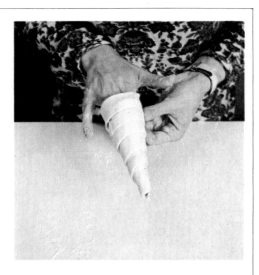

2. However, you may find it easier to start at the bottom and wind towards the top. Make sure that each overlapping strip is at least a third over the previous one.

3. Continue winding round the horn mold, taking care not to stretch the pastry as this will spoil the finished shape.

4. Wind the pastry right to the top of the horn mold, leaving some surplus. Make sure the winding ends at the shallow back part of the mold.

Cream Horns.

Variations:

Cream horns can also be filled simply with plain whipped cream, lightly flavored with vanilla. Add fresh raspberries or strawberries, if in season, for a special treat.

For another alternative filling using whipped cream, add sugar and a dash of rum instead of vanilla, and stir in a little grated chocolate before filling the cream horns.

Jelly Roll

¾ cup flour
½ cup sugar
3 eggs
confectioners' sugar for sprinkling

For filling
red jam or jelly or butter cream

1. Set the oven at 425°F.

2. Line a jelly roll pan measuring 10 by 14 by ¾ inches with waxed paper, cut to fit. Brush the paper lightly with oil. Prepare a work surface of several layers of newspaper topped with a sheet of waxed paper. All papers should be about 3 inches larger than the jelly roll pan. Sift a little flour over the waxed paper.

3. Sift the sugar onto a piece of foil and heat in the pre-set oven for about 6 minutes. Sift the flour. Whisk the eggs with the hot sugar until pale and foamy. Fold in the flour quickly but gently so the air bubbles are not lost.

4. Pour the batter into the prepared pan, spreading it evenly, and bake in the pre-set oven, just above center, for 8 minutes or until golden. Take out of the oven and flip the sponge over and carefully place on the prepared waxed paper. Leave to cool.

5. Trim the sides and spread with jam. To roll up, grip the ends of paper nearest you at either side, lift up and start to roll the sponge away from you. Put one hand behind the papers and push firmly on the sponge as you roll. Ease the paper away from the sponge, keeping it taut and at an angle above the sponge. Keep rolling until the jelly roll is completed. Brush off any surplus flour and sprinkle with confectioners' sugar.

1. Make waxed paper fit your jelly roll pan by drawing round the pan onto the paper, cut through and place the pencilled side downwards.

2. Lay paper on the pan and brush all over – including the sides – with oil.

6. Stop whisking, then shake the sifted flour over the surface of the egg and sugar mixture.

7. Using a spatula, gently fold and cut the flour into the mixture until completely blended. Take care not to lose any of the air bubbles which you have just been whisking up.

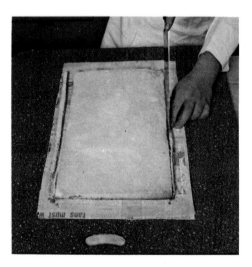

9. Trim the sides of the cooled sponge with a sharp knife. This gives a neat finish to the end result.

10. Pick up the papers nearest you and hold them in the way shown above. Press the edge firmly onto the jam.

3. Prepare a work surface with newspaper and waxed paper, then sift a little flour onto the waxed paper.

4. Heat the sifted sugar in the oven for 6 minutes. Break the eggs into a large bowl and when the sugar is really hot, quickly tip it onto the eggs and start whisking immediately.

5. Continue whisking until the mixture looks like this. It should almost have doubled its bulk and be pale and foamy.

8. Turn the mixture into the prepared pan and spread with the spatula right over the surface, taking care to reach right into the corners of the pan.

11. Roll up quickly, using one hand to hold the papers taut and the other to push from behind.

Jelly Roll filled with butter cream instead of the usual jam. Fillings of whipped cream or confectioners' custard also make a pleasant change.

Cakes and bread

Chocolate Layer Cake

2 eggs plus 1 egg yolk
½ cup plus 1 tbsp confectioners' sugar
½ cup flour
2 tbsp drinking chocolate powder
2 tbsp coffee syrup
coffee butter cream for filling

For chocolate frosting and decoration
½ cup sugar
3 tbsp water
6 oz semi sweet chocolate
1–2 drops of olive oil

1. Set the oven at 350°F.

2. Beat together the eggs, egg yolk and sugar in a mixing bowl until thick and creamy. Sprinkle over the flour together with the drinking chocolate, then fold in lightly. Stir in the coffee syrup.

3. Line a greased and floured baking pan with greased waxed paper cut to fit.

4. Turn the mixture into the prepared pan and bake just below the center of the pre-set oven for about 30 minutes or until risen and the sponge springs back when pressed lightly with a fingertip. Turn out onto a wire rack to cool, then trim the sloping edges.

5. With a sharp knife cut the sponge in 3 equal pieces lengthwise. Cover one piece with coffee butter cream, place the second piece of sponge on top, then cover with more butter cream and top with the third piece of sponge.

6. Make the chocolate frosting by dissolving ½ cup sugar in the water in a pan over a moderate heat; then bring to the boil, reduce heat at once and simmer until the sugar syrup is a light yellow color.

7. Take the pan from the heat and cool until the syrup is tepid. In a heavy based pan heat the chocolate until just liquid. Stir the sugar syrup into the chocolate, add

the olive oil and continue stirring until the frosting is of a spreading consistency. Spread the frosting over the top and sides of the cake to cover them completely and leave to set.

8. When icing is cold and firm, melt the remaining chocolate in a pan over a low heat until liquid, fill into a pastry bag fitted with ¼ inch plain nozzle and pipe thin lines of chocolate at random all over the top and sides. Leave to set.

Viennese Torte

1 packet round Vienna wafer cookies
13 coffee beans for decoration

For coffee butter cream
5 tbsp softened sweet butter
1½ cups sifted confectioners' sugar
1–2 tsp coffee liqueur
2–3 drops coffee syrup

For coffee confectioners' sugar icing
2¼ cups sifted confectioners' sugar
2 tbsp warmed coffee syrup

1. Make the coffee butter cream by creaming the butter in a mixing bowl until soft and light, then beat in the confectioners' sugar and the coffee liqueur. Gradually stir in enough coffee syrup to flavor it delicately and still retain a fairly firm mixture. Spread butter cream over all the wafers except for one. Carefully sandwich them together, topping with the remaining plain wafer.

2. Make the coffee confectioners' sugar icing. Sift the confectioners' sugar into a bowl and gradually add coffee syrup. Mix until smooth and of a thick spreading consistency. Smooth icing over the top and sides of the wafer cake, using a palette knife dipped in hot water.

3. Before the icing sets, mark off 12 portions with a sharp knife and place a coffee bean at the edge of each one; place remaining coffee bean in the center.

Chocolate Layer Cake.

Cream Slices

puff pastry made from 3 cups flour
1¼ cups confectioners' custard
strawberry or raspberry jam
⅔ whipped heavy cream
confectioners' sugar icing
3 oz melted semi sweet chocolate

1. Set the oven at 425°F.

2. Roll out the pastry to a thickness of no more than ¼ inch. Using a rectangular metal flan frame measuring 14×4½ inches, cut out, inside the frame, a wide strip of pastry. Reroll remaining pastry and repeat this process until you have 4 equal pastry rectangles.

3. Lightly flour a cookie sheet; place one pastry rectangle on the prepared cookie sheet, fit over flan frame and bake above the center shelf in the pre-set oven for about 10 minutes or until the pastry is golden and well risen. Take out and cool, then carefully split in half lengthwise. Repeat this process with remaining 3 rectangles to give 8 pieces in all.

4. Choose 7 of the neatest rectangles (the eighth piece isn't required for this recipe, so use up in another way), reserving the thickest and smoothest for the top piece.

5. Layer the first strip with confectioners' custard, the second with jam, the third with whipped cream, then repeat this layering with next 3 strips.

6. Top with the reserved strip of pastry, cover with confectioners' sugar icing and before it sets pipe on melted chocolate, using a pastry bag fitted with a fine nozzle, in 2 parallel lines. Feather the chocolate by drawing through it a skewer or needle, if you like. Leave to firm before cutting into slices for serving.

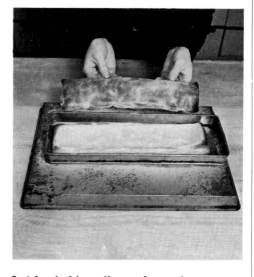

1. Cut panels of pastry with a metal rectangular frame. Transfer each panel to a lightly floured cookie sheet, leaving the frame in position whilst baking. This helps to keep the shape of the pastry.

2. After baking, slice each panel horizontally in half so that you have 8 panels out of the original 4.

3. When you have assembled the layers of pastry, and filled and iced them, decorate with melted chocolate along the length and, using a skewer, draw out branches.

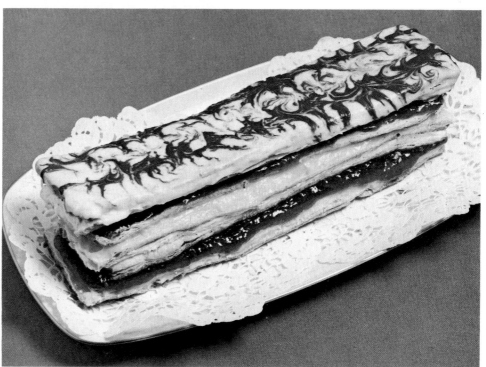

Cream Slice.

Cakes and bread

Rich Sponge Cake

4 egg yolks
⅓ cup plus 1 tbsp sugar
¾ cup plus 1 tbsp flour
confectioners' sugar to finish

1. Set the oven at 350°F.

2. In a mixing bowl beat the egg yolks well until creamy. Beat in the sugar until the mixture is thick and frothy. Sift the flour and fold in.

3. Line a 9 inch diameter layer pan with greased and floured waxed paper cut to fit.

4. Turn the cake batter into the prepared pan and bake just above the center of the pre-set oven for 20 minutes or until brown and firm to the touch. Turn out and cool on a wire rack. Sprinkle thickly with confectioners' sugar.

Cheesecake

7 tbsp sweet butter
2 cups crushed graham crackers
1⅓ cups curd cheese
1 egg
juice and finely grated rind of ½ lemon
2 tbsp vanilla flavored confectioners' sugar

For choux pastry topping
¼ cup sweet butter
⅔ cup cold water
½ cup plus 1 tbsp flour
2 eggs

1. Set the oven at 350°F.

2. Line a rectangular metal flan case measuring 4½ by 11 inches with well greased and floured waxed paper so that it stands at least an inch above the rim.

3. Melt the fat and stir in the cracker crumbs in a pan over a moderate heat until they bind together. Press the mixture into the prepared case.

4. In a mixing bowl work the curd cheese until soft, then beat in the egg, lemon juice and rind and the flavored confectioners' sugar. When well blended turn into the lined case and smooth the top.

5. Make the choux pastry. In a heavy based pan over a moderate heat melt the

Rich Sponge Cake.

butter in the water until dissolved and the mixture comes to the boil. Add the flour at once and as the mixture bubbles up turn off the heat immediately. Using a wooden spoon beat until the mixture forms a smooth paste and comes away cleanly from the sides of the pan. Beat in an egg, until the mixture becomes smooth again, then beat in the remaining egg. Place a plate over the pan and leave at room temperature until the choux paste is completely cold.

6. When cold fill choux paste into a pastry bag fitted with ¼ inch plain nozzle and pipe a trellis pattern over the top. Bake cheesecake in the pre-set oven for 20 minutes, take out and cool. Then refrigerate for about 6 hours before serving. To serve, carefully remove metal case and peel away the paper.

Variations:
Instead of covering the top with a trellis of choux pastry leave cheesecake plain, then after baking spread over ½ cup cultured sour cream, top with rosettes of stiffly whipped heavy cream and sprinkle with either confectioners' sugar or browned almonds.

Coffee Syrup

Basic Recipe

*2¼ cups black coffee, preferably
made from freshly ground
coffee beans for the best flavor*

Despite its name, no sugar is added to the coffee syrup because there will be sufficient natural sweetness in other ingredients according to the recipe.

1. Bring coffee to the boil in a pan over a medium heat; reduce by boiling to about ¼ cup to concentrate its flavor.

2. Remove pan from heat, leave to cool, then pour into container or jar to store and use according to recipe.

Mocha Cake

*3 eggs plus 1 egg yolk
⅔ cup sugar
½ cup flour
4 oz semi sweet chocolate, broken into
    pieces and melted until just liquid*

*For coffee almond paste
1 cup finely ground almonds
2¼ cups sifted confectioners' sugar
1 lightly whipped egg white
1 tsp coffee syrup
cornstarch for dusting*

*To decorate
apricot glaze
chocolate flakes
drinking chocolate powder for sprinkling*

1. Set the oven at 350°F.

2. In a mixing bowl over a pan of hot water whisk together the eggs, egg yolk and sugar until thick, creamy and almost doubled in volume. Remove the bowl from the heat and continue whisking until just tepid. Sprinkle over the flour, then fold in lightly with a metal spoon until blended. Stir in the melted chocolate.

3. Well grease and flour sides of 8 inch diameter layer cake pan and line with greased and floured waxed paper cut to fit. Turn the mixture into the prepared pan and bake in the pre-set oven for about 25 minutes or until risen and the cake just pulls away from the sides of the pan. Take out and turn onto a wire rack to cool; remove paper from the base.

4. Meanwhile make the almond paste. In a mixing bowl work together the ground almonds and the confectioners' sugar with your hand. Make a well in the center and pour in half the egg white and the coffee syrup. Work again until a smooth paste is formed. Turn onto a work surface dusted with cornstarch and knead to a soft dough. Only add remaining egg white or part of it if the paste stays stiff and crumbly. Roll out to a round large enough to cover the top and sides of the chocolate cake.

5. To decorate: Brush the cake with warmed apricot glaze, then cover with the almond paste. Tie a satin ribbon around the sides of the cake. Pile chocolate flakes on top and sprinkle with drinking chocolate powder.

APPLYING CONFECTIONERS' SUGAR ICING

1. Stand the cake to be iced on a wire rack or cake board or any other flat surface. Pour all the icing into the middle of the cake, scraping every bit from the bowl.

2. Dip the palette knife in the hot water, shaking off all the drips, and run the flat of the blade quickly through the icing, working it from the center to the sides and down to give an even layer overall.

3. Keep dipping the knife blade in and out of the hot water so that it runs freely, and smooth off any remaining ridges around the edges of the cake. Smooth the icing on the sides and leave to set until hard. Place chosen decorations for top of the cake on just before the icing sets completely.

Wedding Cake

6 cups softened butter
6 cups firmly packed, light brown sugar
12 cups flour
2 tbsp powdered nutmeg
2 tbsp cinnamon
2 tbsp powdered cloves
2 tbsp ginger
4 cups roughly chopped candied cherries
6 cups chopped, mixed candied peel
4 cups chopped seed raisins
12 cups currants
12 cups seedless raisins
1½ cups finely ground almonds
1½ cups chopped walnuts
18 eggs
1½ cups brandy
1 bottle port
4 tbsp orange flower water
finely grated rind and juice of 6 oranges
finely grated rind and juice of 6 lemons
6 tbsp light corn syrup
6 tbsp molasses

To decorate
apricot glaze
almond paste made from 10 cups finely
 ground almonds
royal icing made from 36 cups
 confectioners' sugar

These quantities are too large to mix in one batch, so divide ingredients into 2 or 3 and make up smaller batches. Quantities given above are enough for 3 round tiers, measuring 9 by 4 inches, 11 by 4 inches and 13 by 4½ inches respectively.

1. Set the oven at 325°F.

2. In a mixing bowl cream the butter until light and soft, then gradually beat in the light brown sugar. In another bowl mix together the flour, spices, candied cherries, mixed peel, dried fruits and nuts. In a third bowl beat the eggs, then beat in the brandy and port, orange flower water, fruit juices and rinds.

3. In a pan over a low heat gently warm the syrup and molasses until blended, then stir into the egg mixture. Beat the flour mixture into the creamed butter and sugar, gradually blending in the egg and syrup mixture from time to time until a smooth mixture is formed.

4. Line the well greased cake pans (as sizes above) with waxed paper cut to fit. Transfer into the prepared cake pans, having same depth of mixture in 9 and 11 inch pans and a little greater depth in the largest pan. Bake just below center of the pre-set oven for an hour for the 9 inch cake, 1½ hours for the 11 inch cake, and 2 hours for the 13 inch cake; then reduce the oven temperature to 300°F and bake for a further 3–4 hours, according to the size of the cake, until dark brown (but not burnt) and a heated thin skewer inserted in the center comes away clean. Take out of the oven and cool on a wire rack. This mixture can be kept in the pan, overnight in the refrigerator when it is not possible to cook all cakes on the same day.

5. To complete the wedding cake, first brush the top and sides of each cake with warmed apricot glaze, then cover with almond paste. To ice the cakes, stand the largest cake on a silver cake board about 16 inches in diameter; thickly coat the top and sides with royal icing and smooth off; leave to harden before proceeding with the decoration. Stand the other 2 cakes on cake boards or an icing table if you have one and coat with royal icing as for the base cake. Leave to harden before proceeding with the decoration as given below. When the decoration is hard, put the 3 tiers together, the smallest cake being the top tier, and decorate the top according to choice.

1. On a large piece of paper trace 3 11-pointed stars, their diameters equalling those of each of the cakes to be decorated i.e. 13 inches for the 13 inch cake. Place the paper star on top of the cake and, using a fine needle, prick round the star shape to leave a star design on the icing.

3. Fill in a side outline of linked half circles, using the same writing nozzle. Each half circle meets directly below each star point, and these half circles should arc to a depth of 1 inch on the 13 inch cake, ¾ inch on the 11 inch cake, and ½ inch on the 9 inch cake.

5. Change the nozzle for a finer one. Then pipe directly on top of the first series of arcs that formed the basis of the trellis pattern to give a raised effect and make the lines stand out.

2. Fill a quantity of royal icing into a pastry bag fitted with a plain nozzle and pipe a thin line along the pin pricks to form the frame of the star design.

4. The next step is to fill in the triangular spaces between the points of the star with a simple trellis pattern. Using the same writing nozzle, pipe a series of fine arcs across each space, and complete the trellis effect.

6. Fill royal icing into a pastry bag fitted with a star nozzle and pipe tiny rosettes along the outline of the star, concealing the beginnings of the trellis pattern. Repeat this pattern on the smaller cakes and when hard, assemble the tiers.

Wedding Cake.

APPLYING ALMOND PASTE

1. Brush the top of the cake generously with sieved apricot jam.

2. Roll out the almond paste and place the cake, jam side down, in the middle.

3. Cut off the almond paste round the cake, using a sharp knife.

4. The neat almond paste top will adhere to the jammy cake.

5. Gather up the trimmings and roll out the paste again in a strip which is slightly longer than the circumference of the cake and exactly the depth. Brush the cake sides with jam and roll the cake over the paste to coat the sides.

Gâteau St. Honoré

For sweet shortcrust pastry
4½ cups flour
salt
1¼ cups butter
½ cup sifted confectioners' sugar
1 lightly beaten egg
⅔ cup cold water

For sweet choux paste
2 tbsp sweet butter
⅔ cup milk
1 sugar cube
¾ cup flour
2½ eggs

To finish
⅓ cup sugar
3 tbsp water
1¼ cups confectioners' custard
1¼ cups chantilly cream

1. Set the oven at 350°F.

2. Make the shortcrust pastry. Sift the flour and a dash of salt onto a work surface, make a well in the center and into this put the butter, sugar and egg. Using 2 knives, gradually blend the flour into the other ingredients, adding a little water from time to time, until a soft but not sticky dough is formed. Wrap in waxed paper and chill in the refrigerator for 30 minutes before rolling out to an 8 inch diameter, ½ inch thick, round. Put on a greased and floured cookie sheet and bake in the pre-set oven for 20–25 minutes or until golden. Take out and cool on a wire rack.

3. Increase the oven temperature to 400°F. Make the sweet choux paste. In a heavy based pan over a low heat melt the butter in the milk and heat until the milk starts to bubble. At once add the sugar and stir until it is dissolved. Increase the heat and bring the mixture to the boil, then stir in the flour at once and let the mixture bubble up quickly. Take off the heat immediately and beat in the eggs until a smooth paste is formed and it comes away cleanly from the sides of the pan. Set aside to cool.

4. When cold fill the choux paste into a pastry bag fitted with a medium or small plain round nozzle and pipe about 16–18 choux buns onto the prepared cookie sheets, spacing them wide apart. Bake in

Gâteau St. Honoré.

the pre-set oven for 10–15 minutes or until puffed and golden. Take out and cool on a wire rack. Split in half when cold and fill with a little confectioners' custard. To finish the cake, place pastry base on a serving dish. In a heavy based pan over a low heat dissolve the sugar in the water, then bring to the boil and boil until the syrup starts to go straw colored at the edges. Remove from the heat at once.

5. Dip the choux buns in the syrup, using a pair of kitchen tongs, and arrange in 2 circles, one on top of the other, around the pastry base. Use the syrup to anchor them in position. Spoon confectioners' custard into the center of the cake, then cover with about two thirds of the chantilly cream. Fill the remaining chantilly cream into a

pastry bag fitted with a star nozzle and pipe rosettes on top and over the cake to decorate.

Royal Icing

Basic Recipe ☆

6¾ cups sifted confectioners' sugar
juice of ½ lemon
several egg whites
food coloring if required

1. In a mixing bowl work the confectioners' sugar with the lemon juice and 1 egg white; continue adding egg white until the mixture is smooth, free from any air bubbles and of a thick spreading consistency. Too much egg white will make the icing

runny, in which case add more confectioners' sugar; too little egg white will make the icing stiff and dry to work.

2. To color royal icing, spoon a little of the mixture onto the work surface; work in a few drops of chosen color so icing is vividly colored, then blend this into the main quantity of icing; this will tone down the brightness and the icing will gradually assume a pastel shade.

Cakes and bread

Fruit Loaf Cake

2¾ cups mixed dried fruits or seedless raisins
1 cup plus 2 tbsp firmly packed light brown
  sugar
1¼ cups strained cold tea
4 cups flour
salt

1 lightly beaten egg
confectioners' sugar icing to finish

1. Set the oven at 375°F.

2. In a mixing bowl stir together the
dried fruits or white raisins and the sugar.
Stir in the tea and sift the flour with a dash
of salt. Add to mixture with the egg.

3. Combine together until the mixture
forms a cake batter, then turn into a
greased and floured, 9 by 5 by 3 inch pan.

4. Bake in the pre-set oven for 1 hour,
then take out and cool slightly on a wire
rack before removing from the pan. If
liked, cover with a thin topping of plain
confectioners' sugar icing.

Cherry Cake

¾ cup softened sweet butter
finely grated rind of 1 small lemon
1 cup plus 2 tbsp sugar
4 cups flour
4 eggs
2 cups candied cherries

1. Set the oven at 325°F.

2. In a mixing bowl cream the butter with
the lemon rind until very soft. Sift and stir
in ¼ cup flour and 1 egg; beat well. Continue adding the flour a little at a time,
with an egg each time, and beating well.
Then beat in the remaining flour until a
smooth, creamy batter is formed.

3. Coat the candied cherries with a little
flour and fold them into the cake batter.

4. Line the bottom and sides of a loose
bottomed, deep 8 inch cake pan with a
piece of greased and floured waxed paper.
Turn the mixture into the pan. Bake in the
pre-set oven for about 1½ hours. Take out
and cool in the pan for a while before
turning out onto a wire rack to cool completely.

Apricot Glaze

1 cup apricot jam
1¼ cups water
¾ cup sugar

1. Gently heat together the jam,
water and sugar in a heavy based pan over
a low heat until all are completely dissolved. Increase the heat until the mixture
just starts to bubble gently and becomes
fairly thick but still of a pouring consistency.

2. Work through a sieve, and use the
glaze while still warm. Store in clean dry
jars if not using immediately.

Moist Tea Bread

2 eggs
¾ cup sugar
2 tbsp butter
2½ cups flour
1 cup chopped candied peel
¼ cup currants
1 tsp powdered mixed spice
2 tsp baking powder
milk to mix

For topping
½–¾ cup crushed sugar cubes or apricot
  glaze,
1¼ cups crystallized fruits and
1 cup roughly chopped walnuts

1. Set the oven at 325°F.

2. In a mixing bowl beat the eggs and
sugar together until well blended. Sift the
flour into another bowl. Rub the butter
into the flour until the mixture resembles
fine breadcrumbs, then stir in the rest of
the ingredients except the milk.

3. Beat portions of the flour mixture into
the egg mixture, together with just enough
milk to form a soft cake batter. Turn into a
greased and floured 6–7 inch deep cake
pan and bake for about an hour or until a
skewer comes away clean. Take out of the
oven, turn out of the pan, upside down, on
a wire rack to cool.

4. When cold either cover with a topping
of crushed sugar lumps and caramelize
under a hot broiler or brush with warmed
apricot glaze and cover with crystallized
fruits and chopped walnuts.

Kugelhopf

¾ cake fresh yeast
1¼ cups sugar
¼ cup lukewarm water
4 cups flour
½ tsp salt
1 tsp vanilla powder
⅓ cup seedless raisins
¾ cup blanched flaked almonds
finely grated rind of 1 lemon
2 beaten eggs
5 tbsp melted butter
1 cup warm milk
confectioners' sugar for sprinkling

1. In a bowl blend together the yeast and
2 tbsp sugar until completely dissolved
and liquid. Stir in the lukewarm water and
set aside yeast mixture to prove in a warm
place for 30 minutes. Well grease a
kugelhopf pan.

2. Warm a mixing bowl and sift the flour
and salt into it; stir in the remaining sugar,
vanilla powder, raisins, almonds and
lemon rind. Make a well in the center of
the mixture, tip in the yeast liquid and
blend. Stir in the eggs a little at a time,
then add the melted butter. Blend in
enough of the warm milk to form a smooth
dough. Lightly sprinkle with flour, cover
with a warm cloth and stand the bowl in a
warm place so the dough can prove for
about 2 hours or until doubled in size.

3. Place the risen dough on a floured
work surface; using your fist knock down
the dough several times, then place in the
prepared pan. Cover again with a warm
cloth, put in a warm place and leave to rise
for about an hour. Set the oven at 350°F.

4. When risen put the cake into the pre-
set oven and bake for about an hour or
until a rich brown. If the top browns too
quickly cover with a piece of waxed paper.
When baked take out of the oven and cool
on a wire rack.

5. Leave for 24 hours before cutting and
sprinkle with confectioners' sugar before
serving.

MAKING BREAD

1. Warm a crock or a deep bowl and put half the flour into it. Beat the yeast and sugar together and pour this mixture over the flour.

2. Add milk and water. Mix to a batter.

3. Cover the crock with a clean cloth and leave to prove.

4. Add the remaining flour and mix.

5. Knead the dough thoroughly; pull the dough toward you.

6. Press the dough down and forward with the palms of the hands.

7. Leave in a warm place to prove, make cuts on the surface with scissors.

8. Press dough into baking pans.

9. After baking for 5 minutes, quickly brush beaten egg over the bread and return it to the oven.

Cakes and bread

White Bread

6 cups strong bread flour
2 tsp salt
1 tbsp lard rubbed in either ¾ cake fresh
  yeast dissolved in 2 cups warm water or
  dissolve 1 tsp sugar in 2 cups warm water
  and sprinkle on 2 tsp dried yeast and
  leave 10 minutes until frothy

1. Add the yeast liquid to the dry mix and work to a firm dough that leaves the bowl clean.

2. Turn the dough onto a lightly floured surface and knead by folding the dough towards you, then pushing down and away from you with the palm of your hand. Give the dough a quarter turn and repeat the kneading process. Knead until the dough feels firm and elastic and no longer sticky – about 10 minutes. If you have a mixer follow the manufacturers instructions for using the dough hook. Place yeast liquid and dry ingredients in the bowl and turn onto lowest speed and mix for 1 minute. Increase speed and mix for a further 2 minutes to knead dough.

3. Shape the dough into a round ball and place in a lightly oiled polythene bag.

4. Leave it to rise to suit your convenience: 45–60 minutes in a warm place 2 hours at average room temperature, 12 hours in a cold room, 24 hours in a refrigerator, the colder the dough is kept and the slower it rises the better your finished bread will be.

5. When it has doubled in size, springs back when lightly pressed with a floured finger and is back to room temperature, knock it back by flattening each piece with the knuckles to knock out the air bubbles. Knead again to a firm dough.

6. Shape into a desired shape and place on a lightly greased and floured cookie sheet or half fill a greased and floured pan.

7. Set the oven at 450°F.

8. Leave to prove inside an oiled polythene bag for about 1 hour at room temperature until the dough rises just above the tops of the pan. Remove the polythene bag. Brush tops with egg wash if a shiny crust is desired.

9. Bake in the center of the pre-set oven for 30–40 minutes when the loaves should sound hollow when tapped on the base.

Sally Lunn

1 cup milk
2 tbsp butter
3 cups flour
½ tsp salt
1 egg
1 cake fresh yeast
1 tsp sugar

For glaze
1 tbsp sugar
1 tbsp milk

1. Place the milk and butter in a pan and heat gently until the butter melts. Cool until just warm.

2. Warm the flour slightly, then sift into a bowl with the salt. Beat the egg and add to the cooled mixture.

3. Cream the yeast and sugar, and add to the milk.

4. Make a well in the flour and strain the liquid into it. Mix to make a dough. Turn into a floured board and knead lightly.

5. Grease and warm 2 5 inch diameter cake pans. Divide the dough into the pans. Cover with a cloth and leave to rise for about 30 minutes or until the dough has doubled in size.

6. Set oven at 425°F.

7. Bake in the pre-set oven for 20–25 minutes. Dissolve the sugar in the milk and brush the dough with this mixture. Return to the oven for a few minutes to dry the glaze. Turn out of the pans and leave on a rack to cool.

8. Slice into rounds, toast each side and spread generously with butter. Reshape the Sally Lunn and slice vertically for serving.

White Bread baked in a variety of pans.

dissolve 1 tsp of the sugar in 1½ cups of the water in the recipe. Have the water warm, then sprinkle the dried yeast on top. Leave for about 10 minutes until frothy. Add this to the flour, salt, remaining sugar and water.

3. Knead thoroughly until it is no longer sticky – 5–10 minutes.

4. Shape the dough into a round ball and place in a lightly oiled polythene bag, lightly tied.

5. Leave it to rise to suit your convenience: 45–60 minutes in a warm place, 2 hours at average room temperature, 12 hours in a cold room, 24 hours in a refrigerator. The colder the dough is kept and the slower it rises the better your finished bread will be.

6. When it has doubled in size, springs back when lightly pressed with a floured finger and is back to room temperature, knock it back by flattening each piece with the knuckles to knock out the air bubbles. Knead again to a firm dough.

7. Shape into a desired shape and place on a lightly greased and floured cookie sheet or half fill a greased and floured pan.

8. Set the oven at 450°F.

9. Leave to prove inside an oiled polythene bag for about an hour at room temperature until the dough rises just above the tops of the pan. Remove the polythene. Brush tops with salt and water to get a good crust.

10. Bake in the center of the oven for 30–40 minutes when the loaves should sound hollow when tapped on the base.

Variation:
Follow the recipe for wholewheat bread using 1½ cups cracked wheat in place of 1½ cups of the flour. When shaping the bread after proving, scatter a little cracked wheat on the board and this will be picked up on the dough. Finally scatter cracked wheat over the surface of the loaf or rolls just before they go in the oven.

Brioches

2 cups plain flour
¾ cake fresh yeast
2–3 tbsp warm water
1 tbsp sugar
1 tsp salt
2 eggs
2–4 tbsp milk
¼ cup butter
extra flour for sprinkling

For brushing
1 beaten egg
1 tbsp milk
salt

1. Sift the flour. Dissolve the yeast in the water and mix with a quarter of the flour to make a small ball of dough. Mark a cross on top of the dough ball and place it in a large bowl of warm water. Leave until the dough has doubled in size and has risen to the surface.

2. Make a well in the remaining flour. Place the sugar, salt and eggs in it and mix to a loose, elastic dough, using the milk as necessary.

3. Cream the butter until soft and work it into the dough. Drain the ball of yeast dough, then cut and fold it into the mixture. Knead the dough. Place in a greased bowl, sprinkle with a little flour, cover with a cloth and leave to rise for about 2 hours at room temperature.

4. When the dough is doubled in size, knock down and knead it. Sprinkle with more flour, cover and leave overnight in the refrigerator.

5. Grease 8 individual brioche pans and divide the dough to fit the pans with a small ball of dough on the top. Leave to rise in a warm place for 20 minutes.

6. Set the oven at 425°F.

7. Mix the beaten egg with the milk and a dash of salt, and brush the brioches with this mixture. Bake in the pre-set oven for 15–20 minutes.

Wholewheat Plaited Loaf and Wholewheat Bread.

Croissants

For butter dough
1½ cups butter
⅓ cup flour

For yeast dough
2¼ cakes fresh yeast
1 tbsp sugar
1 egg
1 cup water
3¾ cups flour

1. Work the flour into the butter and chill in the refrigerator.

2. Mix the yeast with the sugar. Add the egg and beat well. Stir in water.

3. Sift the flour onto a clean work surface. Make a well in the center. Pour the yeast mixture in. Using 2 knives gradually work in the flour to make a smooth dough.

4. Slap the ball of dough from hand to hand until there is a slight rising and falling movement in the dough. This is necessary to activate the yeast.

5. Roll out the dough and place the chilled slab of butter dough in the center. Fold into a parcel. Turn and roll out with a jerky uneven movement so that the surface is corrugated but unbroken.

6. Fold the dough in 3, turn 90°, then roll out again. Repeat this folding, turning and rolling out procedure twice then chill the dough for at least an hour.

7. Set the oven at 400°F.

8. Roll out the rested dough and cut triangles 6 by 6½ inches. Wet the tips and stretch the base slightly before rolling up from the base. Shape into crescents.

9. Place on a cookie sheet, brush with beaten egg and bake in the pre-set oven for 20–25 minutes or until golden brown.

Variations:
Croissants can also be sprinkled with flaked almonds, dusted with sugar, or brushed with apricot glaze before baking.

1. Cut the butter into the flour.

2. Make the butter dough into a slab and refrigerate.

6. Slap the ball of dough from one hand to the other. This reactivates the yeast.

7. Roll out the dough and place the butter dough in the center.

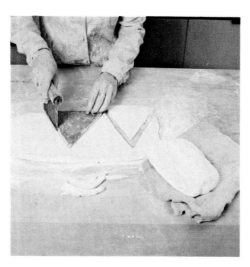

11. Roll out thinly and cut out triangles.

12. Wet the angles with cold water and pull the base to stretch it.

3. Work yeast and sugar together.

4. Make a well in the center of the flour and pour the yeast in.

5. Work together with 2 knives to form a smooth dough.

8. Fold dough into a parcel.

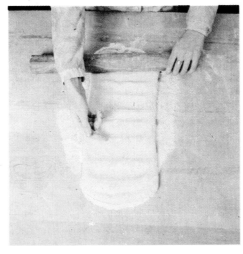

9. Roll out, pressing unevenly, to give the above effect. Fold into a parcel.

10. Turn 90°. Reroll, fold and turn twice more. Refrigerate for an hour or more before using.

13. Roll up from base to top.

14. Make into a curve and flatten ends.

Croissants.

251

Index

Index

Index